This book is dedicated to three friends:
Winifred, Lawn, and Jay,
all physicians who are not made anxious
by their patient's health.

BEYOND CULTURE

EDWARD T. HALL

Anchor Press/Doubleday
Garden City, New York
1976 126-134

ISBN 0-385-08747-0
Library of Congress Catalog Card Number 74-3550

ACKNOWLEDGMENTS

Grateful acknowledgment is made for permission to use excerpts from copyrighted material, as follows:

From pp. 100–1 of A HIGH WIND IN JAMAICA, by Richard Hughes. Copyright 1928, 1929, by Richard Hughes; renewed 1956, 1957, by Richard Hughes. Reprinted by permission of Harper & Row, Publishers, Inc.

From "Conceptual Categories in Primitive Languages," by Edward Sapir, *Science*, Vol. 74, 4 December 1931, p. 578. Reprinted by permission of *Science*.

From LOLITA, by Vladimir Nabokov. Copyright © 1955 by Vladimir Nabokov. Reprinted by permission of G. P. Putnam's Sons, Publishers.

From pp. 16–17 of THE FOX IN THE ATTIC, by Richard Hughes. Copyright © 1961 by Richard Hughes. Reprinted by permission of Harper & Row, Publishers, Inc.

From BILLY BUDD, by Herman Melville. New York: The New American Library, 1961.

From HOW CHILDREN FAIL, by John Holt. New York: Pitman Publishing Corporation, 1964. Reprinted by permission.

From "Paralinguistics, Kinesics and Cultural Anthropology," by Weston La Barre. In APPROACHES TO SEMIOTICS, by T. A. Sebeok, A. S. Hayes, and M. C. Bateson (eds.). The Hague: Mouton & Co., N.V., Publishers, 1962.

From ECOLOGICAL PSYCHOLOGY, by Roger G. Barker. Stanford, Calif.: Stanford University Press, 1968.

Author's Preface

Writing a book is a co-operative effort; while the author is ultimately responsible for the content, form, style, and organization of ideas, he depends upon the assistance of others, without which his task would be immeasurably lengthened.

My first acknowledgment, therefore, with thanks and appreciation, is to Mildred Reed Hall, my friend, partner, and wife, whose unflagging faith in my work frequently kept me going when I might otherwise have given up. Despite full-time professional responsibilities, she made it possible for me to have time for writing by assuming many burdens and shielding me from the demands of others. She has also read and criticized several versions of this book. For editorial assistance, I am indebted to Roma McNickle, whose skill and experience were extremely helpful. My first editor at Doubleday, William Whitehead, provided an extensive and thoughtful critique of the first draft. The second draft of the book was reviewed and strengthened by Elizabeth Knappman. To both these Doubleday editors I express my thanks. My agent, Robert Lescher, also contributed invaluable assistance at many stages in the production of the manuscript.

Special thanks go to the following individuals who performed innumerable tasks essential to publication: Cornelia Lowndes, who deciphered my handwriting, typed several versions of the manuscript, and contributed many helpful suggestions; Lane Ittelson and Cynthia Peters, who helped with library research, checking footnotes and bibliographic references; and Ellen McCoy Hall, who contributed many cogent comments on the manuscript at various stages.

April 7, 1975
Santa Fe, New Mexico

Contents

Introduction

There are two related crises in the world of contemporary man. The first and most visible is the population/environment crisis. The second, more subtle but equally lethal, is man himself—his relationship to himself, to his extensions, his institutions, his ideas, to those around him, as well as between the many groups that inhabit the globe; in a word, his relationship to his culture.

Both crises must be resolved or neither will be solved. For there are no technological solutions to the problems confronting man and his eternal conflicts. At the same time, technical solutions to environmental problems will never be applied rationally until man has begun to transcend the limitations imposed by his institutions, his philosophies, and his cultures. Particularly pressing are the world's hot spots, such as the Middle East.

Politics is part of life—beginning in the home and becoming more and more visible as power is manifest in the larger institutions on the local, the national, and the international levels. We should not be fooled by either politics or political institutions. What we are talking about here is power and its use. But there is more to life than sheer power; at least, one hopes that in time the power motive will diminish. Apart from power, culture still plays a prominent role in the relations between the Russians and the West. Culture has always been an issue, not only between Europe and Russia, but among the European states as well. The Germans, the French, the Italians, the Spanish, Portuguese and English, as well as the Scandinavian and Balkan cultures all have their own unique identity, language, systems of nonverbal communication, material culture, history, and way of doing things. To argue that each culture is not unique is one of the irrationalities discussed in the chapters to follow. Europe is relatively calm now. But what about China and its neighbor Japan? Any Westerner who was raised outside the Far East and claims he really understands and can communicate with either the Chinese or the Japanese is deluding himself.[1] On the horizon are the multiple cultures of Africa and the emerging nations of Latin America demanding to be recognized in their own right. The future depends on man's transcending the limits of individual cultures. To do so, however, he must first recognize and accept the multiple hidden dimensions of the nonverbal side of life.

Exacerbating the world's political and cultural problems are environmental and economic crises. As Hardin[2] showed with wisdom and insight in an article titled "The Tragedy of the Commons,"[3] mankind cannot continue to increase the consumption of the world's finite resources. The classical English pattern of using the village commons (communally owned and used land which was available for pasturing *private* livestock) did not involve a conflict between public and private welfare as long as there was enough land. However, as herds increased, the overgrazed land became less productive, so that herdsmen had to increase their stocks in order to stay even, and thus the commons were destroyed. The tragedy was that profits accrued to the opportunistic herdsmen who exploited the commons the most, while losses were shared by *all* the users. Those who exercised restraint were doubly penalized. Not only did they suffer losses from the overgrazing of neighbors, but they were unable to exploit the market by means of their own production.

Today, the sea, the air, the waterways, the earth, the land and what it produces have *all* become commons, and all are vulnerable to overuse. Appeals to altruism are futile and in one sense foolhardy. Technology alone will not get us out of this dilemma, because these are human problems. Hardin argues that the single-track, Newtonian approach will satisfy only the politicians and the big exploiters of the commons. What is needed, he feels, is a more comprehensive, Darwinian (Dionysian) approach that can be used as a basis for establishing priorities, alternatives, and options. In a word, unless man can learn to pull together and to regulate his own consumption (and production) patterns, he is headed for disaster.

The tragedy of the commons is one of those irrationalities discussed in Chapter 14. The answer lies not in restricting man but in opening up new alternatives, new possibilities, new dimensions, new options, and new avenues for creative uses of man himself that do not use resources and are not ego-dependent. Ego needs, particularly if they are neurotic, almost inevitably are irrational, obsessional, compulsive, gained at the expense of others, and make extensive use of material resources.

This brings us to an important question that has grown in my mind in the process of living. It has to do with man's basic and underlying attitude toward himself. I am not speaking of something superficial, which can be easily observed or experienced, but something else, deeper and more subtle than surface man. The question is: *Why are most people so unnecessarily hard on themselves?* And why do they not make better use of their talents? Why is mankind so hard on mankind? It is as though we nurtured the child that is in all of us and, in being childish, were afraid of each other. This is not a simple problem, and it may be world-wide.

We see evidences of man's putting himself down in folklore, religions, philosophies, institutions, as well as in daily life. The processes certainly are not within the reach of conscious control but deep within us. Freud was so struck by these processes that he posited a death instinct and built his theories around the notion that man inevitably advances at the expense of himself. Freud believed that the basic energies, the libidinal forces of man, had to be repressed in order for man to live in groups, and that the libidinal energy was "sublimated" into the creative, cooperative drives that produced modern institutions. That is, creativity was a by-product of the necessity for man to repress his basic drives and to control himself. Like all of us, Freud was a product of his times, which were characterized by such thinking, and given the times, much of Freud's thinking made sense. Nevertheless, the study of man's past as well as his present—in his many forms—fails to confirm Freud's view that man advances and builds his institutions through a process of sublimation of sexual energy; i.e., by suppressing sex in its widest possible connotation. I would suggest another alternative, namely that once man began evolving his extensions, particularly language, tools, and institutions, he got caught in the web of what I term extension transference (Chapter 2) and was both alienated from himself and incapable of controlling the monsters he had created. In this sense, he has advanced at the expense of that part of himself that he had extended, and as a consequence has ended up by repressing his nature in its many forms. Man's goal from here on out should be to rediscover that self.

Certainly, there are tremendous areas of conflict between Western man and his material as well as his non-material extensions. The instrument he has created is like an ill-fitting shoe. According to some of the most distinguished and thoughtful students of the mind, one of the most devastating and damaging things that can happen to anyone is to fail to fulfill his potential. A kind of gnawing emptiness, longing, frustration, and displaced anger takes over when this occurs. Whether the anger is turned inward on the self or outward toward others, dreadful destruction results. Yet, how man evolved with such an incredible reservoir of talent and such fantastic diversity is not completely understood. Man is not anywhere nearly enough in awe of himself, possibly because he knows so little and has nothing to measure himself against.

People get cast in molds (of status and roles) for which they are variously equipped. The problem lies between man's creativeness and diversity and the rather specific needs of his institutions, for most cultures and the institutions they engender represent highly specialized solutions to rather specific problems. For example, in England during the early days of the industrial revolution,[4] villagers and field hands were brought into the factory to work. These first generations of mill hands were not conditioned to the whistle. Like all preindustrial peoples, when they earned enough to pay off their debts and keep them for a while they quit and went home. This situation could have continued indefinitely if there had not been a hidden trap—children.

There were no child labor laws and no one to care for the children at home, so the children worked with the parents in the factory and became imprinted by the whistle. They then brought up their own children accordingly.

If the totality of man's experiences with factory work and schedules means anything at all, and if current pressure on the part of workers to do something about the monotony is significant, industrialists could hardly have done better at creating an anti-human work situation if they had deliberately set out to do so. Man has put himself in his own zoo. He has so simplified his life and stereotyped his responses that he might as well be in a cage.

The result is that, since people can't fight the institutions on which their lives depend, they unconsciously first turn their anger inward and later outward against the "enemies" of the institutions to which they have sold their souls. Someday, man will no longer need ideological crutches. To coin a phrase, ideologies are the opiate of the people and have taken the place not of religion, but of religious institutions.

But, to continue with our basic theme, many people's sense of worth, the value they place on the image of the self, is directly related to the number of situations in which they are in control, which means that many people have a problem with their self-image, because they are in control of so little.[5] The ultimate in human degradation and the subservience of human needs to institutional forms is shown in Kesey's[6] novel ONE FLEW OVER THE CUCKOO'S NEST. Big Nurse, in Kesey's book, epitomizes all the anti-humanism and destructiveness, all the distortions of the communication process, all the violations of cultural norms that one finds in the bureaucracies that man has created. The book is a statement of the powerlessness and lack of self-affirmation so common in our times.

Powerlessness and lack of self-affirmation lead to aggression, as repeatedly asserted by psychologists and psychiatrists. Psychological powerlessness is the result of past events, but situational and cultural powerlessness are here and now. Blacks and students rioted in recent years not only because they were powerless to make the system work, but because *they saw themselves as powerless.* There is no other way to explain the incredible out-burst of rage triggered by the assassination of Martin Luther King or the "incursion" into Cambodia. The groundwork had been laid long before, but it was suddenly and overwhelmingly apparent to those concerned.

Things are quieter in the ghettos now because the rhythm of black life is in a quiet phase—they are taking a breather. It is quieter on the campus since the winding down of the Viet-nam War. But a major and continuing source of frustration exists because the many gifts and talents of women, black peo-ple, Indians, Spanish Americans, and others are not only unrecognized but frequently denigrated by members of the dominant group. It is the corrosive daily and niggling frustra-tion, the inability to communicate or to establish meaningful relationships that is so soul-shrinking.

The cultural and psychological insight that is important for man to accept is that denying culture can be as destructive as denying evil. Man must come to terms with both. It is man's powerlessness in the face of culture and the limitations placed on the development of self that result in aggression. Paradoxi-cally, the only way that man can escape the hidden constraints of covert culture is to involve himself actively and quite con-sciously in those parts of his life that he takes most for granted.

What is called for is a massive cultural literacy movement that is not imposed but springs from within. Man can benefit from more as well as deeper knowledge of what an incredible or-ganism he is. He can grow, swell with pride, and breathe better for having many remarkable talents. To do so, however, he must stop ranking either people or talents and accept the fact that there are many roads to truth and no culture has a corner on the path or is better equipped than others to search for it. What is more, no man can tell another how to conduct that search.

1. The Paradox of Culture

Two widely divergent but interrelated experiences, psycho-analysis and work as an anthropologist, have led me to the belief that in his strivings for order, Western man has created chaos by denying that part of his self that integrates while enshrining the parts that fragment experience. These examinations of man's psyche have also convinced me that: the natural act of thinking is greatly modified by culture; Western man uses only a small fraction of his mental capabilities; there are many different and legitimate ways of thinking; we in the West value one of these ways above all others—the one we call "logic," a linear system that has been with us since Socrates.

Western man sees his system of logic as synonymous with the truth. For him it is the only road to reality. Yet Freud educated us to the complexities of the psyche, helping his readers to look at dreams as a legitimate mental process that exists quite apart from the linearity of manifest thought. But his ideas were from the outset strenuously resisted, particularly by scientists and engineers, who were still wedded to a Newtonian model. When taken seriously, Freudian thinking shook the very foundations of conventional thought. Freud's followers, particularly Fromm and Jung, undeterred by popular stereotypes and the tremendous prestige of the physical sciences, added to his theories and bridged the gap between the linear world of logic and the integrative world of dreams.[1]

Knowing that the interpretation of dreams, myths, and acts is always to some degree an individual matter,[2] I cannot help asking myself what a psychoanalytically sophisticated reader would

add to my own interpretation of a sequence of events reported
in the New York *Times* concerning a police dog sighted on
Ruffle Bar, an uninhabited island near New York.[3] Visible only
from a distance, the dog, nicknamed the King of Ruffle Bar,
had sustained itself for an estimated two years, was apparently
in good health, and presumably would have survived in his semi-
wild state, barring accidents, for the rest of his natural life. However, some well-meaning soul heard about the dog and reported
him to the American Society for the Prevention of Cruelty to
Animals, thereby setting the bureaucratic wheels in motion.
Since the King could not be approached by people, a baited trap
was set. According to the *Times* report: ". . . every day, a police
launch from Sheepshead Bay takes off for Ruffle Bar, the
uninhabited swampy island of the dog. Every day, a police
helicopter hovers for a half hour or more over Ruffle Bar." A
radio report of the broadcast at the time described how the
helicopter harassed the dog in futile efforts to "catch" (sic) him
(he refused to enter the trap) or at least to get a better view of
him. Police were quoted as saying the dog "looked in good
shape." When questioned, representatives of the ASPCA said:
"When we catch the dog, we will have it examined by a vet, and
if it is in good health, we will find a *happy* home for it."[4] (italics
added)

If this story had been a dream or a myth instead of a news
report, there is little doubt as to its interpretation. Both the latent and the manifest content are quite clear, possibly explaining why this local news item was given national coverage. I find,
as I go over the story, that free associations come to mind on
different levels. The story epitomizes the little man against the
big bureaucracy. There is also a delusional side which cannot be
overlooked. The ASPCA became obsessed with capturing the
dog. Once triggered, the ASPCA involved the police with a
remorseless, mindless persistence that is too terrifyingly characteristic of bureaucracies once they are activated. Interestingly
enough, the police, having known about the dog for two years,
had been content to leave him on the island. Emotionally, they
sided with the King, even while carrying out their orders. "Why

don't they leave the dog alone?" said one policeman. Another observed, "The dog is as happy as a pig in a puddle."[5]

The delusional aspects have to do with the institutionalized necessity to control "everything," and the widely accepted notion that the bureaucrat knows what is best; never for a moment does he doubt the validity of the bureaucratic solution. It is also slightly insane, or at least indicative of our incapacity to order priorities with any common sense, to spend thousands of dollars for helicopters, gasoline, and salaries for the sole purpose of bureaucratic neatness.

Even more recently, a New York *Times* news item[6] reported a U. S. Park Police campaign to stamp out kite flying on the grounds of the Washington Monument. Their charter to harass the kite fliers lay in an old law written by Congress supposedly to keep the Wright brothers' planes from becoming fouled in kite strings.

The psychoanalyst Laing is convinced that the Western world is mad.[7] These stories of the dog and the kite fliers bolster Laing's view and symbolize man's plight as well as any recent events I know.[8] However, it is not man who is crazy so much as his institutions[9] and those culture patterns that determine his behavior. We in the West are alienated from ourselves and from nature. We labor under a number of delusions, one of which is that life makes sense; i.e., that we are sane. We persist in this view despite massive evidence to the contrary. We live fragmented, compartmentalized lives in which contradictions are carefully sealed off from each other. We have been taught to think linearly rather than comprehensively,[10] and we do this not through conscious design or because we are not intelligent or capable, but because of the way in which deep cultural undercurrents structure life in subtle but highly consistent ways that are not consciously formulated. Like the invisible jet streams in the skies that determine the course of a storm, these hidden currents shape our lives; yet their influence is only beginning to be identified. Given our linear, step-by-step, compartmentalized way of thinking,[11] fostered by the schools and public media, it is impossible for our leaders to consider events comprehensively or to weigh priorities according to a system of common good, all of which can be placed like an unwanted waif on culture's doorstep. Yet, paradoxically, few anthropologists are in agreement as to what to include under the general rubric of culture. While it will be denied by some, much depends on the anthropologist's own culture, which exerts a deep and abiding influence not only over how anthropologists think but over where they draw the boundaries in such matters. Frequently, the greater portion of contemporary culture will be excluded or referred to as "mere convention." In a practical sense, the conventions of the field and what one's peers are studying have more to do with what anthropologists define as culture than an appraisal of one's data might indicate. Like everyone else, anthropologists use models, and some models are more fashionable than others. Most of them are handed down and modified periodically.

The reader may well ask, "What is a model?" or "What kind of models are you talking about?" While models and how man uses them are just beginning to be understood, one thing is certain: many different models exist. Mechanical models, such as scale models of airplanes flown in wind tunnels, show how machines and processes work. Models for making molds can reproduce everything from machines to copies of works of art. Life models help the artist fill in gaps in a faulty visual memory. Parents and teachers may be models for the young.

Scientists use theoretical models, often mathematical in nature. These are used to symbolically express certain qualities, quantities, and relationships encountered in life. Econometricians, for example, use these models to investigate how the more measurable aspects of the economic system operate.

Anthropologists use predominantly non-mathematical theoretical models that are rooted in culture. Since culture is itself a series of situational models for behavior and thought, the models anthropologists use are frequently highly abstract versions of parts of models that make up the entire culture (kinship systems, for example).

Man is the model-making organism par excellence. His earliest intellectual endeavors resulted in monuments that mystified and puzzled twentieth-century man until they were figured out. Stonehenge, for example, is a model of the solar system that enabled the early inhabitants of the Salisbury Plain to make accurate observations of celestial events and to keep track of the seasons, order their ceremonial life, and even predict eclipses at a time when no one would have thought such refined calculations and observations were possible (fifteen hundred to two thousand years B.C.!).

Grammars and writing systems are models of language. Any school child who has struggled to make sense of what he is taught knows that some fit reasonably well, others don't. Myths, philosophical systems, and science represent different types of models of what the social scientists call cognitive systems. The purpose of the model is to enable the user to do a better job in handling the enormous complexity of life. By using models, we see and test how things work and can even predict how things will go in the future. The effectiveness of a model can be judged by how well it works, as well as how consistent it is as a mechanical or philosophical system. People are very closely identified with their models, since they also form the basis for behavior. Men have fought and died in the name of different models of nature.

All theoretical models are incomplete. By definition, they are abstractions and therefore leave things out. What they leave out is as important as, if not more important than, what they do not, because it is what is left out that gives structure and form to the system. Models have a half life—some are ephemeral, others last for centuries. There are highly explicit models, while others are so much a part of life as to be unavailable for analysis except under very special circumstances.

In constructing their models of culture, most anthropologists take into account that there are different levels of behavior: overt and covert, implicit and explicit, things you talk about and things you do not. Also, that there is such a thing as the unconscious, although few are in agreement as to the degree to which the unconscious is influenced by culture. The psychologist Jung, for example, hypothecated a "collective" unconscious that was shared by all mankind (a concept many anthropologists might have trouble accepting). Paradoxically, studying the models that men create to explain nature tells you more about the men than about the part of nature being studied. In the West, people are more concerned with the content or meaning of the model than they are with how it is put together, is organized, or performs, and the purpose it is supposed to fulfill.

Anthropologists have studied only those things people could or would talk to them about, with the result that many of the important things—culture patterns that make life meaningful and really differentiate one group from another—have gone unnoticed or been unreported and brushed aside as trivial. If one were to use a linguistic analogy, it would be as though there were data on the vocabulary of culture but very little on either the syntactic (grammar) or phonemic systems (alphabets are based on a phonemic analysis). It is not enough to say that the French believe this and the Spanish believe that. Beliefs can change. Beneath the clearly perceived, highly explicit surface culture, there lies a whole other world, which when understood will ultimately radically change our view of human nature. Writing forty years ago, the linguist Sapir started the ball rolling by demonstrating that in language (an important part of culture) man created an instrument that is quite different from what is commonly supposed. He states:

> The relation between language and experience is often misunderstood . . . [it] actually defines experience for us by reason of its formal completeness and because of our unconscious projection of its implicit expectations into the field of experience. . . . [L]anguage is much like a mathematical system, which . . . becomes elaborated into a self-contained conceptual system which *previsages all possible experience* in accordance with certain accepted formal limitations. . . . [C]ategories such as number, gender, case, tense, mode, voice, "aspect" and a host of others . . . *are not so much discovered in experience as imposed* upon it. . . . (italics added)[12]

Sapir's work, which predates McLuhan by thirty-five years, not only makes a stronger, more detailed case than McLuhan that "the media is the message," but can be extended to include other cultural systems as well. In the process of evolving culture, the human species did much more than was at first supposed.

The usefulness of Sapir's model was demonstrated in a practical way by Kluckhohn and Leighton in their pioneering book *The Navajo*,[13] which illustrates the difficulties the verb-oriented Navajo children experienced when they attended white schools and were confronted by English—a loosely structured, adjective language. Kluckhohn and Leighton's basic point, however, was not only that differences in emphasis on adjectival and verbal forms caused difficulty in school, but that the total orientation of the two languages was different, forcing the two groups to attend and fail to attend entirely different things in nature. Having lived and dealt with Navajos for a number of years, I have no doubt not only that they think very differently from the white man, but that much of this difference is at least initially traceable to their language. Working with other cultural systems, I have found evidence that it is not just in language that one finds such constraints, but elsewhere as well, provided of course that one is fortunate enough to have studied cultures sufficiently different from one's own to bring its latent structures into focus.

In considering the data presented in this book, it is important for the reader to come to grips with his own model of culture in its manifest as well as its latent forms, because my purpose is to raise some of the latent to conscious awareness and to give it form so that it can be dealt with. Technically, the model of culture on which my work is based is more inclusive than those of some of my colleagues. My emphasis is on the nonverbal, unstated realm of culture. While I do not exclude philosophical systems, religion, social organization, language, moral values, art, and material culture, I feel it is more important to look at the way things are actually put together than at theories.

Nevertheless, and in spite of many differences in detail, anthropologists do agree on three characteristics of culture: it is not innate, but learned; the various facets of culture are interrelated—you touch a culture in one place and everything else is affected; it is shared and in effect defines the boundaries of different groups.

Culture is man's medium; there is not one aspect of human life that is not touched and altered by culture. This means personality, how people express themselves (including shows of emotion), the way they think, how they move, how problems are solved, how their cities are planned and laid out, how transportation systems function and are organized, as well as how economic and government systems are put together and function. However, like the purloined letter, it is frequently the most obvious and taken-for-granted and therefore the least studied aspects of culture that influence behavior in the deepest and most subtle ways.

As a case in point, let us examine how white Americans are captives of their own time and space systems—beginning with time. American time is what I have termed "monochronic"; that is, Americans, when they are serious, usually prefer to do one thing at a time, and this requires some kind of scheduling, either implicit or explicit. Not all of us conform to monochronic norms. Nevertheless, there are social and other pressures that keep most Americans within the monochronic frame. However, when Americans interact with people of foreign cultures, the different time systems cause great difficulty.

Monochronic time (M-time) and polychronic time (P-time) represent two variant solutions to the use of both time and space as organizing frames for activities. Space is included because the two systems (time and space) are functionally interrelated. M-time emphasizes schedules, segmentation, and promptness. P-time systems are characterized by several things happening at once. They stress involvement of people and completion of transactions rather than adherence to preset schedules. P-time is treated as much less tangible than M-time. P-time is apt to be considered a point rather than a ribbon or a road, and that point is sacred.[14]

Americans overseas are psychologically stressed in many ways when confronted by P-time systems such as those in Latin America and the Middle East. In the markets and stores of Mediterranean countries, one is surrounded by other customers vying for the attention of a clerk. There is no order as to who is served next,[15] and to the northern European or American, confusion and clamor abound. In a different context, the same patterns apply within the governmental bureaucracies of Mediterranean countries: A cabinet officer, for instance, may have a large reception area outside his private office. There are almost always small groups waiting in this area, and these groups are visited by government officials, who move around the room conferring with each. Much of their business is transacted in public instead of having a series of private meetings in an inner office. Particularly distressing to Americans is the way in which appointments are handled by polychronic people. Appointments just don't carry the same weight as they do in the United States. Things are constantly shifted around. Nothing seems solid or firm, particularly plans for the future, and there are always changes in the most important plans right up to the very last minute.

In contrast, within the Western world, man finds little in life that is exempt from the iron hand of M-time. In fact, his social and business life, even his sex life, are apt to be completely time-dominated. Time is so thoroughly woven into the fabric of existence that we are hardly aware of the degree to which it determines and co-ordinates everything we do, including the molding of relations with others in many subtle ways. By scheduling, we compartmentalize; this makes it possible to concentrate on one thing at a time, but it also denies us context. Since scheduling by its very nature selects what will and will not be perceived and attended and permits only a limited number of events within a given period, what gets scheduled in or out constitutes a system for setting priorities for both people and functions.[16] Important things are taken up first and allotted the most time; unimportant things are left to last or omitted if time runs out.[17]

Space and its handling also signal importance and priorities. The amount of space allocated and where a person is placed within an organization tell a lot about him and his relation to the organization. Equally significant is how he handles his time. In fact, discretion over scheduling—the option of determining

when one will be in the office—indicates that one has arrived.
The exceptions are salesmen, whose jobs demand that they be
away from their desks, or those who hold unusual positions, for
example the city editor of a newspaper, whose job is inherently
polychronic. The importance of place—where the activities are
permitted to occur—has become so much a part of modern bureaucracy that some employees whose performance would be
enormously enhanced if they could get away from their desks
are seldom permitted to do so. For example, American Foreign
Service officers assigned to Latin America should be out interacting with the local people, but because of immutable bureaucratic custom they can't leave their desks. Cut off from the people with whom they should be establishing ties, how can they
ever be effective? In another American-based bureaucracy, an
important and famous research program was threatened because
the space required for the experiments was greater than that appropriate to the rank of the investigator. Mad? Yes, completely
mad; but bureaucratically very real.

For M-time people reared in the northern European tradition,
time is linear and segmented like a road or a ribbon extending
forward into the future and backward to the past. It is also tangible; they speak of it as being saved, spent, wasted, lost, made
up, accelerated, slowed down, crawling, and running out. These
metaphors should be taken very seriously, because they express
the basic manner in which time is conceived as an unconscious
determinant or frame on which everything else is built. M-time
scheduling is used as a classification system that orders life.
With the exception of birth and death, all important activities
are scheduled. It should be mentioned that without schedules
and something very much like the M-time system, it is doubtful
if our industrial civilization could have developed as it has.
There are other consequences, however. Monochronic time seals
off one or two people from the group and intensifies relationships with one other person or, at most, two or three people.
M-time in this sense is like a room with a closed door that en-
sures privacy. The only problem is that you must vacate the
"room" at the end of fifteen minutes or an hour, a day, or a
week, depending on the schedule, and make way for the next

one in line. Failure to make way by intruding on the time of the person waiting is egocentric, narcissistic, and bad manners.

Monochronic time is arbitrary and imposed; that is, *learned*. Because it is so thoroughly learned and so thoroughly integrated into our culture, it is treated as though it were the only natural and "logical" way of organizing life. Yet it is not inherent in man's own rhythms and creative drives, nor is it existential in nature. Furthermore, organizations, particularly business and government bureaucracies, subordinate man to the organization, and they accomplish this mainly by the way they handle time-space systems.

Everything in our lives must be fitted to the Procrustean demands of the schedule. As any American can tell you, there are times when things are just beginning to develop in the desired way; yet they must be stopped to conform to a preset schedule. Example: research funds run out just as the results are beginning to be achieved. How often has the reader had the experience of realizing that he is pleasurably immersed in some creative activity, totally unaware of time, solely conscious of the job at hand, only to be brought back to "reality" with the rude shock of realizing that other, preset, frequently inconsequential commitments are bearing down on him?

From this, we see that many Americans make the common mistake of associating the schedule with reality and one's self or the activity as something that is removed from life. M-time can alienate us from ourselves and deny us the experience of context in the wider sense. That is, M-time narrows one's view of events in much the same way as looking through a cardboard tube narrows vision, and it influences subtly and in depth how we think —in segmented compartments.

Possibly, this restriction of context explains in part the difficulty that American enterprises have in adapting to other time systems. An economist once told me that Eskimos working for a fish cannery in Alaska thought factory whistles were ridiculous. The idea that men would work or not work because of a whistle seemed to them sheer lunacy. For the Eskimo, the tides determined what men did, how long they did it, and when they did it. Tide out meant one set of activities; tide in, another. This same man later worked in a large international agency and observed in himself signs of stress resulting from futile attempts to gear his own productivity, particularly its creative aspects, to a time schedule. Finally, convinced that it was impossible to schedule creativity, he gave up trying and compromised by adopting a schedule in which there were periods when he was tied to a desk and handled trivia, followed by other periods in which he worked around the clock. One wonders how many individuals who have been forced to adjust to eight-hour, nine-to-five schedules have sacrificed their creativity, and what the social and human cost of this sacrifice has been.

Time and space are functions of each other. How can you meet a deadline if you are constantly interrupted, for example? How much you are interrupted depends on how available you are. And how available you are is a matter of how well you are screened from others. Also, how can a doctor listen deeply and carefully to a patient's account of his life without proper screening? It's impossible. I am referring here to ideal patterns. Many people have to put up with spaces that cripple them in the performance of their jobs. Some of this comes about because of the tight way in which space, as well as time, is locked into the bureaucratic ranking system. It is quite clear, for example, that case workers in welfare departments require the privacy of an office, yet the rank of their activity and the low status accorded the needy are such as to make an office bureaucratically unfeasible (offices are for "important" people). Incongruities of this type at all levels, where the requirements of the activity call for one thing and the organizational needs for something else, endow much of life with an Alice in Wonderland quality.

It is in this respect that cultures also contrast with each other; polychronic people, such as the Arabs and the Turks, who are almost never alone, even in the home, make different uses of screening.[18] They interact with several people at once and are continually involved with each other. Scheduling is difficult if not impossible with P-time people unless they have mastered M-time technically as a very different system, one they do not confuse with their own but use when it is situationally appropriate, much as they use a foreign language.

Theoretically, when considering social organization, P-time systems should demand a much greater centralization of control and be characterized by a rather shallow or simple structure. This is because the top man deals continually with many people, most of whom stay informed as to what is happening: they are around in the same spaces, are brought up to be deeply involved with each other, and continually ask questions to stay informed. In these circumstances, delegation of authority and a build-up in bureaucratic levels should not be required to handle high volumes of business. The principal shortcomings of P-type bureaucracies are that as functions increase, one would expect to find a proliferation of small bureaucracies as well as difficulty in handling the problems of outsiders. In fact, outsiders traveling or residing in Mediterranean countries find the bureaucracies unusually unresponsive. In polychronic countries, one has to be an insider or else have a "friend" who can make things happen. All bureaucracies are oriented inward, but P-type are especially so.

There are also interesting points to be made concerning the act of administration as it is conceived in these two settings. Administration and control of polychronic peoples (in the Middle East and Latin America) is a matter of job analysis. Administration consists of taking each subordinate's job and identifying the activities that go to make up the job. These are then named and frequently indicated on the elaborate charts with checks that make it possible for the administrator to be sure that each function has been performed. In this way, it is felt, absolute control is maintained over the individual. Yet, how and when each activity is actually attended to is up to the employee. To schedule his activities for him would be considered a tyrannical violation of his individuality.

In contrast, M-time people schedule the activity and leave the analysis of the parts of the job to the individual. A P-type analysis, even though technical by its very nature, keeps reminding the subordinate that his job is a system and is also part of a larger system. M-type people, by virtue of compartmentalization, are less likely to see their activities in context as part of the larger whole. This does not mean that they are unaware of the

"organization"—far from it; only that the job itself or even
the goals of the organization are seldom seen in larger contexts.
Again, placing the organization above what it is supposedly
doing is common in our culture and is epitomized in our allow-
ing the TV commercial, the "special message," to break the con-
tinuity of even the most important communication. By way of
contrast, in Spain I once counted twenty-one commercials
lumped together at the end of an hour's program. The
polychronic Spanish quite sensibly put the commercials between the major programs, not within them.

Both systems have strengths as well as weaknesses. There is a
limit to the speed with which jobs can be analyzed, although
once analyzed, proper reporting can enable a P-time administrator to handle a surprising number of subordinates. Nevertheless,
organizations run on the polychronic model are limited in size,
depend on having gifted men at the top, and are slow and cum-
bersome when dealing with the business of outsiders. Without
gifted men, a P-type bureaucracy can be a disaster, as many people know. P-type models proliferate bureaucracies as a way of
handling greater demands on the system.

M-type organizations go in the opposite direction. They can
and do grow much larger than the P-type. However, they combine instead of proliferating bureaucracies—e.g., consolidated
schools, the business conglomerate, and the new superdepart-
ments we are developing in government today.

The particular blindness of the monochronic organization is
to the humanness of its members. The weakness of the
polychronic type lies in their extreme dependence on the head
man to handle contingencies and stay on top of things. M-type
bureaucracies, as they grow larger, turn inward, becoming blind
to their own structure; they grow rigid and are even apt to lose
sight of their original purpose. Prime examples are the Army
Corps of Engineers and the Bureau of Reclamation, which
wreak havoc on our environment in their dedicated efforts to
stay in business by building dams or hurrying the flow of rivers
to the sea.

Monochronic and polychronic have to do with the way time
and space are organized and how this organization affects the

very core of existence. We can look at things in such a way as to transcend culture and, in so doing, generalize about how culture is organized. One of these generalizations concerns the subtle but complex relationship between meaning and context described in Chapters 6, 7, and 8. Another deals with man as a producer of extensions which in turn mold his life (Chapter 2). What the ethologist calls action chains (Chapter 10) and the situational frame and situational dialect (Chapter 9) are all structural features of unconscious culture. Possibly because they are so ubiquitous, man's extensions will be taken up next.

2. Man as Extension

Nineteenth-century naturalists suggested that mammals were divided into two groups—man and all other mammals; they also thought that birds should be divided into two groups—bowerbirds and all other birds. These categorizations resulted from the observation that both man and the bowerbird have elaborated their extensions and in so doing have greatly accelerated their evolution. The bowerbird occupies the jungles and thickets of New Guinea and northern Australia and, as its name implies, builds a bower with which to attract and woo its mate. The elaborate bower, constructed of twigs and grass, is decorated with shells, iridescent skeletons of insects, seeds, clay balls, charcoal, pebbles, and brightly colored objects including freshly picked flowers. Actually, the bower and its decoration is not only an extension of once brilliant plumage but also of courtship displays as well. As Gilliard[1] states, ". . . these objects have in effect become *externalized* bundles of secondary sexual characteristics that are psychologically but not physically connected with the males" (italics added). Behind the bower lie some radical changes in social organization and behavior. The bowerbirds belong to a group of birds who no longer pair off (pair bonding) with the opposite sex to mate, nest, and raise the young. Instead, males gather in clans (separate from the females) in which they rank themselves hierarchically. In the spring, the clans are formed around "arenas" in which display and mating take place. Each bird has its own private display court, called a lek. Dominant birds occupy the central position in the arena and only the dominant males mate with females that visit the arena. Reminiscent of wealthy, powerful men, the birds who have colorful bowers with the most baubles are dominant in the bowerbird hierarchy.

A story of the evolution of the bowerbird is complex and subtle. What we learn from it is that once the bird begins to evolve by extension, evolution speeds up, as is the case with man. It is no longer necessary to wait for the slower forces of natural selection to work. In the case of the bowerbird, according to Gilliard it is possible to ". . . cross into a new adaptive zone, . . ."[2] which is precisely what man has done, only more completely.

The evolution of the bowerbird is highly suggestive as an example of how a species, once it begins to use the environment as a tool, sets in motion a whole series of new and often unforeseen environmental transactions that require further adjustments. Until now, only short-lived organisms of very small size could evolve rapidly,[3] but extensions can be evolved much faster than the body. The automobile and the airplane evolved from dreams in men's minds, through many simple and inadequate forms to the complex machines we know today.

More, much more, should be known about the whole process of extension. No other species even approaches man in the elaboration of evolution by extension. Both quantitatively and qualitatively, the gap is too great between man and other species to say much more than, when the process begins, evolution accelerates drastically; therefore, because man is unique in this regard, he can learn only from himself. Unfortunately, studies of material extension as process are rare, because all but a few early anthropologists felt there was little to be learned from material culture—one of our most readily available extension[4] systems. With the exception of those interested in primitive art, the early anthropologists were academicians, facile with words but with little feeling for what material things could tell them.

Inventions and scientific break-throughs are real and have their beginnings in looking at things differently. They do not spring full-blown from Zeus's brow, but evolve slowly from very fragile and imperfect events. Let's take a look at the extension process,[4] keeping in mind that what we are examining is one of several ways of meeting environmental challenges.

No organism can survive without altering its environment in some way, if merely to reorganize the chemicals in its immediate vicinity. Altering the environment can be broken down into two complementary processes, *externalizing* and *internalizing*, which are ubiquitous, continuous, and normal. In man, these processes can be adaptive mechanisms as well as controls. Which one of the two processes is used has important consequences for everything that follows. For instance, the conscience is a good example of an internalized control on which much of Western society depends. If the conscience does not function, we have what is known as a psychopath, dangerous to everyone. However, actions that are under the control of what we call the conscience in one part of the world may be handled by externalized controls elsewhere. The reason a given set of controls is internalized in one culture and externalized in another has not been studied. The difference, however, can be observed even in closely related cultures. For example, in the northern European tradition until very recently, sexual controls were vested in the woman for the most part; i.e., internalized. In southern Europe this was not so. The controls were in the situation—people—and in physical structures—doors and locks. For years, people in middle- and upper-class Latin America believed that the sexual drive was so strong in men and the capacity of women to resist was so weak, that if a man and a woman were alone together behind closed doors neither could be expected to be able to resist the overwhelming power of the man's drive. Walls, doors, and locks were a physical extension of morality —externalizations of processes handled internally by middle-class North Americans.

It is also paradoxical that extensional systems—so flexible at first—frequently become quite rigid and difficult to change. Confusion between the extension and the processes that have been extended can explain some but not all of this rigidity. Older readers may remember when English teachers tried to convince them that the real language was the written language, of which the spoken language was merely a watered-down, adulterated version. Actually, the spoken language is the primary extension. The written language is a second-generation extension.

The spoken language is a symbolization of something that happened, could have happened, or is in the process of happening, while the written language is a symbolization of the spoken language. The fact that the written language is a symbolization of a symbolization does not mean that the writing system is not something in its own right, just as mathematics is a system in its own right, independent of computations in the head.

Extension transference (ET) is the term I have given to this common intellectual maneuver in which the extension is confused with or takes the place of the process extended. The ET factor, and the stresses it engenders both actual and conceptual, have occupied some of the most brilliant minds in Western culture. James Joyce,[5] for example, dedicated his life to trying to close the gap between the two systems. In *Finnegans Wake*, Joyce portrays in writing the workings of the verbal parts of the brain. Many of Picasso's paintings and Moore's sculptures provide visual as well as tactile analogues of Joyce, i.e., externalizations of the visual processes of the brain. If Picasso and Moore had not been brilliant and insightful and had not set their sights on piercing the ET screen—if there had not been something there that was real—they would have been treated as cranks instead of as geniuses. Extension transference takes many forms and can be dealt with in many ways. Alfred Korzybski and Wendell Johnson,[6] founders of semantics, identified the ET factor in the use of words and published extensively on the profound effects of mistaking the symbol for the thing symbolized while endowing the symbol with properties it does not possess. Worshiping idols, common to all cultures, represents one of the earliest examples of the ET factor. In the Bible, we see this when men are directed to give up the worship of "graven images."

Extensions often permit man to solve problems in satisfactory ways, to evolve and adapt at great speed without changing the basic structure of his body.[7] However, the extension does something else: it permits man to examine and perfect what is inside the head. Once something is externalized, it is possible to look at it, study it, change it, perfect it, and at the same time learn important things about oneself. The full implications of the extension as lesson and the extension as mirror have yet to be fully realized.

The extension can also serve as a form of prosthesis when something happens to the processes that lie behind the extension. The Russian scientist Luria[8] probably has as deep an understanding of the marvels and complexities of the human brain as any man alive. Luria's genius lies in his ability to recognize the significance of what might otherwise be taken as trivial. His experiments and tests of loss of brain function are so clear, direct, and simple, they can be understood by children; yet somehow he manages to put everything together in such a way that the whole can be grasped. The relationship of brain to extension is the central issue of the processes described in this chapter, and we are fortunate enough to have one of Luria's cases to illustrate the extension as prosthesis. In *The Man with a Shattered World*,[9] Luria has collected and commented on the writings of a Russian engineer, named Zasetsky, whose brain was shattered by a German bullet in World War II. Zasetsky's frontal lobe was left intact, which gave him the will to overcome—in the course of twenty-five years—some of the dreadful damage he had suffered. When the bullet struck, it wiped out the past, the brain's ability to organize sensory perceptions into meaningful wholes, the ability to analyze the feedback systems that told him what his extremities were doing, middle- and long-term memory, the logic of grammar, and the relationship of words to their referents (the actual objects referred to). To Zasetsky it was like being without a mind. Fortunately, he still had a reservoir of words and was able, with help, to begin to use them. Painfully and with great difficulty, he put sentences together. The sentences became his world, and writing his way of thinking!

Now, writing as a way of thinking is not extraordinary. Many of us, who do not carry words in our heads, think this way by translating our thoughts into written words. For Zasetsky, however, it was the *only* way he could think. His case simply drives home the point because there was no other way. Because the written text stands still—like a block of marble being carved by a sculptor—it is then possible to work on a thought until it takes form and can stand on its own feet and in the process tell us something about ourselves.

Descriptive linguists in the tradition of Sapir and Whorf were the first to hint at some of the newer variants on the close relationships between language and thought. Whorf,[10] who was also a chemist and insurance investigator, became initially interested in language because of the frequently disastrous consequences that misuse of words had on people. "Empty" gasoline drums caused fires and explosions; instead of being empty, the drums were "full" of gasoline fumes! Whorf's greatest contribution to Western thinking lay in his meticulous descriptions of the relationship of language to events in a cross-cultural context. He demonstrated that cultures have unique ways of relating language to reality of all sorts, which can be one of man's principal sources of information concerning cultural differences. Nothing happens in the world of human beings that is not deeply influenced by linguistic forms. The Hopi, for example, who are rather pragmatic, exacting people, had difficulty understanding the mythical world of Christianity because they had no abstract, empty spaces without reference to other sensory experience. Heaven as a concept just didn't fit Hopi thought.

While few discoveries are ever really lost, Whorf, a hundred years ahead of his time, carved out an entire field, which has, sadly, been abandoned. His work, as well as that of his mentor, Edward Sapir,[11] while not currently fashionable, was truly brilliant and opened up entire new vistas concerning the incredible diversity of mankind. However, in spite of their brilliance, both Whorf and Sapir apparently fell into the ET trap. That is, they believed that language *was* thought. In a sense, they were correct if one looks only at the incredible influence that language exerts on thought. To escape this particular trap, we must take into consideration people such as Einstein, who did not think with words,[12] but in visual and even muscular terms, a topic that is discussed in Chapter 12.

A variation of the extension-transference theme is that if the ET process in second- and third-generation extensions has gone far enough, the first-generation extension is overshadowed and frequently viewed as though it had had no structure. This was discovered by Charles Ferguson, one of America's leading descriptive linguists and Arabic specialists, while he was working on an orthography and grammar for colloquial Arabic. In the Arab world, classical Arabic (which is also the written language) is sacred. Classical Arabic is almost as distinct from colloquial Arabic as French is from Latin. The educated Arabs learn classical Arabic in schools, speak it on certain formal occasions, and are ranked by how fluently and beautifully they write and speak. At other times, they use the colloquial form of the language.

The fact that there was no written colloquial language meant that children going to schools had the task of not only learning a new language but learning to read and write as well. Ferguson was working at the Foreign Service Institute of the State Department, where it was felt that at least a few U.S. personnel could benefit from being able to speak "the language of the people." Experts and Middle Eastern specialists, of course, had always been expected to learn the "prestige" language, the "real" language—classical Arabic.

Since there were no colloquial grammars, it was necessary to derive one from the living language—which is one of the things that descriptive linguists can do. Ferguson went to work. His first discovery was the common belief among Arabs that colloquial Arabic was not a language at all and that it had no structure! So how could he possibly study it? Ferguson's informants told him that it didn't really matter how one used colloquial Arabic. Nevertheless, thirty minutes with a native speaker would reveal that there were correct and incorrect ways of saying everything. The rules, though unstated, were just as binding as though set in concrete.

Labov[13] *et al.* have described a comparable but not identical situation in regard to black English. Lower-class black children in the United States would come to school equipped with a rich and *different* dialect ideally suited to the multiple needs of black culture, only to be told that what they spoke was a degraded, substandard form of English.

Everywhere I have been in the world, the ET factor was discovered to be a principal source of alienation from self and heritage (the two are often synonymous). When a teacher tells a student that what he learns in school is valid and real and what he grew up with is wrong, the student may have vague misgivings and experience momentary anxiety. But what is he to do? From that moment on, there is an ever-deepening chasm that permanently separates perceived life from reality.[14] The reader will undoubtedly have examples of his own to illustrate the extension-transference process.

Another frequently dysfunctional characteristic of ET systems is that they can be moved around and inappropriately applied. This is understandable, because it takes years and even lifetimes to develop a good extension system. (Sometimes we call them paradigms when they take a grammatical or rule-making or modeling form.) In the days following the opening of Japan to the outside world, American missionaries wrote their own grammars for teaching Japanese to each other. Anyone who has seen one of these early grammars knows that the missionaries projected their own, Indo-European grammatical forms onto Japanese without any reference to the actual structure of the Japanese language. Nominative, genitive, dative, and ablative cases all appear in the grammars with identical Japanese words under each. A characteristic of transference phenomena is that people will treat the transferred system as the only reality and apply it indiscriminately to new situations. I once knew an American woman in Tokyo who became so resentful of the Foreign Service Institute language drill designed to reinforce the learning of proper Japanese that she simply struck out on her own. She said, "The devil with all these honorifics. I'm not going to learn them. I will simply learn vocabulary." What she spoke, of course, was a most dreadful, unintelligible mélange of Japanese words and English grammar.

Something similar has happened to significant blocks of social science. Not only has there been extension transference (not data, but methodology is thought of as the real science), but because physical science has been so successful, the paradigms of the so-called hard sciences were transferred intact to social science, where they are seldom, if ever, appropriate. Garrett Hardin, a professor of ecology at the University of California at

Santa Barbara, has explained the situation in social science as a consequence of a world view borrowed from physics. He states that the physicist ". . . sees the world as composed of isolated atomic units with no real relations to one another . . ."[15] except mere side-by-side juxtaposition and external bumpings. That is, the world of the physicist leads him to think linearly. This approach has been successful and is so prestigious that it is doubly seductive to other disciplines.

The ET factor in social science has also been recently and elegantly described by Martin[16] and Andreski.[17] Ultimately, when ET distortions become too great and the discrepancy between reality and the extension system is so evident that it can no longer be ignored, people become uncomfortable and begin to do something about it. However, the discontinuities can be horrendous before a revolution occurs.

Now popularly acclaimed, the ET process is at work in technology as well, with the result that technology has become an end in itself and is viewed as *the* arena of study and problem solving in today's troubled world—problem solving not by social scientists but by engineers. World problems such as food and housing are seen as technological by even such advanced thinkers as Buckminster Fuller.[18] While I agree with Fuller that we should do "more with less," the story does not end there, nor is the future of Alvin Toffler[19] inevitable.

Recently, people have turned away from technological solutions toward the more integrated study of the dynamics of living processes. The case of insecticides is an example. Nowadays when a pest causes too much damage, one finds biologists and ethologists beginning to look for the pest's natural enemies. Rather than killing everything in sight (as many pesticides do), scientists now try to develop a specific program that zeros in on the pest and does not leave a residue to be concentrated ten millionfold as it ascends the food chain.[20]

Public and private education is another example of the lengths to which ET distortions can go. Not only children but people of all ages have the capacity to learn naturally. What is more, learning can be its own reward. Like eating and sex, the drive to learn is powerful indeed. Yet the process has been distorted in the minds of the educators, who have confused what they call education with learning. The popular notion is that the schools contain the learning and their job is somehow to get the learning into the child. In the United States, the process of distortion in education has progressed to a point comparable to sex in Freud's nineteenth-century Vienna. A natural, powerful, pleasureful drive that binds people to each other is not only feared but hated, which may explain some of the attitudes toward the intellectual in our country.

There are, however, many, many ways as well as conditions in which people learn. For millions of years, man and his predecessors learned without the benefit of schools.[21] Modern education has left us with the illusion that a lot is known about learning, that real learning goes on in the school, and that if it doesn't happen in a school or under the aegis of a school (like the year abroad), it has no validity. Holt,[22] Kozol,[23] Illich,[24] and others have written about this process. Education is simply one more instance of man's having developed an elaborate extension (in this case, complex institutions) to do and presumably enhance what he once did for himself quite naturally.

One purpose of an extension is to enhance a particular function of the organism: the knife does a much better job of cutting than the teeth (but not of chewing). Language and mathematics enhance certain aspects of thinking. But, like the knife, they don't do the whole job. The telescope and the microscope extend the eye, while the camera extends the visual memory system. Wheels enable man to get around faster, but they can't dance or climb cliffs, and when they are powered by motors, atrophy of important body functions can result.

Possibly most important of all, an extended function reveals something of the process from which it springs. There is a discovery factor as well as an emergent property to extensions. Language is a prime example. The linguist Chomsky[25] has used language to tell him something of how he thinks certain portions of the brain are organized, and while Chomsky's main conclusions are not in my mind supported by what is known about either language or the brain, he is correct in looking to language for a map of a particular part of the brain.

Man's mechanical extensions tell us not only about man's brain, but about his body as well. At this point, the reader may have some trouble personalizing what has just been said. Many of man's extensions really are expressions of his basic nature, but we also learn from this that man has *many* basic natures. From our extensions, we begin to get a picture of the incredible diversity of human talent. Consider the people who have neither feeling for nor understanding of machines, and confront them with people who do. Or consider the miracle of composing music and writing poetry, or the beauty of mathematics to those who understand it, compared to the mystery of it all to those who do not. Science and art are direct products of the human central nervous system. Yet the ET factor frequently blinds us to the miracle of it all. If there ever was an example of the externalization process, it is the institution called science. To experience some of the impact of this process, one must think back upon the times when Egyptian and Sumerian priests were attempting for the first time to systematize quantities and magnitudes—systems for measuring and recording plots of land—in the Middle East deltas, just as the Phoenician traders were beginning to record the position of the stars to navigate by. In terms of my earlier formulations,[26] those shared systems that are carried in the head are informal. The technical ones are externalized, i.e. extended, and carried on outside the body. The process of externalizing is continuous and is illustrated by Einstein's efforts to transform his mental insights into either words or mathematics[27]—two extensional systems that were ready-made and waiting at the time of Einstein's birth. What captivated Einstein was the incredible beauty of mathematics. He felt a deep kinship with this picture of the mind, though I am not sure that he realized that this is what mathematics is. The exciting thing about mathematics and science and music and literature is what they can tell us about the workings of the human mind. For these disciplines are literally models of at least certain parts of the mind. Just as the knife cuts but does not chew, while the lens does only a portion of what the eye can do, extensions are reductionist in their capability. No matter how hard it tries, the human race can never fully replace what was left out of extensions in the first place. Also, it is just as important to know what is left out of a given extension system as it is to know what the system will do. Yet the extension-omissions side is frequently overlooked.

It is the characteristic of all extension systems to be treated as distinct and separate from the user and to take on an identity of their own. Religions, philosophies, literature, and art illustrate this. After a time, the extended system accretes to itself a past and a history as well as a body of knowledge and skills that can be learned. Such systems can be studied and appreciated as entities in themselves. Culture is the prime example.[28]

Another important feature of extensions is that they make possible the sharing of human talents that could be accomplished in no other way. One does not have to be able to write poetry, compose music, or paint in order to derive pleasure from the arts. The technically gifted who design and produce automobiles, radios, and TV sets multiply their talent a millionfold: every time a viewer turns on his TV set, he shares the creative talents of hundreds of other minds.

The study of man is a study of his extensions. It is now possible to actually see evolution taking place, an evolution that occurs outside the organism and at a greatly accelerated pace when compared to intrinsic evolution. Man has dominated the earth because his extensions have evolved so fast that there is nothing to stand in their way. The risk, of course, is that by enormously multiplying his power, man is in the position of being able to destroy his own biotope—that part of the environment that contains within it the basic elements for satisfying human needs. Unfortunately, because they do have a life of their own, extensions have a way of taking over. The mathematical genius Norbert Wiener,[29] shortly before he died, saw the danger of his brain child, the computer, and warned against letting it play too prominent a role in human affairs. The automobile is another mechanical system that has so many people and so much of the American economy dependent on it that it is difficult to see, short of catastrophe, any possibility of reversing the take-over trend. Everything has fallen to the automobile —the livability of cities, the countryside, clean air, healthy bodies, etc.

Extensions fragment life and dissociate man from his acts. This is serious. Modern warfare is a dreadful example of how mechanical systems can be used to kill at a distance without any involvement in the process. It is so easy for a president to say, "Drop more bombs, and that will bring them in line."

The characteristic of extension systems that is potentially most harmful and requires constant vigilance is illustrated by this example of a young psychotherapist who is talking to his mentor following a lecture in which certain basic psychiatric connections were made in a new way: Seeking practical advice on the application of his guru's thinking, the younger man brings up the case of one of his patients. His request for help is rebuffed with an impatient gesture and the comment, "That doesn't count, that's real life." In this instance, the two men are struggling with the difficulty of reconciling the complexity of real life with theory—a third or fourth step in a long process of abstraction from life. The danger is that real-life problems are dismissed while philosophical and theoretical systems are treated as real. I see this every day in my students. It has been my experience that after students have spent sixteen or more years in our education system they have been so brainwashed that it is impossible to get them to go out and simply observe and report back what they heard, what they felt, or what went on before their eyes. Most of them are helpless in the face of real life, because they have to know beforehand what they are going to discover and have a theory or a hypothesis to test. Why? Because that is the way they have been taught. What is more, for those who go on for advanced degrees, that is the way they will get their money for research and their "brownie points" for publication.

If people are to live wisely on this earth, they must be more aware of how different kinds of extensions work and the influence they exert upon all of us. For instance, the way in which information is stored in a given social system and how it flows influences how mechanical extensions are integrated. In cultures in which people are deeply involved with each other, and cultures such as the American Indian, in which information is widely shared—what we will term high-context cultures—simple messages with deep meaning flow freely. Such cultures are likely to be overwhelmed by mechanical systems and lose their integrity.[30] The low-context cultures, those highly individualized, somewhat alienated, fragmented cultures such as the Swiss and the German, in which there is relatively little involvement with people, can apparently absorb and use man's mechanical extensions without losing their cultural integrity. In these cultures, people become more and more like their machines. Even here in the United States one can see what technology has done to rural areas. The small community of a hundred years ago, while it has not vanished, is becoming more and more rare as young people go to towns and cities, where there are work and action.

People learn to speak their language, to read, skate, ride bicycles, fly, and ski. Man learns to use his extensions but pays little attention to what lies behind them. Some of them can be extraordinarily complex, such as the tools of "science" or the weapons of war. But they can all tell us a great deal about ourselves. There was a time (two to four million years ago) when man's extensions were limited to a few crude tools and the rudiments of language. Man's basic nature has changed very little since then. All of culture is a complex system of extensions. Therefore, culture is subject to the ET syndrome and all that it implies. That is, culture is experienced as man, and vice versa. What is more, man is frequently seen as a pale reflection of his culture or as a shoddy version that never quite measures up, and man's basic humanness is frequently overlooked or repressed in the process.

From now on, how one arrives at a definition of the relationship of man's basic nature to his culturally conditioned control systems is of crucial importance. For in our shrinking globe man can ill afford cultural illiteracy.

3. Consistency and Life

Man's nervous system evolved before the time of mass media, mass transportation, airplanes, and automobiles. For over a million years, our forefathers knew the significance of every act of all the individuals around them. Like the body language of a dog who wags his tail and prances with forepaws spread out, saying, "Let's play," or raises the hair on his back, saying, "Stay away," the physical signs as well as the behavioral cues of people who were known were easy to read. Stability and predictability were essential if human society was to prosper, develop, and evolve to its present point. Living today in a rapidly changing, ever-shrinking world, it is hard for most of us to conceive what it would be like to grow up and live in a world that did not change, and where there were few strangers because one always saw and dealt with the same people. Those who were raised in the now-disappearing small town have some notion of what it must have been like during the major portion of man's past— quite comfortable and reassuring, but very public. People knew what was coming next before you did something or even knew that you were going to do it. "Jake's going to get a new horse." "Yup. He always fattens up the old one before he trades. Too cheap to feed 'em the rest of the time."

"You can always tell when Mike's getting ready to take somebody apart. First, he gets up and walks around, then he looks out the window with his back to everyone, pulls out his pocket comb and gets every hair in place. When he turns around and looks at them, you know it's going to happen."

Unlike animals, many of whose responses are innate, much of

man's communicative behavior evolved independently of his physiology, and like the spoken language, it cannot be read with assurance if one is dealing with a new culture or even a subculture one does not know well. Man's body is recognizably human everywhere, even though such superficial characteristics as skin color, hair form, physiognomy, and body build may vary. Unless we start tampering with it, this panhuman form will be with us for thousands of generations to come. What has changed, what has evolved, and what is characteristically man— in fact, what gives man his identity no matter where he is born—is his culture, the total communication framework: words, actions, postures, gestures, tones of voice, facial expressions, the way he handles time, space, and materials, and the way he works, plays, makes love, and defends himself. All these things and more are complete communication systems with meanings that can be read correctly only if one is familiar with the behavior in its historical, social, and cultural context.[1]

Everything man is and does is modified by learning and is therefore malleable. But once learned, these behavior patterns, these habitual responses, these ways of interacting gradually sink below the surface of the mind and, like the admiral of a submerged submarine fleet, control from the depths. The hidden controls are usually experienced as though they were innate simply because they are not only ubiquitous but habitual as well.[2]

What makes it doubly hard to differentiate the innate from the acquired is the fact that, as people grow up, everyone around them shares the same patterns. This is not true, of course, if one grows up in a bicultural or tricultural situation, which can be a tremendous asset because it accustoms one to the fact that people are really very different in the ways they behave. In bicultural cases, I have seen people shift from a Spanish to a German way of interacting without knowing that the shift occurred. Also, I have seen others start with a Greek pattern and slip automatically into a German-Swiss pattern as the situation demanded.

Fantastic? Yes, but reasonably common—a function of the way the information-processing and control mechanisms of the brain operate, points that will be described in Chapter 12. In fact, according to Powers,[3] man's nervous system is structured in such a way that the patterns that govern behavior and perception come into consciousness only when there is a deviation from plan. That is why the most important paradigms or rules governing behavior, the ones that control our lives, function below the level of conscious awareness and are not generally available for analysis. This is an important point, one that is often overlooked or denied. The cultural unconscious, like Freud's unconscious, not only controls man's actions but can be understood only by painstaking processes of detailed analysis. Hence, man automatically treats what is most characteristically his own (the culture of his youth) as though it were innate. He is forced into the position of thinking and feeling that anyone whose behavior is not predictable or is peculiar in any way is slightly out of his mind, improperly brought up, irresponsible, psychopathic, politically motivated to a point beyond all redemption, or just plain inferior.

A comment one frequently hears in cross-cultural situations is: "Oh, I just try to be myself and take them as they are. After all, they are adult human beings, aren't they?" Fine and dandy. In superficial social situations, the be-yourself formula works. But what if you are an Anglo schoolteacher with a Spanish American class and are confronted with what appears to be a lack of motivation on the part of your students? You, as a non-Spanish American take it for granted that a certain percentage of children want to do well and to get ahead. So it comes as a shock when you learn that, to many New Mexican Spanish, to stand out from one's peers is to place oneself in great jeopardy and is to be avoided at all costs. Suddenly, your old stereotypes take on a new meaning.

Today, man is increasingly placed in positions in which culture can no longer be depended upon to produce reliable readings of what other people are going to do next. He is constantly in the position of interacting with strangers, so he must take the next step and begin to transcend his culture. This cannot be done in an armchair.

However, what may at first be experienced as a very difficult chore can turn out to be deeply and personally significant. In this context, it is important to keep reminding oneself that the part of man's nervous system that deals with social behavior is designed according to the principle of negative feedback. That is, one is completely unaware of the fact that there is a system of controls as long as the program is followed. Ironically, this means that the majority of mankind are denied knowledge of important parts of the self by virtue of the way the control systems work. The only time one is aware of the control system is when things don't follow the hidden program. This is most frequent in intercultural encounters. Therefore, the great gift that the members of the human race have for each other is not exotic experiences but an opportunity to achieve awareness of the structure of their *own* system, which can be accomplished only by interacting with others who do not share that system—members of the opposite sex, different age groups, different ethnic groups, and different cultures—all suffice. I never would have understood the degree to which Americans use time, not only to structure their lives but as a contexting communication system as well, if I had not been through the experience of observing my countrymen trying to cope with other time systems. That logic, clear thinking, and nature were not all part of a single bundle became clear to me only after I had been to Japan and again found my countrymen frustrated by what they called "indirection." It was also evident that the Japanese were equally turned off by our insisting on spelling out "logical" steps without reference to context. The Japanese are very consistent once you get to know them, but unpredictable if you don't. Admittedly, it is difficult for hard-nosed American businessmen to deal with indirection and accustom themselves to the fact that in Japan verbal agreements are binding and much preferred to the ironbound written contract of the West, which can always be nullified or abrogated anyway.

Overseas, the picture one gets of Americans is that they are distrustful and frequently paranoid in their relations with each other. Our word is not our bond. One gathers from this that the creative use of intercultural relations exposes some very deep, highly personalized, and sensitive areas of the psyche. This may

explain why the more significant aspects of culture are so
frequently and persistently brushed aside. Take the matter of
not trusting people, so that everything has to be on the dotted
line. If we Americans are honest with ourselves, our experiences
with other cultures could teach us a good deal about what it is
like to live in a trusting world. Perhaps then we would not be
quite so fearful of others.

In studying one's self by the cross-cultural technique, one
starts with the notion that what is known least well and is
therefore in the poorest position to be studied is what is closest
to oneself; as stated above, these are the unconscious patterns
that control one's life. In the past, and at home, it was the
shared patterns that made life predictable and provided the
order that can be observed in all nature.

Those of us who have embarked on the task of understanding
ourselves and others abroad have encountered scenes that are
almost beyond belief—not at all what our own culturally conditioned projective systems led us to expect. The mental maps
that we carry with us, based as they are on our own cultural experience, are little better than those Columbus had when he
sailed west to find India in 1492. There are even great conti-
nents yet to be discovered—vast areas of human experience
about which Western man knows nothing. Remember, our own
maps are of territory known so completely—like one's home-
town neighborhood—that there is no need to make them explicit. The fact that they are in our heads is sufficient. It's only
in strange territory that one needs a true externalized, tangible
chart.

Most cultural exploration begins with the annoyance of being
lost. The control systems of the mind signal that something
unexpected has arisen, that we are in uncharted waters and are
going to have to switch off the automatic pilot and man the
helm ourselves. There's a reef where we least expect it. Sadly
enough, people in real-life situations don't actually see it this
way, because the almost inevitable response is to deny that the
reef is there until one has run aground.

I once had occasion to decipher a rather extraordinary pattern
in a small country in the Far East where there were very few

Americans. The members of the U.S. official missions were the only Americans in the country. Exquisitely beautiful, and populated with people who were kind, friendly and gentle, the country was as close to a tropical paradise as one could find. But there was a fly in the ointment. On official visits, the Americans were kept waiting inordinately long. It was almost as though they weren't there. Some waited for hours. Even the newly appointed U.S. ambassador was kept waiting! In ordinary diplomatic circumstances such treatment would constitute an official insult to our government. Yet something told the Americans that this might not be the case; there were too many cues to the contrary. Besides, relations between the two countries were friendly and there was no reason to insult everyone indiscriminately, even before the first meeting. The Americans were mystified, of course. For those familiar with Southeast Asia, horoscopes will come to mind, because there was always the added complication of horoscopes which had to be cast before all important events. In fact, the astrologer's reading prefaced every form of involvement. Yet the horoscope did not seem to be the significant variable in the long, heel-cooling reception-room delays, because the neighboring countries, where horoscopes were also used, did not keep officials waiting.

Using its own bureaucratic paradigm and characteristic American attention to time, the U. S. Embassy finally instructed all employees that if they were on official business they should wait only twenty minutes and, if they had not been received, they should leave and return later. That way, they would be showing respect but they could avoid the personal insult of having to wait thirty to forty-five minutes or even an hour. This procedure took care of the Americans' anxiety, anger, and guilt but did little to inform them of the reasons behind the protracted delays. In response to an obviously strange and puzzling communication, the Americans produced in a typically human way a solution that fit the larger paradigm of their own culture, which is what people generally do. However, by so doing they managed to block any learning either about themselves or their hosts.

The case was interesting to me because it reaffirmed earlier observations of how Americans unconsciously structure time: For official business between people who are not on intimate terms, the eastern-seaboard middle-class pattern holds; it's expected that one will be prompt. Five minutes late calls for a small apology; ten minutes, a bit more must be said; fifteen minutes requires a definite apology plus an explanation; thirty minutes is insulting; and so on.[4] Waiting time is similarly structured. For Americans, these are not "mere conventions," which function at the higher levels of consciousness (as is the case for the English middle and upper classes), but constitute an entire communication system as well as a basic pattern for organizing activities. The twenty-minute waiting limit set for official visits was not an accidental figure pulled out of a hat by some bureaucrat. Knowing the circumstances, it was precisely what could have been predicted and entirely consistent with American informal norms. (Long enough to be polite and short enough to preserve official face.) Behavior of this type is so stereotyped that once the pattern is perceived, observing it is a little bit like pressing a button on a machine and watching the lights go on. The machine—if it is working properly—will always produce the same response; so will the members of a given culture. Otherwise, life cannot continue.

Clearly, analogies between cultures and machines must be taken very lightly, because no machine (even the most advanced complex of computers) can even begin to compare with the complexity of human beings, to say nothing of their transactions with each other. Then again, there is the extension-omission factor. This is an expression of the incapacity of any extension to reproduce all the functions of the organ or activity that is extended. Nevertheless, if the nature of a given mythical machine or organism is unknown, one way to discover what it will do is to vary the inputs and see how it responds. Imagine for a minute an organism so designed that it controls its own inputs according to a program and a series of reference signals of which it is completely unaware. The only way it could discover the nature of the control system used to maintain constancy of input would be to change things systematically in a series of steps in such a way that the organism would have to bring things back to normal. For purposes of a thought experiment, the particular organism is very simple; it swims in a tank of water and during certain hours of the day it stays at a given level just below the surface. If we depress the nose a bit, it corrects itself. But maybe it only responds in one way, will only raise its nose, so we devise another test and get underneath and push the nose up. Again it corrects itself. If the level-swimming organism were to be compared to a man who has so arranged his life that he does everything according to schedule, he will, after a while, if he arranges things properly, lose his awareness both of the schedule and of his need for the schedule until something happens to throw things out of line, at which point his attention will be directed more toward the disruption than toward his own need for scheduling.

This is basically what has happened to the peoples of the world. If the early white settlers in North America couldn't make the Indians conform to the European paradigm, the response was to destroy what could not be controlled and what did not perform in a predictable manner.

The cost of controlling one's inputs by destroying others eventually gets too high to maintain, although there may be (and often is) little awareness of the fact that the cost is too great, because of a preoccupation with the job of trying to maintain control in an unpredictable situation.

A second strategy is to ignore the possibility of another pattern or to delude oneself by saying that all the patterns in the world are basically the same or that the differences don't matter or are mere conventions. This avoids the issue very nicely but creates the added difficulty of setting the two systems on a collision course.

To give some idea, in physical terms, of the processes being discussed, I will describe another thought experiment in which the action changes as things happen. First, let us imagine ten blindfolded men in a room playing blindman's buff. These men have been hypnotized into the belief that they can see. The result is a series of unexpected collisions. Next, tell these same men that, in order to avoid the unexpected collisions they must work harder, intensify their efforts, move faster, swing their arms more. Furthermore, with each unexpected encounter they must increase the tempo and intensity of the swings. They will, of course, end up battered, frustrated, and enraged.

Now let's see what happens if the instructions are changed by telling the men, "You are blind but don't know it because everyone around you is blind. In spite of being blind, you have all learned to stay out of each other's way by a system of devices and signals of which you are unaware. So, for all intents and purposes, you have no way of knowing that you can't see. Now we are going to introduce some people into the room who are also blind and, like yourselves, unaware of their blindness. The difference is that they do not stay out of each other's way, because they use human contact as a way of orienting themselves. They prefer bumping to staying out of each other's way."

If we watch the experiment in our mind's eye, we will see that each group finds the other frustrating. The first group is unexpectedly bumped and fondled. The second group has trouble orienting itself because people keep avoiding contact. Since neither group is aware that they are blind nor do they know how to keep in contact or from being bumped, neither will ever think that it is worthwhile testing for vision. Until the two different groups meet, they will not pay close attention to the cues needed either to keep out of each other's way or to make contact in order to keep oriented. Paradoxically, the cues will become known only in a situation in which they won't work. And while it is not essential, in fact superfluous, to define the nature of a substitute visual system as long as everyone is using the same system, the only way to avoid being bumped and escalating into a swinging match is to be able to identify those aspects of the two signal systems that are in conflict. This means that, for the first group, instead of increasing speed and swinging their arms every time they are bumped, they must now slow down and become acutely aware of signals being emitted and received so that they can be consciously read and controlled. The lesson is fourfold:

1. One has an unconscious, very effective avoidance system at one's command.

2. There are other people in the world, whose goal is to seek human beings, not avoid them.
3. Like yourself, these people are neither aware of the fact that they are blind nor
4. that their behavior is systematic, highly consistent, and pre-dictable.

As a matter of fact, the blindman's-buff analogy is a much oversimplified example of the situation we face when we interact with members of other cultures or even variants of our own culture. This means that if one is to prosper in this new world without being unexpectedly battered, one must transcend one's own system. To do so, two things must be known: first, that there is a system; and second, the nature of that system. What is more, the only way to master either is to seek out systems that are different from one's own and, using oneself as a sensitive recording device, make note of every reaction or tendency to escalate. Ask yourself questions that will help define the state you were in as well as the one you are escalating to. It is impossible to do this in the abstract, because there are too many possibilities; behavioral systems are too complex. The rules governing behavior and structure of one's own cultural system can be discovered only in a specific context or real-life situation.

With this background, let us return to the case of the Americans in the small Asian country and discuss what was actually happening as they were kept waiting. I eventually was able to identify a pattern that explained the puzzling behavior of their hosts. The Americans were kept waiting because they were not known and had not taken on substance. A newly arrived official in someone's outer office was like an undeveloped film; there was no tangible, experiential image of the man. No one knew him as a friend or a human being. You could see him and hear him bellowing about being kept waiting and how important he was, but in terms of relationships in a social system he was at best a shadow and one that didn't look too promising at that. Americans who were willing to come back repeatedly and to meet their hosts socially outside the office had a chance to become flesh-and-blood, active members in a social system. Ultimately, they had no trouble being ushered into offices. Americans saw people in terms of their status, whereas the hosts saw them in a larger frame that took more time to integrate.

Two points about this case stand out: first, the fact that neither party could shed any light on the situation when questioned directly, because both assumed the other was familiar with the workings of his own system without realizing there was a system; second, the incredible differences in the systems that emerged once they were revealed. In working out the explanation to this particular paradox, I was aided by the knowledge that I was initially blind to the inner workings of my own culture and hence had already forced myself to learn a good deal about how American behavioral paradigms work. I also knew, for example, that all over the Far East, people's behavior toward each other is guided by their relationships in a quite stable, long-persisting social system.

The question is: How could the American continue to control his inputs in a situation as basically different from his own as the one just described? First, he must give up some of his narcissism and make adjustments in his own program, such as freeing himself of the binding grip of preset schedules that determine the rate at which human transactions must progress. Instead, he must build relationships with his hosts according to their schedules, make himself real, and allow time to take on substance as a human being, to be believable and predictable, before he tries to do anything else. This is something that hard-nosed bureaucrats who pride themselves on maintaining schedules, and businessmen obsessed with saving time, have found impossible to practice or tolerate in others. They see building a relationship as an expensive personal indulgence, a waste of time, or, even worse, indicative of "going over to the other side." (The Foreign Service keeps people moving precisely so they won't establish lasting relationships with the local people.)

In my experience, the two systems just discussed both require time; it is all a matter of where it is spent. Time spent getting to know people is saved later, because it is possible to cover so much more ground in a shorter time with a friend. The two systems are representative of what I have termed high- and low-context cultures (Chapters 6 and 7). In general, high-context cultures—those which call for considerable programming of individuals to each other—have greater mass and are therefore more predictable, if, and only if, one is familiar with the system. On the other hand, to the observer who doesn't know there is another system, a strange high-context culture can be completely mystifying, although he may not know or accept the fact that he is mystified. Why? The force of his own cultural stereotypes will be so strong that it will distort what he sees; he will delude himself that he knows what's going on before his eyes. This, of course, is a most dangerous and risky situation and one that unfortunately is all too common.

No one likes to give up his stereotypes, but to have to admit that one does not know the local ground rules even though competent or expert at home is more than most people can tolerate. Having spent significant segments of my professional life translating behavior of one culture into another, I have learned that translating is one thing, getting people to believe it is another. To date, there are two, only partially effective means of overcoming the granite-like persistence of an individual's control system. One is to spend a lifetime in a foreign country, dealing on a day-to-day basis with the reality of its system; the other is a very extensive, highly sophisticated training program that includes not only the language but the culture. Such training must take into account these facts:

1. People's nervous systems are organized according to the principles of negative feedback; that is, the whole thing works so smoothly and automatically that the only time the control system is consciously brought into play is when the input signals deviate from the norm. Therefore, people individually and collectively are for the most part unaware of the patterns and reference signals governing behavior.
2. People primarily spend their lives managing their inputs (the reverse of the popular notion).
3. The reality and structure of a person's own paradigms become available only in bits and pieces and in very special

cases, usually after repeated unsuccessful attempts to maintain constancy of input in the face of a foreign culture.

4. Reading the behavior of well-known friends and relatives is like covering thoroughly familiar ground without a mental map or talking before writing systems had even been heard of. One does not need a writing system to talk (or technical awareness of the rules governing speech either). To abstract such a system from the living data where none existed before, however, is a formidable task, an intellectual achievement that can equal the great accomplishments in chemistry, physics, and astronomy.

5. Until recently, man did not need to be aware of the structure of his own behavioral systems, because, staying at home, the behavior of most people was highly predictable. Today, however, man is constantly interacting with strangers, because his extensions have both widened his range and caused his world to shrink. It is therefore necessary for man to transcend his own culture, and this can be done only by making explicit the rules by which it operates.

A portion of what is involved in this complex process is described in the succeeding chapters. To tackle this job, one must consider the nature of man's central nervous system, his several brains, how he images, the role of context in determining behavior, and how some of the basic cultural systems such as time and space are used to organize behavior.

4. Hidden Culture

The paradox of culture is that language, the system most frequently used to describe culture, is by nature poorly adapted to this difficult task. It is too linear, not comprehensive enough, too slow, too limited, too constrained, too unnatural, too much a product of its own evolution, and too artificial. This means that the writer must constantly keep in mind the limitations language places upon him. He is aided, however, by one thing which makes all communication possible and on which all communication and all culture depend; namely, that language is not (as is commonly thought) a system for transferring thoughts or meaning from one brain to another, but a system for organizing information and for releasing thoughts and responses in other organisms. The materials for whatever insights there are in this world exist in incipient form, frequently unformulated but nevertheless already there in man. One may help to release them in a variety of ways, but it is impossible to plant them in the minds of others. Experience does that for us instead—particularly overseas experience.

I can think of few countries Americans are likely to visit and work in in significant numbers where it is more difficult to control one's inputs and where life is more filled with surprises than Japan. Clearly, the above observation does not apply to short visits and the like, because all over the world suitable environments have been created for tourists that shield them from the reality of the life of the people. Tourists seldom stick around for long, and they are happier insulated from the full impact of the foreign culture. Businessmen, educators, government officials, and Foreign Service personnel are something else again. It is to this group that my thoughts are directed, because they stand to gain the most from understanding cultural processes in living contexts. Understanding the reality of covert culture and accepting it on a gut level comes neither quickly nor easily, and it must be lived rather than read or reasoned. However, there are times when examples of what is experienced most intimately can illustrate certain basic patterns that are widely shared. The events described below are taken from my own experiences in Japan and with the Japanese in other countries, and are designed not only to illustrate differences between cultures but to provide a natural history of insights into the contexting process. For no matter how well prepared one is intellectually for immersion in another culture, there is the inevitability of surprises.

A few years ago, I became involved in a sequence of events in Japan that completely mystified me, and only later did I learn how an overt act seen from the vantage point of one's own culture can have an entirely different meaning when looked at in the context of the foreign culture. I had been staying at a hotel in downtown Tokyo that had European as well as Japanese-type rooms. The clientele included a few Europeans but was predominantly Japanese. I had been a guest for about ten days and was returning to my room in the middle of an afternoon. Asking for my key at the desk, I took the elevator to my floor. Entering the room, I immediately sensed that something was wrong. Out of place. Different. I was in the wrong room! Someone else's things were distributed around the head of the bed and the table. Somebody else's toilet articles (those of a Japanese male) were in the bathroom. My first thoughts were, "What if I am discovered here? How do I explain my presence to a Japanese who may not even speak English?"

I was close to panic as I realized how incredibly territorial we in the West are. I checked my key again. Yes, it really was mine. Clearly they had moved somebody else into my room. But where was my room now? And where were my belongings? Baffled and mystified, I took the elevator to the lobby. Why hadn't they told me at the desk, instead of letting me risk embarrassment and loss of face by being caught in somebody else's room? Why had they moved me in the first place? It was a nice room and, being sensitive to spaces and how they work, I was loath to give it up. After all, I had told them I would be in the hotel for almost a month. Why this business of moving me around like someone who has been squeezed in without a reservation? Nothing made sense.

At the desk I was told by the clerk, as he sucked in his breath in deference (and embarrassment?) that indeed they had moved me. My particular room had been reserved in advance by somebody else. I was given the key to my new room and discovered that all my personal effects were distributed around the new room almost as though I had done it myself. This produced a fleeting and strange feeling that maybe I wasn't myself. How could somebody else do all those hundred and one little things just the way I did?

Three days later, I was moved again, but this time I was prepared. There was no shock, just the simple realization that I had been moved and that it would now be doubly difficult for friends who had my old room number to reach me. *Tant pis*, I was in Japan. One thing did puzzle me. Earlier, when I had stayed at Frank Lloyd Wright's Imperial Hotel for several weeks, nothing like this had ever happened. What was different? What had changed? Eventually I got used to being moved and would even ask on my return each day whether I was still in the same room.

Later, at Hakone, a seaside resort where I was visiting with friends, the first thing that happened was that we were asked to disrobe. We were given *okatas*, and our clothes were taken from us by the maid. (For those who have not visited Japan, the okata is a cotton print kimono.) We later learned, when we ventured out in the streets, that it was possible to recognize other guests from our hotel because we had all been equipped with identical okatas. (Each hotel had its own characteristic, clearly recognizable pattern.) Also, I noted that it was polite to wave or nod to these strangers from the same hotel.

Following Hakone, we visited Kyoto, site of many famous temples and palaces, and the ancient capital of Japan.

There we were fortunate enough to stay in a wonderful little country inn on the side of a hill overlooking the town. Kyoto is much more traditional and less industrialized than Tokyo. After we had been there about a week and had thoroughly settled into our new Japanese surroundings, we returned one night to be met at the door by an apologetic manager who was stammering something. I knew immediately that we had been moved, so I said, "You had to move us. Please don't let this bother you, because we understand. Just show us to our new rooms and it will be all right." Our interpreter explained as we started to go through the door that we weren't in that hotel any longer but had been moved to *another* hotel. What a blow! Again, without warning. We wondered what the new hotel would be like, and with our descent into the town our hearts sank further. Finally, when we could descend no more, the taxi took off into a part of the city we hadn't seen before. No Europeans here! The streets got narrower and narrower until we turned into a side street that could barely accommodate the tiny Japanese taxi into which we were squeezed. Clearly this was a hotel of another class. I found that, by then, I was getting a little paranoid, which is easy enough to do in a foreign land, and said to myself, "They must think we are very low-status people indeed to treat us this way."

As it turned out, the neighborhood, in fact the whole district, showed us an entirely different side of life from what we had seen before, much more interesting and authentic. True, we did have some communication problems, because no one was used to dealing with foreigners, but few of them were serious.

Yet, the whole matter of being moved like a piece of derelict luggage puzzled me. In the United States, the person who gets moved is often the lowest-ranking individual. This principle applies to all organizations, including the Army. Whether you can be moved or not is a function of your status, your performance, and your value to the organization. To move someone without telling him is almost worse than an insult, because it means he is below the point at which feelings matter. In these circumstances, moves can be unsettling and damaging to the ego. In addition, moves themselves are often accompanied by great anxiety, whether an entire organization or a small part of an organization moves. What makes people anxious is that the move usually presages organizational changes that have been coordinated with the move. Naturally, everyone wants to see how he comes out vis-à-vis everyone else. I have seen important men refuse to move into an office that was six inches smaller than someone else's of the same rank. While I have heard some American executives say they wouldn't employ such a person, the fact is that in actual practice, unless there is some compensating feature, the significance of space as a communication is so powerful that no employee in his right mind would allow his boss to give him a spatial demotion—unless of course he had already reached his crest and was on the way down.

These spatial messages are not simply conventions in the United States—unless you consider the size of your salary check a mere convention, or where your name appears on the masthead of a journal. Ranking is seldom a matter that people take lightly, particularly in a highly mobile society like that in the United States. Each culture and each country has its own language of space, which is just as unique as the spoken language, frequently more so. In England, for example, there are no offices for the members of Parliament. In the United States, our congressmen and senators proliferate their offices and their office buildings and simply would not tolerate a no-office situation. Constituents, associates, colleagues, and lobbyists would not respond properly. In England, status is internalized; it has its manifestations and markers—the upper-class received English accent, for example. We in the United States, a relatively new country, externalize status. The American in England has some trouble placing people in the social system, while the English can place each other quite accurately by reading ranking cues, but in general tend to look down on the importance that Americans attach to space. It is very easy and very natural to look at things from one's own point of view and to read an event as though it were the same all over the world.

I knew that my emotions on being moved out of my room in Tokyo were of the gut type and quite strong. There was nothing intellectual about my initial response. Although I am a professional observer of cultural patterns, I had no notion of the meaning attached to being moved from hotel to hotel in Kyoto.

I was well aware of the strong significance of moving in my own culture, going back to the time when the new baby displaces older children, right up to the world of business, where a complex dance is performed every time the organization moves to new quarters.

What was happening to me in Japan as I rode up and down in elevators with various keys gripped in my hand was that I was reacting with the cultural part of my brain—the old, mammalian brain. Although my new brain, my symbolic brain —the neocortex—was saying something else, my mammalian brain kept repeating, "You are being treated shabbily." My neocortex was trying to fathom what was happening. Needless to say, neither part of the brain had been programmed to provide me with the answer in Japanese culture. I did have to put up a strong fight with myself to keep from interpreting what was going on as though the Japanese were the same as I. This is the conventional and most common response and one that is often found even among anthropologists. Any time you hear someone say, "Why, *they* are no different than the folks back home—they are just like I am," even though you may understand the reasons behind these remarks you also know that the speaker is living in a single-context world (his own) and is incapable of describing either his world or the foreign one.

The "they are just like the folks back home" syndrome is one of the most persistent and widely held misconceptions of the Western world, if not the whole world. There is very little any outsider can do about this, because it expresses views that are very close to the core of the personality. Simply talking about "cultural differences" and how we must respect them is a hollow cliché. And in fact, intellectualizing isn't much more helpful either, at least at first. The logic of the man who won't move into an office that is six inches smaller than his rival's is *cultural* logic; it works at a lower, more basic level in the brain, a part of the brain that synthesizes but does not verbalize. The response is a total response that is difficult to explain to someone who doesn't already understand, because it is so dependent on context for a correct interpretation. To do so, one must explain the entire system; otherwise, the man's behavior makes little sense.

He may even appear to be acting childishly—which he most definitely is not.

It was my preoccupation with my own cultural mold that explained why I was puzzled for years about the significance of being moved around in Japanese hotels. The answer finally came after further experiences in Japan and many discussions with Japanese friends. In Japan, one has to "belong" or he has no identity. When a man joins a company, he does just that— joins himself to the corporate body—and there is even a ceremony marking the occasion. Normally, he is hired for life, and the company plays a much more paternalistic role than in the United States. There are company songs, and the whole company meets frequently (usually at least once a week) for purposes of maintaining corporate identity and morale.[1]

As a tourist (either European or Japanese) when you go on a tour, you *join* that tour and follow your guide everywhere as a group. She leads you with a little flag that she holds up for all to see. Such behavior strikes Americans as sheeplike; not so the Japanese. The reader may say that this pattern holds in Europe, because there people join Cook's tours and the American Express tours, which is true. Yet there is a big difference. I remember a very attractive young American woman who was traveling with the same group I was with in Japan. At first she was charmed and captivated, until she had spent several days visiting shrines and monuments. At this point, she observed that she could not take the regimentation of Japanese life. Clearly, she was picking up clues, such as the fact that our Japanese group, when it moved, marched in a phalanx rather than moving as a motley mob with stragglers. There was much more discipline in these sightseeing groups than the average Westerner is either used to or willing to accept.

It was my lack of understanding of the full impact of what it means to belong to a high-context culture that caused me to misread hotel behavior at Hakone. I should have known that I was in the grip of a pattern difference and that the significance of all guests being garbed in the same okata meant more than that an opportunistic management used the guests to advertise the hotel. The answer to my puzzle was revealed when a Japanese friend explained what it means to be a guest in a hotel. As soon as you register at the desk, you are no longer an outsider; instead, for the duration of your stay you are a member of a large, mobile family. *You belong.* The fact that I was moved was tangible evidence that I was being treated as a family member— a relationship in which one can afford to be "relaxed and informal and not stand on ceremony." This is a very highly prized state in Japan, which offsets the official properness that is so common in public. Instead of putting me down, they were treating me as a member of the family. Needless to say, the large, luxury hotels that cater to Americans, like Wright's Imperial Hotel, have discovered that Americans do tenaciously stand on ceremony and want to be treated as they are at home in the States. Americans don't like to be moved around; it makes them anxious. Therefore, the Japanese in these establishments have learned not to treat them as family members.

While there are a few rare individuals who move along in the current of life looking around with innocent wonder regardless of what happens to them, most of mankind are not that relaxed. The majority are like men on a raft tossed about in a turbulent sea, who get only an occasional orienting glimpse of surrounding landmarks.

In the United States, the concern of the large middle class is to move ahead in the system, whichever part of it we happen to be in. With perhaps the exception of the younger generation just now entering the job market, we are very tied to our jobs. In fact, the more successful a man or a woman is, the more likely his or her life will revolve around a job to which home and personal relations assume secondary importance. We are only peripherally tied to the lives of others. It takes a long, long time for us to become deeply involved with others, and for some this never happens.

In Japan, life is a very different story, one that is puzzling in the extreme to Americans who interact regularly with the Japanese. Their culture seems to be full of paradoxes. When they communicate, particularly about important things, it is often in a roundabout way (indirection is a word that one hears often in the foreign colony). All of this points to a very high-context approach to life; yet, on the other hand, there are times when they swing in the opposite direction and move to the lower end of the context scale, where nothing can be taken for granted— "Be sure to put *brown* polish on the shoes." This was discovered by American GI's during the occupation. Years later, I had occasion to send some film to Japan for processing and was told to be *sure* to tell them everything I wanted done, because if I left anything out it would be my fault. Weeks later, after having provided what I thought was a set of instructions that could be followed by a computer, I got the film back. Everything was as I had requested—exquisite work—except that I had forgotten one thing. I didn't tell them to roll the film up and put it in a little can or to protect it in some way. In the process of mailing, the negatives had been folded and scratched, in fact were useless for any further work. I had run afoul of the low-context side of Japanese life.

Remember the woman who refused to practice the Foreign Service language drill and wouldn't learn the honorifics[2]—they were undemocratic! Well, the honorifics perform important functions that go far beyond telling the other person that you acknowledge and respect his position. In many offices, the honorifics are used at the beginning of the day and if things are going well they are gradually dropped, so that at the end of the day one is on a more intimate basis with others. Failure to drop the honorifics is a cue that something is wrong. This, along with a lot of other information, enables us to sketch out some dynamics of Japanese life.

The Japanese are pulled in two directions. The first is a very high-context, deeply involved, enveloping intimacy that begins at home in childhood but is extended far beyond the home. There is a deep need to be close, and it is only when they are close that they are comfortable. The other pole is as far away as one can get. In public and during ceremonial occasions (and there are ceremonies of a sort every day, even when people meet), there is great emphasis on self-control, distance, and hiding inner feelings. Like most of Japanese behavior, attitudes toward showing emotion are deeply rooted in a long past. At the time of the samurai knights and nobles, there was survival value in being able to control one's demeanor, because a samurai could legally execute anyone who displeased him or who wasn't properly respectful. This standing on ceremony extended to all levels; not only was the servant expected to be respectful, but the samurai's wife was to show no emotion when she received the news that her husband or son had been killed in battle. Until very recently, there was no public showing of intimacy or touching in Japan.

Still, on the formal, ceremonial side it is very important for the Japanese to be able to place people in a social system. In fact, it is impossible to interact with someone else if this placing has not occurred, hence the requirement that you state who you are on your calling card—first, the organization you work for, second, your position in that organization, your degrees, honors you have received, followed by the family name, the given name, and address, in that order.[3]

When functioning in the low-context mode, the Japanese keeps his mouth shut and volunteers nothing even though he has information that would be very useful. Thus, a young man I knew in Tokyo several years ago was completely unstrung when, just as he was leaving for Europe via Hong Kong he received a telephone call informing him that his flight had been canceled. Due to the scarcity of hotels and infrequency of flights (sometimes only one or two a week), to get off schedule used to be catastrophic, if for no other reason than the matter of hotel reservations. Assuming that the Japanese low-context mode was being used, I advised him to call the airlines immediately and ask if there was another flight to Hong Kong and, if so, could he get on it. The same clerk answered the phone and was very pleased to say yes, there was another flight leaving one hour later than the one that had been canceled. The clerk was of course being solicitous of my friend's status and would not have dreamed of suggesting the other flight. To do so would be to presume to do his thinking for him.

Through all these experiences, I was eventually able to discern the common thread that connected everything, which began to put Japanese behavior in context. The pattern is one that it is important to understand: In Japan there are the two sides to everyone—his warm, close, friendly, involved, high-context side that does not stand on ceremony, and the public, official, status-conscious, ceremonial side, which is what most foreigners see. From what I understand of Japanese culture, most Japanese feel quite uncomfortable (deep down inside) about the ceremonial, low-context, institutionalized side of life. Their principal drive is to move from the "stand on ceremony" side toward the homey, comfortable, warm, intimate, friendly side. One sees this even at the office and the laboratory, where the honorifics are dropped as the day progresses. By this, I do not mean to imply that the Japanese are not tough businessmen or that they aren't well organized, etc. Anyone who has had anything to do with them can only admire their capacity to get things done. The point is that their drive to be close and get to know other people is very strong—in some cases, more than the detached European is either used to or can stand. The record is very clear on this. Consider their practice of men and women sleeping side by side crowded together on the floor in a single room, and the camaraderie of communal bathing.

The American provides a real contrast. He is inclined to be more oriented toward achieving set goals and less toward developing close human relations. It is difficult for him to understand and act on the basis that once a customer in Japan "has been sold," that is just the beginning. He must be "massaged" regularly; otherwise he goes somewhere else. There are of course many other sides to the Japanese, such as their great dependence on tradition—as well as their group, rather than individual, orientation.

The message of this chapter is simple on the surface but does depend somewhat on the reader's being already contexted in cross-cultural communication. Two things get in the way of understanding: the linearity of language and the deep biases and built-in blinders that every culture provides. Transcending either is a formidable task. In addition, the broad base on which culture rests was laid down millions of years ago, long before man appeared on this earth, and for better or worse it ties man forever to the rest of nature. This base is rooted in the old, mammalian brain—that part of the brain that treats things as wholes—which constantly synthesizes and comes up with solutions based on everything that happened in the past. Paradoxically, this old brain that can understand and integrate one's own culture on a preverbal level frequently gets in the way of understanding and integrating new cultural experiences.

This means that if one is to *really* understand a given behavior on the basic level I am referring to, one must know the entire history of the individual. It is never possible to understand completely any other human being; and no individual will ever really understand himself—the complexity is too great and there is not the time to constantly take things apart and examine them. This is the beginning of wisdom in human relations. However, understanding oneself and understanding others are closely related processes. To do one, you must start with the other, and vice versa.

5. Rhythm and Body Movement

"There is no absolute knowledge, and those who claim it, whether they are scientists or dogmatists, open the door to tragedy."

J. Bronowski.[1]

What can the body tell us? Plenty—if we observe how people actually move: whether they move together in synchrony or not, the kind of rhythm they are moving to, as well as the many tiny, unnoticeable events that make up any transaction. The publication of Birdwhistell's *Introduction to Kinesics*, in 1952, marked the beginning of the technical study of body movement; since then, many people have been stimulated and influenced by Birdwhistell's work. One of the several offshoots of these studies reveals highly significant data on synchrony (moving together) that are of relevance to all of us.

Syncing, or "being in sync," may be a new concept to some readers, but for others it is very familiar.[2] People in interactions either move together (in whole or in part) or they don't and in failing to do so are disruptive to others around them. Basically, people in interactions move together in a kind of dance, but they are not aware of their synchronous movement and they do it without music or conscious orchestration. Being "in sync" is itself a form of communication. The body's messages (in or out of awareness), whether read technically or not, seldom lie, and come much closer to what the person's true but sometimes unconscious feelings are than does the spoken word. A number of scientists have worked on the subject of kinesics and synchrony and its significance. Since the field is growing more extensive and complex every day, the work of only one man will be discussed here.

In the early sixties, William Condon,[3] working then at Pennsylvania's Western State Psychiatric Institute, began a frame-by-frame analysis of 16mm films of people talking to each other. Each movement, no matter how minor, was recorded on a large sheet of paper along a time line, so that it was possible to identify all movements that were occurring at a given instant in time. From these studies, we learn that everything that man does can be shown to be under the control of the "body snychronizers."[4]

Moving pictures are normally taken at 18, 24, and 64 frames per second, so that the events being measured are somewhat less than 1/18, 1/24, and 1/64 of a second apart. At intervals of less than 1/64 of a second Condon found it impossible to detect body synchrony. However, within this rather narrow range it is possible to see remarkable characteristics of human interaction. Movies by Condon[5] and Birdwhistell,[6] as well as my own, taken in a variety of settings and circumstances, reveal that when two people talk to each other their movements are synchronized. Sometimes this occurs in barely perceptible ways, when finger, eyelid (blinking), and head movements occur simultaneously and in sync with specific parts of the verbal code (the words, with pitches and stresses) as it unwinds. In other cases, the whole body moves as though the two were under the control of a master choreographer who has written what Lawrence Halprin calls "an open score."[7] Viewing movies in very slow motion, looking for synchrony, one realizes that what we know as dance is really a slowed-down, stylized version of what human beings do whenever they interact.

Syncing is panhuman. It appears to be innate, being well established by the second day of life, and may be present as early as the first hour after birth. What is more, stop motion and slow motion studies of movies of newborn children made by Condon and his associates[8] revealed that the newborn infants initially synchronized the movement of their bodies to speech regardless of the language. American children, for example, synced with

Chinese just as well as they did with English. From this, it appears that synchrony is perhaps the most basic element of speech and the foundation on which all subsequent speech behavior rests.

Condon[9] was so struck by the fact that people's every movement was "in sync" with the words, down to and including eye blinks and syllables, that he thought there might be a semantic score. To test for this possibility, his subjects were given nonsense syllables to read. The synchrony was the same. Sense or nonsense, it made no difference. The only thing that destroyed synchrony was if one of the people was called out of the conversation by a third party. Synchrony stopped, and a new chain was set up with the new interlocutor.

In an attempt to find how this was accomplished, Condon devised a number of experiments. After more than a decade of work with a time/motion analyzer (a projector that can be run at any speed and stopped at any frame), he thinks of the process as operating at many levels in which two nervous systems "drive" each other. In one striking experiment,[10] two people in conversation were wired to electroencephalographs to see if there was any comparability in brain waves. Two cameras were set up so that one focused on the speakers, the other on the EEG recording pens. When the two people talked, the recording pens moved together as though driven by a single brain. When one of the individuals was called out of the conversation by a third person, the pens no longer moved together. Fantastic, isn't it? Yet the data are incontrovertible. What is now known represents a preface, with the rest of the book yet to be written. I say this because Condon did his work with average white subjects. As of this writing, similar movies of black subjects showed such a different pattern as to represent an entirely new language to Condon, indicating that while infants will sync with the human voice regardless of language, they later become habituated to the rhythms of their own language and culture.

As a consequence of years of microanalyses of film, Condon is convinced that it no longer makes sense to view human beings as ". . . isolated entities sending discrete messages" to each other. Rather, it would be more profitable to view the "bond" between humans as the result of participation within shared organizational forms. This means humans are tied to each other by hierarchies of rhythms that are *culture-specific* and expressed through language and body movement.

The results of one of my own research projects support Condon's conclusions. Several years ago, when my students and I were working with blacks under controlled conditions, we uncovered great differences in the kinesic and proxemic,[11] linguistic and other behavior patterns between working-class blacks and a wide range of whites (working class to upper middle class). Such unconscious differences may well be one of the sources of what blacks feel is the basic racism of white society.

The subject of racism on the unconscious behavioral level is touchy, complex, often oversimplified, and frequently treated improperly. For example, it is the practice of my regional subculture to avoid direct eye contact with strangers in public when they are closer than twelve to fourteen feet. A member of any group that is used to visual involvement inside that distance will automatically misread my behavior. When miscuing of this sort is added to feelings of rejection, prejudice, or discrimination on the conscious level, the results can be overwhelming, for it is natural to lump all behavior together and not to distinguish between conscious, deliberate racism and structural differences in cultural systems. To categorize all behavior as racist sidesteps the issue that not every white is consciously or even unconsciously racist but will, regardless of how he feels, use white forms of communication (both verbal and nonverbal), if for no other reason than he simply does not know any others. While blacks could teach whites to use black nonverbal forms, this is very difficult to do, because of a built-in tendency for all groups to interpret their own nonverbal communicative patterns as though they were universal.

Whites do not move the way working-class blacks do or the way Puerto Ricans move or Mexicans or Pueblo or Navajo Indians, Chinese or Japanese. Each culture has its own characteristic manner of locomotion, sitting, standing, reclining, and gesturing. To demonstrate this, one has only to take one of the small, popular Super-8 cameras and record people walking in public where ethnicity can be identified with certainty. Then record another group, and view the movies over and over at slow speed. After these repeated viewings, the differences will become clear. One of my students, a young black woman, was able to identify some fifteen differences in walking behavior between whites and Pueblo Indians by using this very simple procedure.[12]

Syncing, tempo, and rhythm are all related. But most people are unaware when these are happening. When they become aware, they are unable to pay attention to anything else. Also, paying attention to one's own unconscious behavior will usually disrupt that behavior.

Birdwhistell has defined kinesics as the way one moves and handles one's body. One of the most basic of all modes of communication, kinesics as communication was well established before the emergence of mammalian life. Lizards, birds, and mammals communicate this way among themselves and, to some extent, to animals of different species. People recognize posture and body movement even at a distance. But unlike other mammals, we have specialized the language of the body so that it is integrated and congruent with everything else we do. It is therefore culturally determined and must be read against a cultural backdrop. That is, the significance of a posture or act is only partially readable across cultural boundaries. In new and unknown situations, in which one is likely to be most dependent on reading nonverbal cues (NVC), *the chances of one's being correct decrease as cultural distances increase.* Even two people as closely related as the Americans and the English have problems reading each other's kinesics. I do not want to give the impression that there are not innate responses such as the smile (Ekman and Friesen[13] and Eibl-Eibesfeldt[14]). But even smiles must be seen in context. The reassuring smile of the used-car salesman as he unloads a lemon is a deliberate deception. Yet, Ekman and Friesen have shown, he gives himself away—there is leakage.[15] However, the specific form the leakage takes is not universal but must be read culturally.

Kinesics and posture are easy to see. Synchronous movement

occurs on another, deeper level; while the actual rhythms may be different, they are represented in all groups. A striking example of group sync was once captured by one of my students on film as a seminar project. Using an abandoned car as a blind, he photographed children dancing and skipping in a school playground during their lunch hour. At first, they looked like so many kids each doing his own thing. After a while, we noticed that one little girl was moving more than the rest. Careful study revealed that she covered the entire playground. Following procedures laid down for my students, this young man viewed the film over and over at different speeds. Gradually, he perceived that the whole group was moving in synchrony to a definite rhythm. The most active child, the one who moved about most, was the director, the orchestrator of the playground rhythm! Not only was there a rhythm and a beat, but the beat seemed familiar. Seeking help from a friend deeply involved in rock music, who also viewed the film several times, we found a tune that fit the rhythm. Then the music was synchronized with the children's play and once synchronized remained in sync for the entire 4½ minutes of the film clip!

However, when some people actually saw the film and heard the explanation of the experiment, they had trouble understanding that an unconscious undercurrent of synchronized movement tied the group together. Because they didn't understand this, they felt compelled to invent explanations. One school principal who heard the explanation and saw the film after it had been synchronized with music spoke of the children as "dancing to the music"; another person who read the description wanted to know if all the children were "humming the tune." Both were wrong. The children were screaming and yelling and laughing and making all the playground noises that children make. Without knowing it, they were all moving to a beat which they generated themselves. This did not mean that they were all moving at the same time, just as there are times when different sections of an orchestra are silent. They even had a conductor who kept the beat going continuously.

The process is not easy to understand, because most of us are much too used to dealing with second-, third-, or fourth-generation communication systems such as language and writing. My student had identified the source—where the written music that gets composed and played came from. I am sure that there will be composers who will know immediately what I am talking about just as there will be those who won't, because they have been taught to look to other musicians for their music and to disregard the ocean of rhythm in which they are immersed in everyday life. Yet people swim in different oceans. Those of us brought up in the northern European tradition are underdeveloped rhythmically. We have a single beat that we dance to, whereas the Tiv of Nigeria have four drums, *one for each part of the body*. Each drummer beats out a different rhythm; talented dancers move to all four.[16]

Discoveries of this sort have far-reaching implications. Music and dance, for instance, can be seen in a new light. While others will fill in the details, it is worthwhile to sketch in the broad outlines of the general significance of man's rhythms here. Once, on the island of Mykonos, I noticed a group of young people around a table in a sidewalk cafe listening to their portable radio tuned to rock music. Close observation from the next table revealed that they were not consciously listening to the music but were using it instead as a sort of sine wave with which to synchronize their own movements as a way of heightening or strengthening the group bond.

Even the spoken language can be used for syncing, as I discovered a few years ago while building an office addition to my house. I had hired some of my Spanish American neighbors to do the actual labor and, for a variety of reasons, spent most of my working day with them. Soon several things became apparent. Conversation was continuous. It never stopped. Yet the content was not highly relevant. They were talking to be talking. If the conversation lagged, the work lagged. Two or three men could work in a very small area without ever seeming to interfere with each other, and they worked very close together. Whether adobe bricks were being laid, plaster was being applied to the walls, or cement was being smoothed, the whole operation was like a ballet, with the rhythm of the conversation providing the unconscious score that strengthened the group bond and kept them from interfering with each other.

On quite a different level, most Americans are familiar with the working songs of blacks that were (and still presumably are) used to synchronize physical labor. I am convinced that most people saw these songs—since they were so obviously used as syncing devices—as the black man's way of making labor less onerous. Very few realized that they, themselves, did the same thing but in a much less noticeable way.

What struck me first when working with different cultures in different parts of the world was how everybody moved. If one wanted to fit in, or not appear too conspicuous, it was helpful to begin to move to the local rhythm and conform to the local beat. All living things internalize and respond to dozens of rhythms—night and day, lunar, seasonal, annual, as well as the shorter cycles and rhythms such as breathing rate, heart beat, and the various brain waves—to say nothing of the rhythms of hunger and of sex. Despite the studies that demonstrated that women living in groups in dormitories and sorority houses tend to phase their periods and that patients on wards phase metabolism if they are together long enough, I was not prepared for the fact that man probably syncs everything he does and when he is out of phase this is a sign that something is very, very wrong.

In high-context cultures, syncing is very noticeable. It functions on a high level of awareness, and is consciously valued. Perhaps a source of alienation in the members of high-sync, high-context cultures when interacting with low-sync, low-context cultures is the fact that they do not know how to deal with people who are out of phase.

All of this suggests that:

1. The way in which people handle synchrony is both rooted in biology (bio-basic) and modified by culture.
2. Synchrony or lack of it is an index of how things are going and can be an unconscious source of great tension when synchrony is low, absent, or of the wrong kind.
3. On a practical level, absence or disturbances of synchrony can interfere with work and any group activity—in sports,

on production lines, etc. Perhaps one of the things that is wrong with production lines is that they are impossible to sync with and are out of sync with the workers.

4. Music and dance, by extension transference, are looked upon as activities that are produced by artists and are independent of the audience. The data on synchrony strongly suggest that this is not so. The audience and artist are part of the same process.

When one encounters an art form or style one does not like or finds repulsive, four things are possible: the artist may have done a poor job in capturing the perception or the rhythm; he may be representing an unconventional aspect of behavior or perception (Mondrian's portraits of the visual cortex of the brain)[17] or he may have a style that is unfamiliar; he may be expressing a dissociated aspect of behavior, which makes everyone uncomfortable; or he may be foreign and be presenting us with an unfamiliar pattern to which we do not "vibrate." There are other reasons, of course, such as poor technique, incomplete text or message, incongruities between levels, etc. When one thinks of the number of things that can go wrong, it is a wonder that the artist succeeds at all.

In a sense, the new light on synchrony in man reveals that man's relationship to all the art forms is much more intimate than is commonly supposed; man is art and vice versa. There is no way the two can be separated. The whole notion that the two are separate is another example of extension transference (and probably an aberration of Western culture).

While everything that man is and does has significance, rhythms and synchrony of the type I have been describing are classed as having little meaning in the West. However, this could simply be because Western cultures are relatively low-context. For high-context, highly involved cultures, rhythm does have meaning.

Recently, there has been a spate of books about nonverbal communication; it's fashionable and everybody's doing it. Opportunistic writers who collect samples and examples from the experts, exploiting the timeliness of the subject, only manage to describe part of the picture, and a distorted part at that. While the new interest in the subject is gratifying to some who have been trying to achieve deeper understanding of nonverbal processes, popularization has done the field a great disservice and may have even made some people somewhat more tense, for fear that they will reveal unknown or undesirable aspects of themselves by the way in which they move. When the whole process was unconscious, nobody was seen as having an advantage. Those who are fearful feel that their own behavior may be used against them and that NVC insights have put a tool in the hands of people who want to manipulate them.

Like anything else, knowledge of NVC can be misused. The danger is that people will (as they've already done) attach a specific meaning to parts of unconscious nonverbal systems—"crossing the legs means you're uptight," or "crossing your arms means you are shutting people out," or touching or caressing the nose means you think the other person or what he said stinks, etc. Book titles such as How to Read a Person Like a Book[18] are thoroughly misleading, doubly so because they are designed to satisfy the public's need for highly specific answers to complex questions for which there are no simple answers. Nobody reads anybody else like a book at first. And while a person may touch the end of his nose when speaking, it's impossible to tell what stimulated this action. It could be an association released by something in the perceived field at the time, his interlocutor's necktie which he just notices, his tone of voice, something about his posture that reminded him of his father—in fact, any of a hundred different things. NVCs must always be read in context; in fact, they are often a prominent part of the context in which the verbal part of the message is set. Context never has a specific meaning. Yet the meaning of a communication is always dependent upon the context.

The language of behavior is extraordinarily subtle. Most people are lucky to have one subcultural system under control—the one that reflects their own sex, class, generation, and geographic region within a country. Because of its complexity, efforts to isolate out "bits" of nonverbal communication and generalize from them in isolation are doomed to failure. All articles and books on "body language" that purport to turn the reader into an instant expert from watching people's behavior at cocktail parties are totally misleading. The principal defect in the recent popularizations of body language is that it is presented as independent of the person, as though it were pasted on, something that can be doffed and donned like a suit of clothes or an item of vocabulary. Far from being a superficial form of communication that can be consciously manipulated, NVC systems are interwoven with the fabric of the personality and into society itself, even rooted in how one experiences oneself as a man or a woman. Without these unwritten subtle systems for managing the tremendous diversity of encounters in everyday life, man would be nothing but a machine.

Nonverbal systems are closely tied to ethnicity—in fact, they are of the essence of ethnicity. This creates problems for Americans, who have been slow to accept our ethnicities primarily because we are intolerant of differences and believe that if something is different it is therefore inferior.

Nowhere have I found this to be more apparent than in relations between blacks and whites. For years, blacks have been regarded as underdeveloped whites, when in fact black culture is very rich[19] and has its own unwritten rules governing behavior. Recognition of black culture has always been important. Now it is critical.

In any encounter, particularly intercultural or interethnic, the correct reading of the other person's verbal and nonverbal behavior is basic to transactions at all levels. In fact, the correct reading of all sensory inputs and their integration into a coherent picture is one of the most important things we do. There are times when this is not easy, because behavioral systems are tied directly to the self-image system. It is therefore difficult for most of us to accept the reality of another's system, because it involves a different image and may require us to change our own. However, ethnic diversity can be a source of great strength and an invaluable asset, provided people can develop the desire to learn from each other (one of the principal ways of learning about oneself). An intercultural or interethnic encounter can be used to highlight otherwise-hidden structure points of one's own behavior at a rate many times faster than the normal exigencies of life will reveal that same hidden structure. At home, people make mistakes and violate norms; they just don't make as many or as serious mistakes as they do when they are overseas. I would never have been able to identify points in the temporal and spatial behavior of Americans as described in THE SILENT LANGUAGE and THE HIDDEN DIMENSION if I had not been able to observe Americans overseas, struggling to adjust their behavior to people who kept them waiting, came an hour early to dinner (out of respect), or stood too close ("frosting their glasses"). How the cultural interference mode works is illustrated in the following example.

I was once visiting a colleague and friend engaged in interesting research on the Navajo reservation. In this research, portions of the Navajo Indian's unstated world were revealed by how untutored Indians made movies of different events in which they were interested. ("Unstated" or "hidden" is not to be construed as "secret," because no one was interested in secrets or wanted to become involved in them.) The idea was to learn the structure of the implicit, unverbalized grammar of the Navajo visual world. As it turned out, the researchers faced with the Navajo movie method learned more about the unwritten, unspecified structure of their own cinematographic and editing techniques than they did about the Navajo. I played a small role in this experiment when my friend asked me to go over his notes, which were laden with remarks about what the Indians weren't doing. My comment was something like this: "You seem to have a system here, and every time the Navajos violate that system you respond by noting what they aren't doing. How about doing us all a favor, now that you have been through this experience, by making your own system explicit?" The result was reported in a valuable, highly original book[20] on some of the cinematographic conventions of the Western world.

What we learned was that in order to really understand a Navajo movie one had to be a Navajo Indian who was brought up in the traditional Navajo way of life. Differences between white and Navajo visual perception as applied to movie making occurred at almost every level. For example, editing is a big thing among white cinematographers. We think in bits and try to put the bits together in a coherent whole, so that teaching people to edit film is an important part of their training. Not so the Navajo. They have whole sequences in their heads before they begin shooting, and they edit in their heads as they go along! Navajo rhythms are more integrated than our own—they certainly move that way—which makes it possible for them to experience life (even filming) in a more integrated, holistic manner. We, by contrast, cut things up into little pieces, and it can be tough to live in a fragmented world.

6. Context and Meaning

One of the functions of culture is to provide a highly selective screen between man and the outside world. In its many forms, culture therefore designates what we pay attention to and what we ignore.[1] This screening function provides structure for the world and protects the nervous system from "information overload."[2] Information overload is a technical term applied to information-processing systems. It describes a situation in which the system breaks down when it cannot properly handle the huge volume of information to which it is subjected. Any mother who is trying to cope with the demands of small children, run a house, enjoy her husband, and carry on even a modest social life knows that there are times when everything happens at once and the world seems to be closing in on her. She is experiencing the same information overload that afflicts business managers, administrators, physicians, attorneys, and air controllers. Institutions such as stock exchanges, libraries, and telephone systems also go through times when the demands on the system (inputs) exceed capacity. People can handle the crunch through delegating and establishing priorities; while institutional solutions are less obvious, the high-context rule seems to apply. That is, the only way to increase information-handling capacity without increasing the mass and complexity of the system is to program the memory of the system so that less information is required to activate the system, i.e., make it more like the couple that has been married for thirty-five years. The solution to the problem of coping with increased complexity and greater demands on the system seems to lie in the preprogramming of the individual or organization. This is done by means of the "contexting" process—a concept introduced in Chapter 1.

The importance of the role of context is widely recognized in the communication fields, yet the process is rarely described adequately, or if it is, the insights gained are not acted upon. Before dealing with context as a way of handling information overload, let me describe how I envisage the contexting process, which is an emergent function; i.e., we are just discovering what it is and how it works. Closely related to the high–low-context continuum is the degree to which one is aware of the selective screen that one places between himself and the outside world.[3] As one moves from the low to the high side of the scale, awareness of the selective process increases. Therefore, what one pays attention to, context, and information overload are all functionally related.

In the fifties, the United States Government spent millions of dollars developing systems for machine translation of Russian and other languages. After years of effort on the part of some of the most talented linguists in the country, it was finally concluded that the only reliable, and ultimately the fastest, translator is a human being deeply conversant not only with the language but with the subject as well. The computers could spew out yards of print-out but they meant very little. The words and some of the grammar were all there, but the sense was distorted. That the project failed was not due to lack of application, time, money, or talent, but for other reasons, which are central to the theme of this chapter.

The problem lies not in the linguistic code but in the context, which carries varying proportions of the meaning. Without context, the code is incomplete since it encompasses only part of the message. This should become clear if one remembers that the spoken language is an abstraction of an event that happened, might have happened, or is being planned. As any writer knows, an event is usually infinitely more complex and rich than the language used to describe it. Moreover, the writing system is an abstraction of the spoken system and is in effect a reminder system of what somebody said or could have said. In the process of abstracting, as contrasted with measuring, people take in some things and unconsciously ignore others. This is what intelligence is: paying attention to the right things. The linear quality of a language inevitably results in accentuating some things at the expense of others. Two languages provide interesting contrasts. In English, when a man says, "It rained last night," there is no way of knowing how he arrived at that conclusion, or if he is even telling the truth, whereas a Hopi cannot talk about the rain at all without signifying the nature of his relatedness to the event—firsthand experience, inference, or hearsay. This is a point made by the linguist Whorf[4] thirty years ago. However, selective attention and emphasis are not restricted to language but are characteristic of the rest of culture as well.

The rules governing what one perceives and is blind to in the course of living are not simple; at least five sets of disparate categories of events must be taken into account. These are: the subject or activity, the situation, one's status in a social system, past experience, and culture. The patterns governing juggling these five dimensions are learned early in life and are mostly taken for granted. The "subject" or topic one is engaged in has a great deal to do with what one does and does not attend. People working in the "hard" sciences, chemistry and physics, which deal with the physical world, are able to attend and integrate a considerably higher proportion of significant events observed than scientists working with living systems. The physical scientist has fewer variables to deal with; his abstractions are closer to the real events; and context is of less importance. This characterization is, of course, oversimplified. But it is important to remember that the laws governing the physical world, while relatively simple compared to those governing human behavior, may seem complex to the layman, while the complexity of language appears simple to the physicist, who, like everyone else, has been talking all his life. In these terms it is all too easy for the person who is in full command of a particular behavioral system, such as language, to confuse what he can *do* with a given system, with the unstated rules governing the way the system operates. The conceptual model I am using takes into account not only what one takes in and screens out but what one does not know about a given system even though one has mastered that system. The two are *not* the same. Michael Polanyi[5] stated this principle quite elegantly when he said, "The structure of a machine cannot be defined in terms of the laws which it harnesses."

What man chooses to take in, either consciously or unconsciously, is what gives structure and meaning to his world. Furthermore, what he perceives is "what he intends to do about it." Setting aside the other four dimensions (situation, status, past experience, and culture), theoretically it would be possible to arrange all of man's activities along a continuum ranging from those in which a very high proportion of the events influencing the outcome were consciously considered to those in which a much smaller number were considered. In the United States, interpersonal relations are frequently at the low end of the scale. Everyone has had the experience of thinking that he was making a good impression only to learn later that he was not. At times like these, we are paying attention to the wrong things or screening out behavior we should be observing. A common fault of teachers and professors is that they pay more attention to their subject matter than they do to their students, who frequently pay too much attention to the professor and not enough to the subject.

The "situation" also determines what one consciously takes in and leaves out. In an American court of law, the attorneys, the judge, and the jury are impelled by custom and legal practice to pay attention only to what is legally part of the record. Context, by design, carries very little weight. Contrast this with a situation in which an employee is trying to decipher the boss's behavior—whether he is pleased or not, and if he is going to grant a raise. Every little clue is a story in itself, as is the employee's knowledge of behavior in the past.

One's status in a social system also affects what must be attended. People at the top pay attention to different things from those at the middle or the bottom of the system. In order to survive, all organizations, whatever their size, have to develop techniques not only for replacing their leader but for switching the new leader's perceptions from the internal concerns he focused on when he was at the lower and middle levels to a type of global view that enables the head man or woman to chart the course for the institution.

The far-reaching consequences of what is attended can be illustrated by a characteristic fault in Western thinking which dates back to the philosophers of ancient Greece. Our way of thinking is quite arbitrary and causes us to look at ideas rather than events—a most serious shortcoming. Also, linearity can get in the way of mutual understanding and divert people needlessly along irrelevant tangents. The processes I am describing are particularly common in the social sciences, although the younger scientists in these fields are gradually beginning to accept the fact that when someone is talking about events on one level this does not mean that he has failed to take into account the many other events on different levels. It is just that one can talk about only a single aspect of something at any moment (illustrating the linear characteristic of language).

The results of this syndrome (of having to take multiple levels into account when using a single-level system) are reflected in a remark made by one of our most brilliant and least appreciated thinkers in modern psychiatry, H. S. Sullivan,[6] when he observed that as he composed his articles, lectures, and books the person he was writing to (whom he projected in his mind's eye) was a cross between an imbecile and a bitterly paranoid critic. What a waste! And so confusing to the reader who wants to find out what the man is really trying to say.

In less complex and fast-moving times, the problem of mutual understanding was not as difficult, because most transactions were conducted with people well known to the speaker or writer, people with similar backgrounds. It is important for conversationalists in any situation—regardless of the area of discourse (love, business, science)—to get to know each other well enough so that they realize what each person is and is not taking into account. This is crucial. Yet few are willing to make the very real effort—life simply moves too fast—which may explain some of the alienation one sees in the world today.

Programming of the sort I am alluding to takes place in all normal human transactions as well as those of many higher mammals. It constitutes the unmeasurable part of communication. This brings us to the point where it is possible to discuss context in relation to meaning, because what one pays attention to or does not attend is largely a matter of context. Remember, contexting is also an important way of handling the very great complexity of human transactions so that the system does not bog down in information overload.

Like a number of my colleagues, I have observed that meaning and context are inextricably bound up with each other. While a linguistic code can be analyzed on some levels independent of context (which is what the machine translation project tried to accomplish), *in real life the code, the context, and the meaning can only be seen as different aspects of a single event.* What is unfeasible is to measure one side of the equation and not the others.[7]

Earlier, I said that high-context messages are placed at one end and low-context messages at the other end of a continuum. A high-context (HC) communication or message is one in which most of the information is either in the physical context or internalized in the person, while very little is in the coded, explicit, transmitted part of the message. A low-context (LC) communication is just the opposite; i.e., the mass of the information is vested in the explicit code. Twins who have grown up together can and do communicate more economically (HC) than two lawyers in a courtroom during a trial (LC), a mathematician programming a computer, two politicians drafting legislation, two administrators writing a regulation, or a child trying to explain to his mother why he got into a fight.

Although no culture exists exclusively at one end of the scale, some are high while others are low. American culture, while not on the bottom, is toward the lower end of the scale. We are still considerably above the German-Swiss, the Germans, and the Scandinavians in the amount of contexting needed in everyday life. While complex, multi-institutional cultures (those that are technologically advanced) might be thought of as inevitably LC, this is not always true. China, the possessor of a great and complex culture, is on the high-context end of the scale.

One notices this particularly in the written language of

China, which is thirty-five hundred years old and has changed very little in the past three thousand years. This common written language is a unifying force tying together half a billion Chinese, Koreans, Japanese, and even some of the Vietnamese who speak Chinese. The need for context is experienced when looking up words in a Chinese dictionary. To use a Chinese dictionary, the reader must know the significance of 214 radicals (there are no counterparts for radicals in the Indo-European languages). For example, to find the word for star one must know that it appears under the sun radical. To be literate in Chinese, one has to be conversant with Chinese history. In addition, the spoken pronunciation system must be known, because there are four tones and a change of tone means a change of meaning; whereas in English, French, German, Spanish, Italian, etc., the reader need not know how to pronounce the language in order to read it. Another interesting sidelight on the Chinese orthography is that it is also an art form.[8] To my knowledge, no low-context communication system has ever been an art form. Good art is always high-context; bad art, low-context. This is one reason why good art persists and art that releases its message all at once does not.

The level of context determines everything about the nature of the communication and is the foundation on which all subsequent behavior rests (including symbolic behavior). Recent studies in sociolinguistics have demonstrated how context-dependent the language code really is. There is an excellent example of this in the work of the linguist Bernstein,[9] who has identified what he terms "restricted" (HC) and "elaborated" (LC) codes in which vocabulary, syntax, and sounds are all altered: In the restricted code of intimacy in the home, words and sentences collapse and are shortened. This even applies to the phonemic structure of the language. The individual sounds begin to merge, as does the vocabulary, whereas in the highly articulated, highly specific, elaborated code of the classroom, law, or diplomacy, more accurate distinctions are made on all levels. Furthermore, the code that one uses signals and is consistent with the situation. A shifting of code signals a shift in everything else that is to follow. "Talking down" to someone is low-contexting him—telling him more than he needs to know. This can be done quite subtly simply by shifting from the restricted end of the code toward the elaborated forms of discourse.

From the practical viewpoint of communications strategy, one must decide how much time to invest in contexting another person. A certain amount of this is always necessary, so that the information that makes up the explicit portions of the message is neither inadequate nor excessive. One reason most bureaucrats are so difficult to deal with is that they write for each other and are insensitive to the contexting needs of the public. The written regulations are usually highly technical on the one hand, while providing little information on the other. That is, they are a mixture of different codes or else there is incongruity between the code and the people to whom it is addressed. Modern management methods, for which management consultants are largely responsible, are less successful than they should be, because in an attempt to make everything explicit (low-contexting again) they frequently fail in their recommendations to take into account what people already know. This is a common fault of the consultant, because few consultants take the time (and few clients will pay for the time) to become completely contexted in the many complexities of the business.

There is a relationship between the world-wide activism of the sixties and where a given culture is situated on the context scale, because some are more vulnerable than others. HC actions are by definition rooted in the past, slow to change, and highly stable. Commenting on the need for the stabilizing effect of the past, anthropologist Loren Eiseley[10] takes an anti-activist position and points out how vulnerable our own culture is:

> Their world (the world of the activist), therefore, becomes increasingly the violent, unpredictable world of the first men simply because, in lacking faith in the past, one is inevitably forsaking all that enables man to be a planning animal. For man's story,[11] in brief, is essentially that of a creature who has abandoned *instinct* and replaced it with cultural tradition and the hard-won increments of contemplative thought. The lessons of

the past have been found to be a reasonably secure construction for proceeding against an unknown future.[12]

Actually, activism is possible at any point in the HC–LC continuum, but it seems to have less direction or focus and becomes less predictable and more threatening to institutions in LC systems. Most HC systems, however, can absorb activism without being shaken to their foundations.

In LC systems, demonstrations are viewed as the last, most desperate act in a series of escalating events. Riots and demonstrations in the United States, particularly those involving blacks,[13] are a message, a plea, a scream of anguish and anger for the larger society to *do something*. In China (an HC culture), the Red Guard riots apparently had an entirely different significance. They were promulgated from the top of the social order, not the bottom. They were also a communication from top to bottom: first, to produce a show of strength by Mao Tse-tung; second, to give pause to the opposition and shake things up at the middle levels—a way of mobilizing society, not destroying it. Chinese friends with whom I have spoken about these riots took them much less seriously than I did. I was, of course, looking at them from the point of view of one reared in a low-context culture, where such riots can have disastrous effects on the society at large.

Wherever one looks, the influence of the subtle hand of contexting can be detected. We have just spoken of the effects of riots on high- and low-context political systems, but what about day-to-day matters of perception? On the physiological level of color perception, one sees the power of the brain's need to perceive and adjust everything in terms of context. As any interior designer knows, a powerful painting, print, or wall hanging can change the perceived color of the furnishings around it. The color psychologist Faber Birren[14] demonstrated experimentally that the perceived shade of a color depends upon the color context in which it occurs. He did this by systematically varying the color of the background surrounding different color samples.

Some of the most impressive demonstrations of the brain's ability to supply missing information—the function of contexting—are the experiments of Edwin Land, inventor of the Land camera. Working in color photography using a single red filter, he developed a process that is simple, but the explanation for it is not. Until Land's experiments, it was believed that color prints could be made only by superimposing transparent images of three separate photographs made with the primary colors—red, blue, and yellow. Land made his color photographs with two images: a black-and-white image to give light and shadow, and a single, *red* filter for color. When these two images were projected, superimposed on a screen, even though red was the only color, they were perceived in full color with all the shades and gradations of a three-color photograph![15] Even more remarkable is the fact that the objects used were deliberately chosen to provide no cues as to their color. To be sure that his viewers didn't unconsciously project color, Land photographed spools of plastic and wool and geometric objects whose color would be unknown to the viewer. How the eye and the visual centers of the brain function to achieve this remarkable feat of internal contexting is still only partially understood. But the actual stimulus does only part of the job.

Contexting probably involves at least two entirely different but interrelated processes—one inside the organism and the other outside. The first takes place in the brain and is a function of either past experience (programmed, internalized contexting) or the structure of the nervous system (innate contexting), or both. External contexting comprises the situation and/or setting in which an event occurs (situational and/or environmental contexting).[16]

One example of the growing interest in the relationship of external context to behavior is the widespread interest and concern about our public-housing disasters. Pruitt-Igoe Homes in St. Louis is only one example. This $26-million fiasco imposed on poor blacks is now almost completely abandoned. All but a few buildings have been dynamited, because nobody wants to live there.

Objections and defects in high-rise public housing for poor families are legion: Mothers can't supervise their children; there are usually no community service agencies nearby and no stores or markets; and quite often there is no access to any public transportation system. There are no recreation centers for teenagers and few places for young children to play. In any budget crunch, the first thing to be cut is maintenance and then the disintegration process starts; elevators and hallways turn into death traps. The case against high-rise housing for low-income families is complex and underscores the growing recognition that environments are not behaviorally neutral.

Although situational and environmental context has only recently been systematically studied, environmental effects have been known to be a factor in behavior for years. Such men as the industrialist Pullman[17] made statements that sounded very advanced at the time. He believed that if workers were supplied with clean, airy, well-built homes in pleasant surroundings, this would exert a positive influence on their health and general sense of well-being and would make them more productive as well. Pullman was not wrong in his analysis. He simply did not live up to his stated ideals. The main street of his company town, where supervisors lived, was everything he talked about. But his workers were still poorly housed. Being isolated in a company town in close proximity to the plush homes of managers simply made their inadequate living conditions more obvious by way of contrast, and the workers finally embarked on a violent strike. There were many other human, economic, and political needs, which Pullman had not taken into account, that led to worker dissatisfaction. Pullman's professed idealism backfired. Few were aware of the conditions under which his laborers actually lived and worked, so that the damage done to the budding but fragile environmentalist position was incalculable and gave ammunition to the "hard-nosed," "practical" types whose minds were focused on the bottom-line figures of profit and loss.

Quite often, the influence of either programmed contexting (experience) or innate contexting (which is built in) is brushed aside. Consider the individual's spatial needs and his feelings about certain spaces. For example, I have known women who needed a room to be alone in, whose husbands did not share this particular need, and they brushed aside their wives' feelings, dismissing them as childish. Women who have this experience should not let my talking about it raise their blood pressure. For it is very hard for someone who does not share an unstated, informal need with another person to experience that need as tangible and valid. Among people of northern European heritage, the only generally accepted proxemic needs are those associated with status. However, status is linked to the ego. Therefore, while people accept that the person at the top gets a large office, whenever the subject of spatial needs surfaces it is likely to be treated as a form of narcissism. The status and organizational aspects are recognized while internal needs are not.

Yet, people have spatial needs independent of status. Some people can't work unless they are in the midst of a lot of hubbub. Others can't work unless they are behind closed doors, cut off from auditory and visual distractions. Some are extraordinarily sensitive to their environments, as though they had tentacles from the body reaching out and touching everything. Others are impervious to environmental impact. It is these differences, when and if they are understood at all, that cause trouble for architects. Their primary concern is with aesthetics, and what I am talking about lies underneath aesthetics, at a much more basic level.

As often happens, today's problems are being solved in terms of yesterday's understanding. With few exceptions, most thinking on the man-environment relationship fails to make the man-environment (M-E) transaction specific, to say nothing of taking it into account. The sophisticated architect pays lip service to the M-E relationship and then goes right on with what he was going to do anyway, demonstrating once more that people's needs, cultural as well as individual—needing a room of one's own—are not seen as real. Only the building is real! (This is extension transference again.)

Of course, the process is much more complex than most people think. Until quite recently, this whole relationship had been unexplored.[18] Perhaps those who eschewed it did so because they unconsciously and intuitively recognized its complexity. Besides, it is much easier to deal with such simple facts as a balance sheet or the exterior design of a building. Anyone who begins to investigate context and contexting soon discovers that much of what is examined, even though it occurs before his eyes, is altered in its significance by many hidden factors. Support for research into these matters is picayune. What has to be studied is not only very subtle but is thought to be too fine-grained, or even trivial, to warrant serious consideration.

One hospital administrator once threw me out of his office because I wanted to study the effects of space on patients in his hospital. Not only was he not interested in the literature, which was then considerable, but he thought I was a nut to even suggest such a study. To complicate things further, proxemics research requires an inordinate amount of time. For every distance that people use, there are at least five major categories of variables that influence what is perceived as either correct or improper. Take the matter of "intrusion distance" (the distance one has to maintain from two people who are already talking in order to get attention but not intrude). How great this distance is and how long one must wait before moving in depends on: what is going on (activity), your status, your relationship in a social system (husband and wife or boss and subordinate), the emotional state of the parties, the urgency of the needs of the individual who must intrude, etc.

Despite this new information, research in the social and biological sciences has turned away from context. In fact, attempts are often made to consciously exclude context. Fortunately, there are a few exceptions, men and women who have been willing to swim against the main currents of psychological thought.

One of these is Roger Barker, who summarized twenty-five years of observations in a small Kansas town in his book ECOLOGICAL PSYCHOLOGY.[19] Starting a generation ago, Barker and his students moved into the town and recorded the behavior of the citizens in a wide variety of situations and settings such as classrooms, drugstores, Sunday-school classes, basketball games, baseball games, club meetings, business offices, bars, and hangouts. Barker discovered that much of people's behavior is situation-dependent (under control of the setting), to a much greater degree than had been supposed. In fact, as a psychologist, he challenged many of the central and important tenets of his own field. In his words:

> The view is not uncommon among psychologists that the environment of behavior is a relatively unstructured, passive, probabilistic arena of objects and events upon which man behaves in accordance with the programming he carries about within himself. . . . When we look at the environment of behavior as a phenomenon worthy of investigation for itself, and not as an instrument for unraveling the behavior-relevant programming within persons, the situation is quite different. From this viewpoint the environment is seen to consist of highly structured, improbable arrangements of objects and events which *coerce* behavior in accordance with their own dynamic patterning. . . . We found . . . that we could predict some aspects of children's behavior more adequately from knowledge of the behavior characteristics of the drugstores, arithmetic classes, and basketball games they inhabited than from knowledge of the behavior tendencies of particular children. . . . (italics added) (p. 4)

Later Barker states,

> The theory and data support the view that the environment in terms of behavior settings is much more than a source of random inputs to its inhabitants, or of inputs arranged in fixed array and flow patterns. They indicate, rather, that the environment provides inputs with controls that regulate the inputs in accordance with the systemic requirements of the environment, on the one hand, and in accordance with the behavior attributes of its human components, on the other. This means that the same environmental unit provides different inputs to different persons, and different inputs to the same person if his behavior changes; and it means, further, that the whole program of the environment's inputs changes if its own ecological properties change; if it becomes more or less populous, for example. (p. 205)[20]

Barker demonstrates that in studying man *it is impossible to separate the individual from the environment in which he functions.* Much of the work of the transactional psychologists Ames, Ittelson, and Kilpatrick,[21] as well as my earlier work,[22] leads to the same conclusion.

In summary, regardless of where one looks, one discovers that a universal feature of information systems is that meaning (what the receiver is expected to do) is made up of: the communication, the background and preprogrammed responses of the recipient, and the situation. (We call these last two the internal and external context.)

Therefore, what the receiver actually perceives is important in understanding the nature of context. Remember that what an organism perceives is influenced in four ways—by status, activity, setting, and experience. But in man one must add another crucial dimension: *culture.*

Any transaction can be characterized as high-, low-, or middle-context. HC transactions feature preprogrammed information that is in the receiver and in the setting, with only minimal information in the transmitted message. LC transactions are the reverse. Most of the information must be in the transmitted message in order to make up for what is missing in the context (both internal and external).

In general, HC communication, in contrast to LC, is economical, fast, efficient, and satisfying; however, time must be devoted to programming. If this programming does not take place, the communication is incomplete.

HC communications are frequently used as art forms. They act as a unifying, cohesive force, are long-lived, and are slow to change. LC communications do not unify; however, they can be changed easily and rapidly. This is why evolution by extension is so incredibly fast; extensions in their initial stages of development are low-context. To qualify this statement somewhat, some extension systems are higher on the context scale than others. A system of defense rocketry can be out of date before it is in place and is therefore very low-context. Church architecture, however, was for hundreds of years firmly rooted in the past and was the material focus for preserving religious beliefs and ideas. Even today, most churches are still quite traditional in design. One wonders if it is possible to develop strategies for

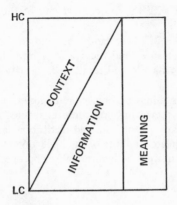

balancing two apparently contradictory needs: the need to adapt and change (by moving in the low-context direction) and the need for stability (high-context). History is replete with examples of nations and institutions that failed to adapt by holding on to high-context modes too long. The instability of low-context systems, however, on the present-day scale is quite new to mankind. And furthermore, there is no reservoir of experience to show us how to deal with change at this rate.

Extensions that now make up most of man's world are for the most part low-context. The question is, How long can man stand the tension between himself and his extensions? This is what FUTURE SHOCK[23] and UNDERSTANDING MEDIA[24] are all about. Take a single example, the automobile, which completely altered the American scene in all its dimensions—exploded communities, shredded the fabric of relationships, switched the rural-urban balance, changed our sex mores and churchgoing habits, altered our cities, crime, education, warfare, health, funerals. (One undertaker recently experimented with drive-in viewing of the corpse!)

In summary:

The screens that one imposes between oneself and reality constitute one of the ways in which reality is structured.

Awareness of that structure is necessary if one is to control behavior with any semblance of rationality. Such awareness is associated with the low-context end of the scale.

Yet there is a price that must be paid for awareness——instability, obsolescence, and change at a rate that may become impossible to handle and result in information overload.

Therefore, as things become more complex, as they inevitably must with fast-evolving, low-context systems, it eventually becomes necessary to turn life and institutions around and move toward the greater stability of the high-context part of the scale as a way of dealing with information overload.

7. Contexts, High and Low

Is there anything more frustrating than being unable to make things work? I am thinking of the child struggling to tie his shoes, or the agony of the man who has suffered a stroke, striving to make himself understood, to get change out of his pocket, or even to feed himself. Equally frustrating though not quite so obvious are the common, everyday problems people face such as disorientation in space or the inability to get from here to there according to plan, or failure to progress in school or on the job or to control the social system of which one is a part. In these circumstances, life turns from an ego-expanding, joyous process to a shriveled, shadow world hardly worth the effort.

In American culture, depending on our philosophical orientation, we blame such failures on either the individual or the social system. Seldom do we look to our lack of understanding of the processes themselves or entertain the notion that there might be something wrong with the design of our institutions or the manner in which the personality and the culture mesh. Much of this frustration stems from people's failure to quite understand the more obvious, superficial manifestations of the institutions they have created. Remember, it is possible to live life with no knowledge of physiology, speak a language well without knowing linguistics or even schoolteachers' grammar, or use a TV set, a telephone, and an automobile without a clue to electronic or mechanical know-how. It is also possible to grow up and mature in a culture with little or no knowledge of the basic laws that make it work and differentiate it from all other cultures.

Cultures, however, are extraordinarily complex, much more so than TV sets, automobiles, or possibly even human physiology. So how does one go about learning the underlying structure of culture? It does not matter much where one makes one's entry as long as one is consistent in what is being observed. Any of the basic cultural systems and subsystems can serve as a focus for observation. These include matters such as material culture, business institutions,[1] marriage and the family, social organization,[2] language, even the military (all armies bear the stamp of their culture), sex (I once knew a man who became fascinated with cultural differences in blue movies), and the law. These activities and many more besides reflect and are reflected in culture. I have chosen to compare some differences in the way the law, as it is observed to function in trials, relates to context in different cultures.

I have chosen the law to make points on contexting for several reasons. First, much of the law as it is administered in the United States has been so decontexted in interpretations that it has been transformed from a positive guiding force into something more akin to gambling than a system of justice.[3] I do not imply that this is always the case or that attorneys and judges willed it so, merely that the larger culture in which the law functions, as well as crucial decisions reinforced by the weight of custom, have created a low-context edifice in which it is extraordinarily difficult to guarantee that the proceedings can be linked to real life. Second, all men are not equal under the law. There are differences in sex, socioeconomic level, power, and ethnicity. Many of our citizens do not trace their cultural antecedents to England and northern Europe but to other parts of the world, where the law is quite different.

In the United States, our ideal is that we have a government of laws, not men, and many Americans generally approve this view. Others, as a result of firsthand experience with the law, have a different idea and see American law as not only discriminatory but cold, impersonal, and unjust. American lawyers I have known see the law as something that is set apart from real life; that is, somehow more perfect (extension transference again). Lawyers, in their own eyes, are endowed with unique ways of thinking not privy to ordinary men. Richard Nixon, when he was Vice-President, was heard to say, "Yes, I can deal with him—he's a lawyer, too."

There are times when lawyers give laymen the impression that there is something special about the law. In American culture, this is true. However, it is true because of the culture, not the law. The culture underlies the law, and many things can be read and understood by studying the way in which the law is handled. Like many aspects of our culture the law is so designed as to operate apart from the rest of life. The common inadmissibility of contexting testimony, including hearsay, sets our courts apart and frequently makes them harsh, inhuman, and impersonal. The culprit, according to Ralph Slovenko,[4] professor of law and psychiatry, is the "opinion rule."[5] According to the opinion rule, only established facts, stripped of all contexting background data, are admissible as evidence. How many times has the reader heard, "Answer the question, Yes or No." Such statements reveal the U.S. courts as the epitome of low-context systems. Those who are interested or well versed in the deeper significance of comparative law and who have a knack for recognizing patterns can get a feeling for other low-context systems by studying how the American legal system actually works, not how it is supposed to work.

One of the shortcomings of low-context systems, particularly in complex societies, is that as their mass increases they become unwieldy. Also, low-context systems are open to manipulation, for as it turns out, it is quite possible for the powerful to build the law that they want by systematically influencing precedents in widely scattered courts. Again, one needs the comparative backdrop of a high-context system to assess this statement properly, because HC systems are not subject to consciously manipulated precedent. Low-context systems do not afford equal treatment but favor those who can enlist the most articulate and skillful lawyers on their side. In addition, if these systems are to operate properly, they must have highly skilled, thoughtful jurists—people who are sufficiently intelligent and skeptical to bring context into the system—to find out what actually transpired, not just what the attorneys and witnesses said took place.[6]

In contrast, the French courts that I have known, the ones that deal with people's problems, allow great leeway in the testimony admitted as evidence. The court wants to find out as much as possible about the circumstances behind the surface acts that brought people before the bench. Everything is heard —facts, hearsay, gossip. The court wants to know what kind of human beings were involved (normally irrelevant prior to determination of guilt in an American court).[7] In a word, the French trial is much higher-context than the United States trial. Paradoxically, the French system places power in the hands of the judge. This is consistent with other highly centralized aspects of French culture, but it removes an added source of contexting balance. In the United States, the law may be LC but juries aren't.

Again, there is no intention to give the impression that one system is better than another, only that they are not only different but representative of the culture and consistent with everything else. It is possible, for example, for juries in the United States to circumvent the anti-contexting biases of the legal system in order to get at essential data, but it is less common than in France. The issue is only that the two systems are structured differently and therefore work differently.

In spite of the French legal system, which permits a certain give-and-take in trials, one discovers that in the culture at large the French are even more subject to the tyranny of bureaucrats than we are in the United States. But in France there is an added quality of involvement in life and with each other which is not common among white Americans. One sees this in business practice. However, many American businessmen have difficulty accepting the fact that French businessmen are very different from their American counterparts. The French as a rule are much more involved with their employees and with their customers and clients as well. They do not feel they can serve them adequately unless they know them well. Even today, in spite of a speeded-up world, once one has established a client or customer relationship in France, one can count on keeping the relationship for generations. The American "high pressure" salesmanship is the direct antithesis to the French. The result, of course, is that if there is an established market in France, Americans will encounter more resistance there than they are used to. One does not move in and win the French overnight.[8]

The Gauls have never been easy for the northern Europeans, the Americans, or the English to understand. The answer may be that French culture is a mixture, a mélange, of high- and low-context institutions and situations. It is not always possible for the foreigner to predict in what proportions they will be found or in what order they occur.

Even more difficult for Americans to fathom are the Japanese, whose language, customs, and dress have captivated and mystified Westerners ever since Commodore Perry's 1853 opening of Tokyo Bay. A friend of mine, a third-generation American-in-Japan who was bilingual in Japanese and English, used to keep a file of items that one must know if he is to function in Japan. My friend never stopped discovering new things; he added to the file almost every day. Japanese courts and law are especially strange to the Westerner, yet they are entirely functional in Japan.

A study of the trial in Japan also gives us appropriate and useful insights into one facet of Japanese culture. Normally, one hears very little about trials in other nations unless they are political. Trials are considered to be an internal matter concerning relations between the people and their government. However, in the early days of the U.S. occupation of Japan following World War II, the Western world had an unusual opportunity to observe Japanese courts in action, to get a glimpse of one of the important paradigms of Japanese behavior. In a move toward normal relations, a Status of Forces Agreement gave the Japanese the right to try United States citizens (including the military) for crimes committed against the Japanese. The inevitable occurred when an army private named Girard, while guarding spent artillery casings left over from practice firing, killed an old Japanese woman. The accident happened because the military had posted guards to prevent the Japanese from scavenging the brass casings. The guards, with nothing else to do, had invented a kind of game using the Japanese scavengers as pawns. Each day when artillery practice was over and the guards were posted, Japanese women would appear and start retrieving the brass casings. The GI guards, using grenade launchers attached to the muzzles of their rifles, would lob these same shell casings at the Japanese, who ducked and scattered as the spent shell casings whistled overhead or thudded into the ground beside them. Girard, an overzealous participant in the "scare the slant-eyes and watch them jump" game, managed to hit the old woman between the shoulder blades, breaking her back and killing her.

This was a clear-cut case for the Status of Forces Agreement. Girard had to be tried by a Japanese court. The Americans were convinced that Girard would be crucified. The case naturally attracted a lot of attention in the United States, where feeling in the press ran high. An American attorney was retained, and the trial finally got under way.

As reported in the press, Girard, instead of being contrite, acted more like a bantam rooster before a cockfight. He strutted and puffed out his chest, waved to the cameras, and clearly reveled in the limelight. Almost without exception, the American press fanned the flames of prejudice by exploiting the natural ignorance and fears of the American public. In a typically bipolar fashion, it was Us against Them.

The Japanese were dumfounded. How do you respond to someone who hasn't the remotest notion of how to behave in court and makes a mockery of your most sacred institutions? Their considered decision, after observing Girard's behavior during the trial and that of his counsel (who was also completely ignorant of either the importance or the subtleties of intercultural relations), was to wash their hands of the entire affair by declaring the accused innocent and asking the United States Government to repatriate Girard and never permit him to set foot on Japanese soil again.

The two systems (the American and the Japanese) exemplify high- and low-context justice. The Japanese trial has an entirely different purpose from the American. Because of the inclusiveness of HC systems, it eschews the protagonist-antagonist conflict which characterizes the American court.

Very high-context systems, by definition, take much more into account, and this has the effect of putting the accused, the court, the public, and those who are the injured parties on the same side, where, ideally, they can work together to settle things. The purpose of the trial is to provide a setting where the powers of government can act as a backdrop for a perform-ance, where the consequences and the impact of the crime are played out before the accused. It also provides an opportunity for the accused to be properly and publicly repentant for dis-rupting the orderly processes of life, for releasing the evil of disorder by failing to observe the regulative norms expected of decent human beings. In a word, the function of the trial is to place the crime in context and present it in such a way that the criminal must see and understand the consequences of his act. It is crucial that the culprit exhibit a high degree of con-trition. Girard's behavior, while gaining him brownie points at home, certainly was a deep, unmistakable affront to the Japanese.

Though he has long since been forgotten, Girard's case illus-trates in almost classic form what happens when high- and low-context systems meet in the same setting, when the unspoken, unformulated, unexplicit rules governing how information is handled and how people interact and relate are at opposite ends of the context scale. There were, of course, both larger and smaller issues at stake in the Girard case. There were deep politi-cal and ethnocentric overtones. Unconsciously, the United States was still defeating the Japanese. To my knowledge, the question of why the United States officers who permitted the grenade-launching game to continue were not brought to trial was never raised—another clue to low-context behavior. If the situation had been reversed, you can rest assured that a high Japanese general would have resigned and, in the old days, committed hara-kiri.

In case the reader is wondering about the difference between the French and the Japanese vis-à-vis context (since courts in both are higher in context than in the United States), the difference is this: The entire French system is a mixture of high- and low-context situations. In Japan, the over-all approach to life, institutions, government, and the law is one in which one has to know considerably more about what is going on at the covert level than in the West. It is very seldom in Japan that someone will correct you or explain things to you. You are supposed to know, and they get quite upset when you don't. Also, Japanese loyalties are rather concrete and circumscribed. You join a business firm and, in a larger sense, you belong to the Emperor. You *owe* each a debt that can never be repaid. Once a relationship is formed, loyalty is never questioned. What is more, you have no real identity unless you do belong.[9] This does not mean that there aren't differences at all levels between people, ranging from the interpersonal to the national. It is just that differences are expressed and worked out differently. As in all HC systems, the forms that are used are important. To misuse them is a communication in itself.

Context, in one sense, is just one of many ways of looking at things. Failure to take contexting differences into account, however, can cause problems for Americans living in Japan, and even at times inconvenience the sheltered tourist. High-context cultures make greater distinctions between insiders and outsiders than low-context cultures do. People raised in high-context systems expect more of others than do the participants in low-context systems. When talking about something that they have on their minds, a high-context individual will expect his interlocutor to know what's bothering him, so that he doesn't have to be specific. The result is that he will talk around and around the point, in effect putting all the pieces in place except the crucial one. Placing it properly—this keystone—is the role of his interlocutor. To do this for him is an insult and a violation of his individuality.

Also in HC systems, people in places of authority are personally and truly (not just in theory) responsible for the actions of subordinates down to the lowest man. In LC systems, responsibility is diffused throughout the system and difficult to pin down—a point that President Nixon exploited in his Watergate defense. Paradoxically, when something happens to a low-context system, everyone runs for cover and "the system" is supposed to protect its members. If a scapegoat is needed, the most plausible low-ranking scapegoat is chosen. In the My Lai incident, a lieutenant took the rap.

Moving from law to literature, one again finds a tremendous resource—a stockpile of cultural data—albeit raw data which must be mined and refined before their meaning is clear. Japanese novels are interesting and sometimes puzzling for Westerners to read. To the uninitiated, much of the richness as well as great depths of meaning pass unnoticed, because the nuances of Japanese culture are not known. Nobelist Yasunari Kawabata provides some excellent examples. In SNOW COUNTRY, the central character, Shimamura, has sought retreat from the pressures of life in a remote country inn, where he meets Komako, a prostitute. Even though Komako never declares her love to Shimamura, she doesn't have to. Only the Western reader might miss the intense passion of her love. In one scene, Komako, mumbling incomprehensible phrases about a party she has left, staggers drunkenly into Shimamura's room, gulps down some water, and staggers back to the party. To the Japanese, the scene is unforgettable, because Kawabata manages to make the reader sense that behind the curtain of Komako's incoherent mumbling lies feelings of a blazing, soul-consuming intensity.[10]

Discussing another of Kawabata's works, "Sleeping Beauties," Donald Keene,[11] a leading authority on Japan, makes a culture-contrasting point that captures the essence of high-context experiences. A portion of his description follows:

A man named Eguchi visits a house of pleasure reserved for men in their 60's and 70's. The men are provided with naked virgins who are drugged so heavily they cannot be awakened from sleep, and are warned by the proprietors of the establishment not to attempt any "mischief." Eguchi spends six nights lying beside six different girls. It is a triumph of Kawabata's virtuosity that he managed to make each of Eguchi's experiences entirely different, even though the six women do not utter a word or reveal anything about themselves but their nakedness. His thoughts as he lies beside these sleeping beauties take in all his life, especially his attachment to the young loveliness of women.

The Western mind boggles at the notion of a man seeking physically passive experiences night after night using the six beautiful, naked virgins only to release a succession of thoughts and memories. Again, in high-context situations, less is required to release the message. It is a sign of Kawabata's genius to use the drugged nakedness of woman to expose all that is in a man.

Anthropologist Weston La Barre[12] has made significant contributions to our knowledge of man, not only by calling our attention to the fact that man evolves his extensions rather than his body, but in his observations of the "human animal" in his natural habitat. One of these is quoted below because it aptly illustrates how much we take for granted even in the most mundane acts, such as "dunking" doughnuts.[13]

> During the last War [WW II] there appeared in the North African edition of *Stars and Stripes* a news picture, purporting to portray an American GI teaching an Arab the gentle art of dunking doughnuts. The American is obviously much self-amused, and the whole context of the picture is "See how good Americans make friends with anybody in the world!" by teaching the foreigner a homely aspect of the American's own culture. But, protests the cultural anthropologist, is this what is actually happening here? Is the GI really teaching . . . the Arab *all there is to know* about doughnut-dunking? For doughnut-dunking also evokes Emily Post, a male vacation from females striving for vertical social mobility, Jiggs and Maggie, the revolt of the American he-man from "Mom" as the introject-source for manners in a neomatriarchate—and much else besides. Underlying it all is the classless American society —in which everyone is restlessly struggling to change his social status, by persuading others that he is a "good guy" and a good average nonconformist-conformist. Doughnut-dunking is all this—and more!

La Barre's commentary on one of the minor culture patterns of U.S. males is an excellent illustration of the fact that behind such apparently inconsequential acts as doughnut dunking, one finds the seeds of social unrest. High-context actions such as these could have been used to predict at least some of the energy and emotional power that lay behind the explosive rebellion of our youth a generation later, not only against Momism but all that they considered to be repressive of the individual's impulses. A generation ago, father figuratively thumbed his nose at his mom by dunking a doughnut. Today, his children overthrow the whole system of parental controls. Today, the dunking example seems ridiculously ineffectual and even timid. However, La Barre's point still holds, that one has to be properly contexted to correctly interpret everyday customs. The soldier who gets a secret bang out of soaking a common piece of pastry in his morning coffee can't tell you why he finds this simple act so psychologically gratifying. The more that lies behind his actions (the higher the context), the less he can tell you.

8. Why Context?

Internal contexting makes it possible for human beings to perform the exceedingly important function of automatically correcting for distortions or omissions of information in messages. This mechanism was investigated by Richard and Roslyn Warren,[1] a psychologist-zoologist team. The Warrens excised portions of words on recorded tape and replaced them with background sounds encountered in everyday life, such as a cough. Subjects listening to the tapes for the first time were unable to detect the excisions; they still actually "heard" the missing sounds and had difficulty localizing the cough. At first, the Warrens simply removed one sound—the central "s" in "legislatures,"[2] used in a normal sentence. They were careful to remove enough of preceding and following sounds so as to eliminate transitional cues. Later, the Warrens eliminated an entire syllable—the "gis" in "legislatures," still used in a sentence—with the same result. Allowed to play the tape as many times as they liked, the subjects would maintain structural integrity of the word and still "hear" the missing syllable. In order to understand this experiment, the reader must visualize a subject using headphones, sitting in a room listening to tapes of sentences. The tapes are of normal conversations with normal background noises; subjects do not at first know that the tapes have been doctored, so they replace the missing sounds because their own auditory contexting processes (of which they are unaware) enable them to do so. Even more remarkable is that when told that a whole syllable was missing from a particular sentence, the subjects had difficulty localizing the cough and were unable to identify even the part of the sentence from which the syllable had been taken. The Warrens state:

> Verbal context . . . *can determine completely the synthesis of illusory speech sounds;* phonemic restorations are heard *when the context is clear* but part of the stimulus is absent. Another illusion arises when the stimulus is clear and the context is absent. (italics added)

However, when a single word without context is repeated over a three-minute period, nothing remains constant—the average subject will hear approximately thirty changes, which involve six different forms. The same word after a time is no longer heard as the same word but several different words. The word "tress" repeated without pause and heard distinctly was soon transformed into "dress," "stress," "Joyce," "floris," "florist," and "purse."[3]

In another, even more recent study of perception as a holistic function, Johnston and McClelland[4] report in *Science* that subjects can perceive and identify a particular letter as part of a word more accurately than they can if the letter is by itself. They state: "The processing of any given stimulus letter must depend critically on the larger stimulus of which it is a part." The words COIN and JOIN were flashed briefly on a screen. It was possible for subjects to read the whole word more accurately and in a shorter time than the letters J and C when projected on the screen separately as single letters.

Contexting is apparently deeply embedded in processes governing the evolution of both the nervous system and the sensory receptors, particularly the eyes and the ears. In fact, it appears that one of the principal consequences of the evolution of the neocortex—the "new brain" that is so highly developed in man—has been to equip the human species so that man can detect and work with patterns to a greater degree than other life forms. This is not "intelligence" as it is measured by educators and psychologists, but an even more basic skill needed by all normal people. Pattern-recognizing ability is what makes it possible to tell that ÂÂâAᴀaAaA are all variants of the same symbol; or to read handwriting that bears only a casual relationship to the standard graphemes used in script; and why it is possible to understand people who have lost important parts of the speech apparatus such as the tongue. If human beings were unable to detect and work with patterns, it is doubtful if complex life could have evolved.

Organisms lower on the phylogenetic scale than man are more easily fooled by mimicry, which is the antithesis of the contexting process. In fact, nature is full of examples of species preyed upon by others who have developed camouflage or other features to outwit the predator. This in turn pushes the compensatory capacity to penetrate camouflage. An example is the several species of hawkmoth that exhibit spots on their wings that look like owls' eyes when disturbed. Mimicry in nature is legion. For example, wasps are very unpleasant eating for birds, because they taste bitter; hence, many insects protectively copy the black-and-yellow markings of wasps.[5] Fly fishermen all know that the flies they tie do not have to imitate the fish's food exactly. They only have to reproduce those features that the fish employs to identify its food. Along this same line, an important set of studies, under the direction of Warren S. McCulloch[6] of the Massachusetts Institute of Technology, which have been devoted to identifying the information sent to the brain by the eye, reveal that the frog is quite easily fooled because of its low-context visual system. Anything that is within a certain size range, is dark, and moves, is going to be treated as a fly by the frog. Live but anesthetized flies that don't move do not get eaten, while the burned head of a match or any small, dark object placed on the edge of a revolving disk will be ingested immediately by any frog within range. As one moves up the phylogenetic scale, more and more contexting (hence greater pattern-recognition capacity) is built into the whole visual apparatus, not only the eye but the brain as well.

Gouras and Bishop[7] have reported on the neural circuitry of the retina as it changes in response to increased needs for information as life forms evolve. They state:

The differences between various vertebrate retinas are not due to new types of synapses but different proportions of the same types, and these differences become most apparent in the output of the retina, the ganglion cells. Ganglion cells of lower order vertebrates are more specific in their stimulus requirements than are those of higher vertebrates. The more specialized a cell becomes, the less potential information it carries, so that by delaying the process of specialization until the more central nervous system—where more nerve cells are available—higher vertebrates gain the advantage of extracting more features from the external world.

By delaying the specialization of stimulus requirements of ganglion cells as they evolve, animals are also less easily fooled and as a consequence have enhanced their survival chances.

Man's visual apparatus enables him to see simultaneously in many different ways, and this is why the eye has yet to be mechanically replicated. The central portion of the retina has two parts or areas. The fovea—which sees with incredible precision—is a small, almost microscopic dot containing some twenty thousand color-sensitive cones, each with its own neuron. Surrounding the fovea is a lozenge-shaped structure, also highly sensitive to color, called the macula. The macula sees clearly but not as sharply as the fovea. It apparently performs a sort of contexting function for foveal vision.

As one moves outward from the center of the retina, the proportion of rods (color-blind cells) to cones (color-sensitive cells) changes. So does the way in which the cells are attached to their respective neurons. The rods increase and are attached in series to single neurons, which has the effect of magnifying movement in the peripheral field. This is an important survival mechanism, since it enabled primitive man to detect danger on either side and is still important in keeping track of speeding automobiles in parallel lanes when driving on today's freeways. The movement-detecting function, however, is only one of the many performed by peripheral vision. At night, rods are more light-sensitive than the cones. Hence, as was discovered during World War II blackouts, it is possible to navigate in the dark using the ultra-light-sensitive rods. Since the central portion of the eye is less light-sensitive than the periphery, a person must try not to look directly at anything at night. If he does, he will not see what he is looking at. When using night vision correctly, one navigates almost entirely by context. It takes time, but as those who have done it know, it is possible to fill in the details from context and memory. Peripheral vision also enables us to find and then fixate with the fovea even very small objects such as a tiny airplane in a large sky. To get a notion of what it is like to do without peripheral vision, try looking through a tube for an hour or so.

Like all mechanical extensions, most photographs and all TV images are low-context. Pictures taken through lenses give a macular view of things.[8] One of the consequences is that the viewer never knows what's going on off camera. This makes it possible to trick him, as in the case with all low-context systems, like the trout going after the fisherman's lure.

Even though a great deal is known about the human visual system, there are still not only popular misconceptions about how that system works, but large areas of ignorance and controversy as well. Moving on from the form, function, and evolution of man's visual systems and keeping in mind what was said earlier about auditory contexting, it is interesting to note how modern science has developed both high-context (rare) and low-context systems and how taxonomies (classification systems) seem to fall into the high- and low-context patterns.

Science and taxonomy go hand in glove. In fact, implicit in every taxonomy is a theory of the nature of the events or organisms being classified. Yet a review of the historical development of taxonomy of living things reveals that, paradoxically, the more Western man classifies, the less useful are his classificatory systems. Folk taxonomies[9] and scientific taxonomies are examples of high- and low-context systems, respectively. For example, in a recent article on the subject, the authors state:[10]

> . . . the taxonomic system we use *appears* to communicate a great deal about the organism being discussed, whereas in fact it communicates very little. Since, in the vast majority of in-

stances, only the describer has seen the named organism, no one with whom he is communicating shares his understanding of it.

In contrast, folk taxonomies perform entirely different functions and are designed not for information retrieval but for communicating *about* organisms with those who already know culturally significant properties of the organisms being discussed. The authors further state:

> In dealing with the vast numbers of organisms that exist, we tend to overemphasize the process of classification and the decisions it involves at the expense of the information *about* the organisms. . . . (italics added)

In other words, modern classification methods provide man with a lot of information that is difficult to integrate into a usable, intelligible pattern. This is a classic example of low-context information. What is more, millions of man-hours have gone into the classification of the million or more species now on record. The classification system cannot handle the vast numbers now involved. A new paradigm is clearly needed.

The reader may well ask how classification systems are relevant to our subject. The classification system is an excellent example of how the majority of Western peoples have been trained to think. Since the days of Linnaeus, the system has been highly respected and occupies a prestigious niche in the edifice of Western thought. Things could not have developed in any other way. The result has been, however, that whichever way we Westerners turn, we find ourselves deeply preoccupied with specifics (remember the neurons in the eye), to the exclusion of everything else. This is true today of our four main institutions, which absorb most of the energy and talent of this country: business, government (including defense), science, and education. Even the ecologists, who should know better, are frequently in dispute because each of the leading figures thinks he has a corner on the truth. The questions that must be answered are: Where do we go for the overview? Who is putting things together? Who are the experts in the high-context integrative systems? Who knows how to make the type of observations necessary to build integrative systems of thought that will tell us where we stand?

We must not only learn how to integrate the two or more systems of observation, but have the courage to underwrite contextual thinking and contextual research. Switching things around will not be easy, because scientific institutions and the committees that referee research grants are set up to deal with and evaluate past research and are miserably equipped to evaluate future research or anything that does not fit the linear paradigms of Western science. To be a recognized HC thinker, one has to be an Einstein or an Albert Szent-Györgyi. Nobelist Szent-Györgyi[11] classifies the two types according to an old Greek system: Apollonian, "which tends to develop established lines to perfection" (LC), and Dionysian, which is more apt to open new lines of research (HC). He says:

> These are not merely academic problems. They have most important corollaries and consequences. The future of mankind depends upon the progress of science, and the progress of science depends on the support it can find. Support mostly takes the form of grants, and the present methods of distributing grants unduly favors the Apollonian. Applying for a grant begins with writing a project. The Apollonian clearly sees the future lines of his research and has no difficulty writing a clear project. Not so the Dionysian, who knows only the direction in which he wants to go out into the unknown; he has no idea what he's going to find there and how he's going to find it. Defining the unknown or writing down the subconscious is a contradiction in absurdum. . . . A great deal of conscious or self-conscious thinking must precede a Dionysian's observations: . . . . . .

A Dionysian scientist must be deeply contexted in his work before he even writes a proposal. Szent-Györgyi goes on to state that in order to get research grants he had to lie about what he intended to do, make up proposals he knew would be acceptable. He states:

. . . while earlier all of my faked projects were always accepted, since I can write down honestly what I think I will do my applications have been invariably rejected.

Continuing in this vein, he states:

. . . sitting in an easy chair I can cook up anytime a project which must seem quite attractive, clear, and logical. But if I go out into nature, into the unknown, to the fringes of knowledge, everything seems mixed up and contradictory, illogical and incoherent. This is what research does; it smooths out contradiction, makes things simple, logical, and coherent. So when I bring reality into my projects, they seem hazy and are rejected. The reviewer, feeling responsibility for the "taxpayers' money," justly hesitates to give money for research, the lines of which are not clear to the applicant himself.

A discovery must be, by definition, at variance with existing knowledge. During my lifetime, I have made two. Both were rejected offhand by the popes of the field.

A footnote to this discussion is Holden's[12] report on the growing feelings of futility and self-doubt among psychologists which she found at a recent meeting of the American Psychological Association. Few psychologists felt that their work was relevant, so perhaps there is still hope for the Dionysian.

There is a paradox in investigating high-context behavioral responses with low-context methods. In fact, the Warrens (referred to earlier) set out neither to investigate nor to demonstrate the role of context in recognition or in the determination of meaning. The results in this case were strictly fortuitous. I would predict, however, that if one could get behind the scenes one would find context-dependent results in the majority of research projects. I would venture that findings of this sort do not get reported as frequently as they might, simply because in most Western science, striving for replicability and rigor in methods is conducted with a view to eliminating context. This is in spite of the fact that there are as models such men as Szent-Györgyi and the brilliant pathologist Dubos,[13] both of whom saw through the fallacy of the usual, Apollonian procedures. Dubos made his reputation by demonstrating that micro-organisms raised in sterile, replicable laboratory environments were not the same organisms but were totally different from those having to meet the challenges of a normal, complex environment. In a sense, what is being discussed is a variation on the physicist Heisenberg's principle of uncertainty, which demonstrates that even in the world of molecular physics the act of observation alters everything.

As one moves from the physicist's world of subatomic particles to living substance, one observes that things become even more uncertain and even less predictable as one ascends the phylogenetic scale. The essence of living substance is uncertainty. If uncertainty were taken seriously, the effect on research methods used in the investigation of complex life forms would be unmistakable. Clearly, the less predictable the performance and the more involvement there is between observer and observed—such as creating entire experimental situations[14]—the more attention must be paid not only to observation but to accuracy and adequacy of description.

Returning to the previous comments concerning the scarcity of comprehensive models, again the field of psychology comes to mind. One does not have to listen for long to hear the complaint that psychology has no comprehensive theoretical model except B. F. Skinner's[15] mechanistic interpretations of Pavlov's behaviorism. Skinner is comprehensive in a single, restricted sense because he reduces behavior to one set of explanations. Following Watson, he holds that everything that man does is determined by his environment. Yet many dislike Skinner's theories, because they are so narrow. It is typical of our culture that we have no way of reconciling or including in one frame of reference such divergent views as Freudian psychoanalysis and Skinnerian environmental determinism. We act as though one *or* the other had to be right, when in fact both work and are relevant when placed in proper perspective. The integration of these two approaches is something behavioral scientists must learn to live with.

Fortunately, some of what is needed is already known. For example, it appears that when one is faced with a high-context system, as in Japan, the power of the system is such that new situations can be learned only if they are approached technically and in the greatest detail. Those of us in the West who are used to having to struggle with the complexities of LC systems can, when we are confronted with something new, be quite creative about it and not require an inordinate amount of detailed programming. HC people can be creative within their own system but have to move to the bottom of the context scale when dealing with anything new, whereas LC people can be quite creative and innovative when dealing with the new but have trouble being anything but pedestrian when working within the bounds of old systems. To all of this there are limits and exceptions, but it is often necessary in an intercultural situation for the LC person to have to go into much more detail than he is used to when he is dealing with HC people. (Remember the example of the GI's stationed in Japan during the Occupation who had to specify the color of the polish to be used when they sent their shoes out to be shined.) If the LC person interacting with a high-context culture does not really think things through and try to foresee all contingencies, he's headed for trouble.

It is easier to foresee trouble or coming confrontations in LC cultures than HC cultures, because in the LC culture the bonds that tie people together are somewhat fragile, so that people move away or withdraw if things are not going well. In the HC culture, according to anthropologist Francis Hsu[16] and others, because the bonds between people are so strong there is a tendency to allow for considerable bending of the system. When the explosion comes, it is likely to come without warning. When the boundaries are overstepped, they must be overstepped so far that there is no turning back. It is sheer folly to get seriously involved with HC cultures unless one is really contexted. This is the danger that the West faces in its dealings with the East, particularly in view of our State Department's head-in-the-sand attitude toward Chinese culture.

While the principle described here applies to the full range of human transactions, from individuals to business to governments, we can only sketch in the basic patterns, because we have not had much experience in looking at cultures in terms of how they structure the information/context equation. While there is a significant difference, one can only guess what the total implications are.

9. Situation—
Culture's Building Block

There are hundreds if not thousands of different situational frames in cultures as complex as our own. These frames are made up of situational dialects, material appurtenances, situational personalities, and behavior patterns that occur in recognized settings and are appropriate to specific situations. Some common settings and situations are: greeting, working, eating, bargaining, fighting, governing, making love, going to school, cooking and serving meals, hanging out, and the like. The situational frame is the smallest viable unit of a culture that can be analyzed, taught, transmitted, and handed down as a complete entity. Frames contain linguistic, kinesic, proxemic, temporal, social, material, personality, and other components.

The framing concept is important not just because it provides the basis for identifying analytic units that are manageable when put in the hands of the expert, but framing can be useful when learning a new culture. In addition, framing will ultimately be the basis upon which towns and buildings are planned in the future. Frames represent the materials and contexts in which action occurs—the modules on which all planning should be based. Learning a new subject or gaining control of a new culture is greatly facilitated if one restricts oneself to natural frames as they occur and does not attempt to go beyond them. The point is subtle but important and one that has been demonstrably successful in overcoming some of the antediluvian methods in the teaching of foreign languages, for example.

Pioneering work in this field was successfully carried out at such places as the Foreign Service Institute of the U. S. Department of State.

In contrast to the situational approach, traditional language learning and unfortunately much of current practice simply reproduce the methods used when the instructor himself was a student. His paradigm is common in the Western world and permeates the teaching field. The student is presented with parts and asked to combine them according to rules which are memorized. For some reason, people reared in the European tradition feel more comfortable if they have a rule to fall back on, even if it doesn't fit. This is important, because people who depend on rules and authorities in order to act are slow to experience the reality of another system. Projecting what they have been told in the past, they fit the world into their own model.

Examples and principles from linguistics will serve to illustrate this point:

1. When an American tries to use his high school French in France, he can neither understand nor be understood. People just don't speak the way he was taught. This is because the rules for language learning, promulgated by some distant, forgotten authority and passed down to the current generation with little change by a more recent authority are almost invariably wrong.[1]
2. People don't learn to perform by combining parts which are memorized according to rules which they must think about in the course of the transaction, whether it is a new language one is learning, or skiing, or spotting enemy planes in wartime. The process is too slow and too complex. Besides, people learn in gestalts—complete units—which are contexted in situations and can be recalled as wholes.
3. Each culture is not only an integrated whole but has its own rules for learning. These are reinforced by different patterns of over-all organization. An important part of understanding a different culture is learning how things are organized and how one goes about learning them in *that* culture. This is

not possible if one persists in using the learning models handed down in one's own culture.

4. The reason one cannot get into another culture by applying the "let's-fit-the-pieces-together" process is the total complexity of any culture. In the West, we cling to the notion that there is such a thing as "the" English language or "the" French language, or "the" Spanish culture or "the" Navajo culture. The "the" model is oversimplified. It does not do justice to either language or culture. Ultimately, use of the model can only lead to frustration, because there is little in language or culture that can be pinned down the way many would like.

These facts were brought home to me several years ago, when my wife (who works with me) and I were asked to evaluate some of the English language tests that were being administered to foreigners in preparation for coming to the United States for various types of training. The theory was that the foreign trainees would need to speak, read, and write English. Therefore, it was decided that before embarking on a training program in this country they should be tested for English competency. It sounds logical enough. The trouble was that those who passed tests given overseas all too frequently were unable to understand what was going on when they were placed in actual classes in the United States or when they had to interact with their American instructors. In fact, they could not communicate in English in even the most basic and simplest situations. Part of the problem lay in the fact that there is no such thing as a basic form of the language that is universally applicable.

During our studies, we concluded that people anywhere in the world master hundreds of what we came to call "situational dialects" which are used in specific situational frames, none of which is the language taught in the classroom. More important, the classroom is the only place where the classroom form of the language will be found.[2] It is a monument to the human intellect that it has been able to overcome the handicap of classroom instruction and move into the living language.

Ordering meals in restaurants represents a class of situational dialects (SD) of moderate complexity, depending upon the circle the speaker travels in as well as on how much of a gourmet he happens to be. If he eats ordinary food or frequents lunch counters in larger American cities, a few properly placed words will do. But if he wants to swing with the Jet Set and be at ease with the maître d'hotel at the Ritz, Maxim's, or La Pyramide, he will need a whole new arsenal of terms as well as strategies and plans for their use.

Properly used, situational frames are relatively high-context. This facilitates and simplifies matters and makes it possible to take advantage of what the other person already knows. However, one must have been given the proper expressions to use in the appropriate contexts, for the situational dialect immediately identifies the speaker as one who belongs, one who is an insider, not an outsider, and therefore as one who knows how the system works. This applies even to such simple situations as boarding a bus or buying a railroad ticket. It is possible for the neophyte to observe and learn the SD from the habitual customer or passenger, as these transactions occur with great speed and little effort. "Two first to Land's End returning" is all that is needed. None of this business about "Would you please sell me two round-trip tickets, first-class, to Land's End for today?" The language used between pilots and control-tower personnel is an excellent example of a very high-context SD, developed in response to the need for a language of great parsimony and low ambiguity. The use of this language is admittedly limited, but to those who know it, it fits the pattern to a T. Situational dialects of these types frequently make use of restricted codes —and remember, restricted codes are for the insider. Everything is condensed: grammar, vocabulary, intonation. All the rules that are so carefully learned in the classroom go right out the window.

What the neophyte or outsider needs to know is: What do I say and what do I communicate by my posture, intonation, gestures, and clothing in this particular situation? He also must be able to read his interlocutor's speech as well as his behavior, regardless of whether he is of the culture or a foreigner. New situations require the learning of new situational dialects—for example, meeting the new in-laws when class or ethnicity is different. In fact, anything that one does for the first time.[3]

At times, the new SD is simply a consequence of joining a new organization. Twenty years ago, I had a job in a research training satellite of an East Coast university. The organization was staffed by two types of people—Ph.D. professors and young women secretaries who kept the place running. I was barely ensconced in my office when I began to pick up some of the tensions. The academicians clearly ranked the women much lower than themselves, while the women felt that many of the obsessions with accuracy and form in written material were narcissistically motivated and unnecessary. My sympathies were with the women. So it was therefore puzzling to me when I noticed that they began acting toward me in a way that verged on being fresh or rude. I wondered what I had done to elicit such behavior. They were still being polite and pleasant to the regular professional staff. Fortunately, the secretary I had brought with me was deeply contexted in a variety of speech and behavior as well as being a more relaxed human being than I. She translated for me. "The girls like you, you ninny. You are the only one around here who treats them like human beings."

In one sense, the notion of situational behavior in speech is not new. Savants ranging from Socrates to Peter Drucker[4] have stressed the necessity of speaking to people in their own language. But one should not only speak to people in their language but in situations with which they are familiar and feel at ease, and which are appropriate to the transaction. Easier said than done, but not all that difficult either, once people accustom themselves to the idea that what makes another individual uncomfortable may not be the result of specific design on the part of the speaker as it is incorrect situational usage. The bus driver, the counterman, and the man in the control tower all appreciate it if you use their particular SD properly.

Faking an SD on the job is another matter. In fact, it can be a form of condescension and frequently has a phony quality unless it was actually learned on the job, as with a man who has worked his way up through the ranks and become president. He is still one of the boys when he wants to be, and uses the situational dialect to indicate how he defines the situation. He is one of the boys when he wants to be, Mr. Smith at other times. People can understand this because his use of the SD is a communication about a communication.

Situational behavior appears to be basic to all vertebrates. No one knows how far down the phylogenetic scale situational behavior can be traced. Possibly it extends as far as single-celled organisms which have active and passive phases, times when they conjugate and when they divide, when behavior alters. It does appear, however, that complexity of the situational inventory is a function of evolution. Play, for example, does not emerge as an identifiable activity below the level of birds and mammals. Play is readily observed in mammals, particularly the young. Though Lorenz[5] claims to have observed jackdaws playing, the difference between play and non-play in birds is more difficult for humans to distinguish than in mammals. However, people do buy "toys" for parakeets, and while there may be an element of anthropomorphism here, the aerobatics of ravens that I have seen in the mountains is a form of play.

Anyone with any experience of animals (even laboratory animals) knows that animals will exhibit a repertoire of species-specific behaviors with accompanying hormonal changes (as with females in heat). These behaviors are frequently associated with specific psychological states as well as specific times and spaces. The hungry animal looking for food or eating is different from one with a full stomach. The animal in the middle of an active sexual cycle exhibits different behavior from one whose sexual drive has subsided. Other "basic archetypical situations" (BAS) are: birth, death, hierarchical behaviors (dominance and submission), agonistic or aggressive behavior, play, territorial behavior, teaching and learning, and various types of communicative behavior.[6]

The suppression of and failure to recognize man's situational needs in the Western world has resulted in untold distortions in the way we live, the meaning we attach to life, and how our personalities develop. Take the sex drive, which lies behind a basic archetypical situation. Without the repression of sex, the aberrations of behavior that led to Freud's theories would not have occurred. Today, there has been a swing in the opposite direction. Sex, instead of remaining situational in character, insinuates itself into everything from the packaging of presidents to automobiles. Play, another BAS, is now pursued like work and turns into a multibillion-dollar industry in the United States, with the result that few white middle-class Americans know how to really play. The effect that this has had on our daily lives and our politics is incalculable—we take ourselves much too seriously.

Consider time. While the time system in American culture has not been developed to the extremes that one finds in Switzerland and Germany, time is the dominant organizing principle in the culture. Time started as a natural series of rhythms associated with daily, monthly, and annual cycles. It is now imposed as an outside constraint and sends its tentacles into every nook and crevice of even our most private acts (bowel movements and sex are regulated by the clock and the calendar). As many of the young have discovered, our time system has done much to alienate Western man from himself. A reason for people getting sick is to escape the shackles of time and to return and re-experience their own rhythms, but at what price!

In THE SILENT LANGUAGE, as well as Chapter 1 of this volume, I described some different time systems developed by other cultures. If there is anything that can change the character of life, it is how time is handled. Time is not a "mere convention," as some English anthropologists would lead us to believe, but one of the most basic organizing systems of life, for all situational behavior has a temporal and spatial (proxemic) dimension.

In discussing time in the West, it is important not to forget that, without schedules, industrial society would be unknown. Dependence on time as an organizing system can be traced to the need to co-ordinate activities when transportation was relatively slow. Now the electronic revolution not only makes for simultaneous diffusion of events throughout the world but the storage of events on video tape so that they can be viewed at any time, and there is no longer the pressure for a time strait-jacket. The assembly line, which has been viewed for years as an anti-human abomination eliciting nothing but anomie, resentment, and boredom, is finally in the process of being slowly altered. The problem has been what to do about it. Fortunately, industry on its own initiative is beginning to consult workers for solutions. In Sweden, auto workers in teams now assemble an entire motor. In other plants, both abroad and in the United States, efforts are being made to switch people around in order to vary not only the job but the rhythm as well.

Aggression and territoriality have received a good deal of attention these days—too much attention. The point is not that man is or is not aggressive. Man, like other animals, is situationally aggressive; but, unlike other species, he handles and channels aggression in many different ways depending upon his culture and how it structures and integrates aggression. The Hopi of Arizona, who live crowded together on their mesas, will tell the white man that they are not aggressive, they are the Peaceful People—this is their ideal. However, when one gets to know them, as I did in living and working with them for a number of years, it is evident that aggression among the Hopi has been dissociated. They are brought up in the belief that it is bad to be aggressive and do not seem to experience their aggression, if we are to believe what they tell us. Yet, evidences of aggression keep cropping up among the Hopi like locusts burrowing their way through asphalt. The town of Awatovi, the easternmost village, was destroyed and the inhabitants murdered by their Hopi neighbors. New Oraibi exists because of a factional split in Old Oraibi. So do Moencopi, Bakavi, Polacca, and other villages at the foot of the mesas. Gossip and slander are a form of aggression which are endemic among the Hopi. My own theory is that the Hopi had to put the lid on aggression because they were crowded in incredibly close quarters on the mesa. (The whole First Mesa, housing three villages, appears to have less space than the deck of a single aircraft carrier.) All of this the Hopi probably could have tolerated if they were not the possessors of an unusually rigid and unyielding culture, one in which there is very little freedom to deviate from cultural norms. Thus, the Hopi are both physically and psychically crowded in their mesa-top towns. Open aggression would tear the place apart, so they simply repress it.

Extreme crowding can be tolerated if everyone behaves, talks, thinks, and feels according to the dictates of a common pattern. Cultural and social rigidity can be hard on people, because mankind is the most diverse species on earth, but it is apparently necessary under crowded conditions. Aggression springing from differences can be dangerous when living in close quarters. In such circumstances, man's energies must be turned to channeling aggression so that it is not continually being triggered. How this is done is illustrated in the life of some of America's Indians. Prior to the time when the white man killed off the buffalo and rounded up the more nomadic Indians, the Plains Indians, living with vast spaces around them, recognized and institutionalized a modified form of aggression in their warfare. They could afford it then, but not now.

One sees evidence of the restricting nature of situational behavior in another minority group, the mentally ill. This was illustrated in a report in *Science*.[7] The author, Rosenhan, and his colleagues presented themselves to twelve mental hospitals in five different states on both coasts. This group of sane scientists simply told the admissions personnel that they heard voices uttering words like "thud," "empty," and "hollow." Otherwise, everything the scientists did and said, including their case histories, was true. In all cases, hearing voices was sufficient cause for admission. Once inside, regardless of their behavior, Rosenhan and his group were judged insane and treated accordingly. The mere fact that they were patients in the actual situation of a mental hospital was enough to distort every perception of the hospital staff. There is no such thing as a patient independent and separate from his hospital situation.

Man is not innately and solely aggressive or co-operative or loving or sexual or hard-working or playful or hierarchical or territorial or bound by time or competitive or materialistic or scholarly or communicative. He is all of these things but usually emphasizes only one or two at a time. Not only is man situationally loving, hard-working, hierarchical, etc., but different individuals seem to be endowed with different proportions of these traits: some are more active, others more energetic, or more social, or more communicative than others. However, if these traits are suppressed by the situational inventories of the culture, this can lead to trouble of a deep, ill-defined nature, like a plant potted in the wrong soil.

This brings us to the convergence of psychiatry (particularly psychoanalysis) and anthropology. The two fields overlap in the study of how man's situational needs are structured, handled, sublimated, repressed, suppressed, experienced, and exploited. An improper balance leads to neurosis; denial of man's nature, to psychosis.

No culture I know or have read about has developed a perfect balance of man's situational needs. This is due in part to the fact that man domesticated himself with very little knowledge of his own basic nature. Some cultures seem to have done better than others at domesticating their members, but whether this is true is impossible to determine. To my knowledge, no comparative studies have been made as to how well man satisfies his basic situational needs in different cultural settings.

Following World War II there was a spate of interest in man's "basic needs." Very little came from a needs approach because of the overriding influence of culture on needs. The fact that so many social scientists were attracted to a needs approach is indicative that there was something there, but we were simply not able to deal with it given the conceptual models available at the time. About the same time, a study of "values" was also fashionable in anthropology, and values studies received extensive and generous support from the foundations. Unfortunately, the study of values is a little like studying vocabulary without reference to grammar, etc. You can learn something, much of it interesting but also at times trivial unless of course the lists of values are so extensive as to provide the basis for a pattern analysis.

The study of situational behavior—basic, archetypal, and derived—differs from both the needs and values studies in that it focuses on a total situation that is made up of elements from all the primary message systems, follows the pattern laws of order, selection, and congruence, and is part of a transaction—that is, where there is feedback. In other words, a situation is a complete entity, just as a sentence is a complete entity. Situational frames are the building blocks of both individual lives and institutions and are the meeting point of: the individual and his psychic makeup, institutions ranging from marriage to large bureaucracies, and culture, which gives meaning to the other two.

In these terms it is interesting to note that Sullivan defined personality in situational terms. An almost overwhelming task lies ahead to classify situational frames and the way in which they build up into larger wholes. Man has had very little experience with this sort of analysis, and I for one have no notion where it will lead us.

10. Action Chains

Borrowed from ethology, the action chain is closely linked conceptually to the situational frame. An action chain is a set sequence of events in which usually two or more individuals participate. It is reminiscent of a dance that is used as a means of reaching a common goal that can be reached only after, and not before, each link in the chain has been forged. Like frames, action chains can be simple, complex, or derived. Every action within a frame has a beginning, a climax, and an end, and comprises a number of intermediate stages. If any of the basic acts are left out or are too greatly distorted, the action must be started all over again. Making breakfast, meeting a friend, becoming engaged, buying something in a store, writing a poem or a book, are all examples of action chains of varying complexity.

There are practical reasons for studying action chains, some of which are particularly relevant to the tasks of the architect and the planner. Thus, research in how space is used reveals that failure to get detailed data on the action chains and the situational frames in which they occur can result in breaking the chain. This happens when architectural spaces don't fit the activities they house. Crowding is so devastating in its consequences not because it is inherently bad, but because it results in disorganization and disruption of action chains. For those who remember Calhoun's experiments with rats,[1] progressively increased crowding resulted in seriously disrupted nest building, courting, and care of the young, all of which represent action chains.

In order to review for the reader the concept of the AC, a description of a well-known simple sequence that has been studied at length by Tinbergen[2] is paraphrased below from one of my earlier books:

Phase A
Steps
1–4

In the spring, each male stickleback [a fish of the family Gasterosteidae] (1) carves out a circular territory, (2) defends it several times against all comers, (3) and builds a nest. (4) His inconspicuous, gray coloring then changes, so that his chin and belly are bright red, his back blue-white, and his eyes blue. The change in coloration serves to attract females and repel males.

Phase B
Steps
5–10

When a female, her belly swollen with eggs, comes within range of the stickleback's nest, (5) the male zigzags toward her, alternately displaying his face and colorful profile. The two-step ceremony must be repeated several times before (6) the female will follow the male and enter the nest. Shifting the visual mode of communication to the more basic one of touch, (7) the male with his nose rhythmically prods the female at the base of her spine until she lays her eggs. (8) The male then enters the nest and fertilizes the eggs, and (9) drives the female away. (10) He repeats this sequence until four or five females have deposited eggs in his nest.

Phase C
Steps
11–15

(11) At this point the mating impulse subsides, and a new set of responses is observed. (12) The male becomes his old, inconspicuous gray. (13) His role now is to defend the nest and (14) keep the eggs supplied with oxygen by fanning water through the nest with his pectoral fins. (15) When the eggs hatch, the male protects the young fish until they are big enough to fend for themselves. He will even catch those that wander too far, carrying them in his mouth carefully back to the nest.

Niko Tinbergen, the Dutch ethologist who first studied the stickleback, notes that the male's zigzag approach to the female is a slightly inhibited urge to attack which must run its course before the sexual urge can emerge. It is the egg-swollen shape of the female that releases the courting response in the male. When she is heavy with eggs, the color red attracts her; once the eggs are laid, this is no longer the case. Yet she will not lay eggs until prodded by the male. Because the sequence is so predictable, Tinbergen was able to conduct several experiments in crowding and its relation to action chains. Too many males meant too many territories too close together and, as a consequence, too many defenses of territory, to the point that there was such disruption that males were even killed on occasion. Too much red in the environment disrupted the courting sequence and broke the chain, so that important steps were omitted. Eggs were not laid in the nest, and if they were laid, were not fertilized. The response to crowding in this instance was identical to that of Calhoun's crowded rats.

On the human level, one finds comparable action chains. In fact, I seriously doubt if man does anything of a social nature that does not involve action chains. Some AC's are incredibly long, requiring more than a lifetime to be played out, while others last only a few seconds.

One example of a short action chain would be shaking hands. One person extends his hand. The hand is taken and the correct grip found—the amount of pressure that is applied in the United States is arrived at by a complex series of extraordinarily rapid responses controlled by feedback from the pressure applied by the other party. There are exceptions, of course—those individuals (usually male) who oversimplify the process, reducing it to a kind of contest of strength. The duration of the shake and the terminal breakaway are determined by situational factors independent of the actual handshake: the degree of eye contact and mutual responses of warmth or lack of it, all of which can transpire in less than ten seconds.

All planning, if it is realistic and not of the armchair variety, constitutes and must take into account an elaborate hierarchy of action chains. Planning that is not thought of in this way is static and doomed to miss the mark.

Action chains represent transactions in the sense that Dewey and the transactional psychologists use the term. These can be divided roughly into three basic categories:

1. Transactions with the inanimate environment and man's extensions, ranging from preparing a meal to building a house, a huge dam, or even a whole city.
2. Transactions with living things, including plants, animals, and other human beings.
3. Intrapsychic transactions involving the various parts of one's psyche. In Freudian terms, there are transactions between the id, the ego, and the superego as well as between life and death wishes, for example. Or, if one is a follower of Harry Stack Sullivan,[3] there are the in-awareness and dissociated aspects of one's personality; i.e., behavior that is consciously experienced as contrasted with that which is experienced only indirectly. Intrapsychic transactions occur in the context of both the first two categories, and since man spends considerable time rolling things over in his mind, transactions can occur in which the contexts are illusory (imagined).

The reader, at this point, should be reminded that the division of nature into inanimate and animate and intrapsychic realms is strictly the product of Western European thinking. Other cultures carve up the universe differently. The Hopi, for example, should have no difficulty recognizing the transactional nature of dealing with plants and animals, for they talk to their crops and their sheep and to all growing things, just as they talk to their children so that they will grow and develop properly.[4] The Hopi tell us that they cannot conceive of anything growing and flourishing except with love, care, and encouragement. In addition, their use of time used to be and probably still is very, very different from that of the white man. The Europeans who inhabited the North American continent imposed their time system on everything, organic and inorganic alike. Whites have concrete notions concerning books, houses, dams, office buildings, etc., all of which have scheduled times for completion, just as children are supposed to walk and talk and go to school at certain ages. For the Hopi, every *living* thing has its own inherent time system; tasks concerned with man's material nonliving extensions therefore have no inherent schedule. Hence, the Hopi feel no compulsion to complete certain jobs within a specified time.

When I was working with the Hopi in the 1930s as a construction foreman, the fact that the white man had schedules for all sorts of projects that the Hopi did not, caused considerable tension. Construction projects such as dams were scheduled to be completed in a given length of time. The Hopi could not understand why they were always being needled to hurry things up and why it was that a dam should be built in any set length of time. Today, of course, some forty years later, things undoubtedly have changed. At the time I am referring to, a house could have taken twenty years to build.

Carlos Castaneda's[5] Yaqui sorcerer of Sonora does not distinguish between the three categories of transactions, but lumps them all into one. To him, man cannot be separated from nature. He conducts his transactions according to an elaborate system of knowledge in which detailed information is required concerning the specific habits, attributes, and characteristics of plants, animals, and people, all of whom fall into categories that are either suitable or unsuitable for a particular person to deal with. A given individual may have to avoid one of the categories of magic, and all the plants and animals as well as the knowledge associated with that magic. Hunters relate to one cluster of living substance, while men of knowledge have another set. It is important for the Yaqui man of knowledge to control the forces in himself and the forces in nature and to balance these forces intelligently. Man has a *personal* relationship with everything. What one needs from life is power, but that power can be used or find its way only in certain directions, which are set by the karma of the particular individual.

Like many of the things we have discussed, action chains can be arranged along a continuum ranging from those in which the commitment to complete the chain is haphazard at best to those in which a relentless progression is set in motion and there is no turning away. A given chain in the continuum can be explained by two factors: the internal state of the organism, and culture.

A cat that has been trained to kill mice does this in a particular and highly predictable way. She sees the mouse, stalks it, pounces at the right point, pins the mouse down, rotates it if necessary, and breaks its neck with a well-directed bite below the base of the skull. However, when the cat is no longer hungry, the chain is altered. The cat will avoid injuring the mouse when pouncing and will play with it instead of dispatching it in the businesslike fashion she uses when she's hungry.[6]

In man, there are psychological drives that are not as easily sated as a basic drive like hunger. A predatory woman will set her cap for a particular man in highly predictable ways. Once the chase is on, there is little doubt, either, as to the steps she will take or the outcome. Similarly, any mother who has stood by helplessly while arguments between her husband and son escalate from a chance remark to a point where it looks as though the two want to kill each other, knows about this relentless action chain. There is, of course, a situational variable that must be taken into account in all cases. Both father and son will generally be less likely to start something when on their good behavior—in the presence of company, for example. Which type of AC is more relentless and binding—the personality or the culture—is not known. But cultures do seem to vary greatly (just as individuals do) in the extent to which action chains, once started, must be played out.

The Kentucky feud is a case in point; so are the vendettas of southern Italy. The Trukese, who occupy islands in a South Pacific atoll, were captives of a system of vengeful warfare that they were unable either to circumvent or stop until outsiders intervened when the islands were annexed by the Spanish and later the Germans in the nineteenth century. When dealing with both Arabs and people of Spanish heritage (the two are culturally related), one has to be very careful to avoid any action that will push them into a "spite pattern," for once the spite syndrome is entered, there is no relief.[7] Logic and persuasion normally fail unless there is strong intervention by a third party.

The Arab-Israeli dispute is a perfect illustration of the processes I am describing. What makes it doubly devastating is that neither side seems to realize that a significant portion of their difficulty is cultural.

The degree to which one is committed to complete an action chain is one of the many ways in which cultures vary. In general, high-context cultures, because of the high involvement people have with each other and their highly interreticular, cohesive nature, tend toward high commitment to complete action chains, all of which makes for great caution and often reluctance to begin something, particularly in fields or relationships that are not well known. White Americans and other low-context people, particularly those who deal primarily with word systems, do not ordinarily feel as bound to complete actions regardless of circumstances as some other cultures. Many white Americans will break a chain at the drop of a hat if they don't like the way things are going or if something or someone better comes along. All of this is very unsettling to people brought up with a different set of expectations. Any culture in which commitments are taken lightly or have to be enforced by law is going to have a problem with the stability of its institutions—a situation that can be very unsettling for everyone.

René Spitz,[8] the Swiss psychiatrist whose insights have contributed so much to an understanding of man's psyche, published a delightful paper called "The Derailment of Dialogue—Stimulus Overload, Action Cycles, and the Completion Gradient." The reader must not be put off by Spitz's title; it was written for other psychiatrists! What he has to say, however, has a relevance that extends beyond psychiatry and is applicable to each of us. Spitz describes some of the traumatic consequences of broken chains and uncompleted acts.[9]

Spitz's theory is that if human beings (or other animals) are put in the position of having to cope with the consequences of too many broken chains, they will compensate. The compensations will ultimately become so numerous as to block or prohibit normal behavior. The culmination of this process, he calls "derailment of dialogue," a term that indicates not only words but actions as well. To such derailment, he attributes many of the ills of our overcrowded cities, including juvenile delinquency, sadistic teen-age crimes, neuroses, and psychosis.

Rollo May,[10] another psychiatrist and philosopher, discussing the apathy of the United States public following the invasions of Cambodia and Laos, sees four types of apathy as steps in an escalating series, starting with withdrawal from life and culminating in violence.

First, there is "withdrawal from the active world to give time to repair the damage to oneself, and to protect oneself from further damage." This is known to the young as dropping out.

Second, there is the apathy of impotence. American students were apparently going through this stage as a consequence of their inability to influence the Washington juggernaut.

Third, is the apathy of hopelessness and despair of the type experienced by the German people following World War I when they were saddled with an impossible economic burden of war reparations and forced to accept the "war guilt." Such apathy is the type that breeds dictators.

Fourth, man reaches a state of numbness and "unfeelingness." May believes that no human being can exist for long in this final state. He does not merely stagnate: ". . . the pent-up potentialities turn into morbidity and despair, and eventually into destructive activity. . . . It develops in him a readiness for wild aggression and violence . . . without thought of whom he will hit." Many ghetto dwellers in this country evidently had reached this stage when they burned and pillaged their own neighborhoods in the late sixties.

Clearly, May's scheme is somewhat different from Spitz's theories. The two focus on opposite ends of the political spectrum. While Spitz is oriented toward the individual in an interpersonal encounter, May concentrates on the individual's feeling of being powerless to influence the vital factors that control his own life, particularly at the national level. The drive toward responsive government is a basic one stemming from the need to be heard and to influence the outcome of events that control one's very existence. Failure to achieve this goal hits at one of the basic political action chains in men's lives. In his books,

May describes what he believes to be the consequences of varying degrees of failure in the democratic process.

The term action chain has been frequently used in my own household for the past few years. I find that my wife, like all monochronic people with strong drives to do well, is particularly sensitive to interruptions. This brings up another point in regard to intercultural relations. While I mentioned earlier that high-context people have a greater commitment to complete action chains than low-context people, I must now amend this statement somewhat. High-context people also tend to be polychronic; that is, they are apt to be involved in a lot of different activities with several different people at any given time, a pattern that characterizes most Mediterranean cultures. Monochronic peoples, in part because of the way they schedule their lives, are more comfortable if they can take up one thing at a time.[11] It is the high involvement factor, of course, that produces the greater degree of context. To the low-context, monochronic, one-thing-at-a-time person, polychronic behavior can be almost totally disorganizing in its effect, *which is identical in its consequences to overcrowding.* Action chains get broken, and nothing is completed. The two systems are like oil and water: they do not mix.

Furthermore, polychronic cultures often place completion of the job in a special category much below the importance of being nice, courteous, considerate, kind, and sociable to other human beings. Remember, polychronic people are much more vulnerable to anger once it gets started. As a consequence, their action chains are built around human relations. To be too obsessional about achieving a work goal at the expense of getting along is considered aggressive, pushy, and disruptive. In effect, two people engaged in the same task, one of them monochronic and the other polychronic, will view the entire process from very different angles and will have not only a different set of objectives but different priorities as well.

Courting, in both man and animals, is a series of interdependent AC's. In man, the chains are both explicit and implicit, but the latter are more binding. Because of my interest in young people in our own culture, I once decided to study the processes whereby young men and women get to know each other on a university campus. A single setting, the library, was selected for study because it was known to be an area that students used to pick each other up. The library was ideally situated to the needs of the study, for there were places where one could observe the process without intruding on it. Two students were assigned the task of observing on a regular schedule between 7 and 10 P.M. for a period of six weeks. At first, they observed every night. Later, when the pattern had been recognized, they found that Monday and Tuesday were the most active nights, but regular checks were made at other times. Their report is summarized below.

First, boys preceded girls and staked out their territory, taking every other seat at study tables, leaving opposite seats open. As decoys, books on law, medicine, and business were spread out so that girls could ascertain boys' career interests. Second, thirty-five to forty minutes after the boys were positioned, the girls would show up and make their selections. Third, within fifteen to forty-five minutes of the girl's being seated, the boy would ask a question, make a comment on what she was studying, or ask to borrow something—a pencil, a piece of gum. The female would respond or comply and act pleasant, but no more. Fourth, in forty-five minutes to an hour, a conversation was initiated *by the female*, which elicited information from the male. At that time, if the female closed her book, leaned back, or stared at the male, he would ask her to go on a study break, where the second phase of getting acquainted began.

The chain could be broken by either party at several points. However, in *no* case in which the female initiated the first encounter did the couple leave together. Nor did this occur if the female failed to observe the 45–60-minute period between encounters. (Time is no mere convention.) Much more transpired than has been recorded here, such as visual appraisal on the sly and unconscious syncing. What was interesting was that the same paradigm occurred over and over again, week after week. And if the chain was broken, one party would leave and start again the next night. There were those who never caught on, both male and female. These unsuccessful ones constituted our controls. Elsewhere, my students and I have been investigating courtship in the United States, in Barbados, and among the Spanish Americans in New Mexico. As a result of these investigations, we have found that the steps in courtship, once identified, are extraordinarily stable.

Courtship is not restricted to couples but is also found in the business and academic worlds when people are being considered for important jobs. The higher the position, the more elaborate the ritual.[12] The same pattern occurs when a business decides to purchase a subsidiary or set up a joint venture. I have heard both businessmen and politicians say, without batting an eye, "I would be perfectly willing to jump into bed with them."

Spelling out the rules for the courtship progression (AC) is difficult for people, and their ability to be specific varies greatly. Most people can give only the barest outlines. Even after working with students at Northwestern University who had been made aware of unconscious patterning, my assistants and I have found that there are great discrepancies between one group and another. In one study, the boys were able to produce six times as much concrete information on courtship as the girls, just the opposite of what we had predicted. This, of course, is only a single study, and it is very likely that at another time the ratio would be reversed. Nevertheless, in such an important area of life as choosing a mate the process is still safely guarded by being relegated to that part of the consciousness over which people have little or no control. There is clearly a pattern, but most people rebel at the notion of making it explicit. Like Freud's unconscious, the cultural unconscious is actively hidden and, like Freud's patients, one is forever driven by processes that cannot be examined without outside help.

11. Covert Culture and Action Chains

> "If I could have found my tongue, I would not have struck him. . . . I could say it only with a blow."
>
> *Billy Budd*

Being inarticulate, Billy Budd would have felt it but not said it. It took Melville to put it in words. People avoid verbalizing what they take for granted—their basic modes of interacting with each other. One reason for this is that much of the truly integrative behavior that falls under the rubric of culture is under the control of those parts of the brain that are not concerned with speech. What we are discussing are super gestalts, so important and so centrally located in the scheme of things that they are almost impossible for us to formulate verbally. This is because much behavior is not experienced on the verbal level but on the emotional. I once watched a highly intelligent Pueblo Indian engaged in intercultural education programs struggle and sweat to put into words a problem he and his people were having to cope with. Whenever a white man is put down in the middle of a pueblo, the Indians must cope with his narcissism as expressed by his almost total preoccupation with how *he* is doing (providing he is well motivated) or how he is being treated (if he is less idealistic). Regardless of motives, behavior of this sort is threatening and disruptive to Pueblo life, because the Indians are just the opposite. Their concern is not with themselves but the group and how the group is faring. The

Indians see what we call narcissism in all whites—a trait that goes far beyond and is much more inclusive than self-love and individual differences. Since the Pueblo Indians themselves are not this way, how can they describe what they themselves do not include in their experience? And what does the well-motivated, concerned white man do when he has devoted much of his life to "helping" the Indians only to discover that cultural insight reveals him as a disruptive force in Pueblo life, even though he considers himself an ally? Why hadn't any of his Pueblo friends told him this?

Many of the deeper, more significant features that characterize a given culture may be experienced as threatening when first encountered. The action chain is no exception, because in a culture that prides itself on freedom and individuality, the AC reveals that the actor, instead of being autonomous, is directly and intimately bound up in the behavior of others. Furthermore, people often aggressively preserve the folklore of everyday life. They stubbornly resist the notion that there is anything about themselves that they don't already know. Some of these responses can be traced to extension transference, some to the tremendous power of the grip of culture, and some to the natural resistance on the part of most people to rearranging their thinking. I also suspect that in the United States we are somewhat ambivalent about taking a long, careful look at anything we ourselves are doing. Low-context cultures seem to resist self-examination.

Information on human action chains is therefore scarce. But as people learn more about how the AC functions and begin to look at behavior in this new light, the solutions to problems in intercultural relations wherever they are found (inside or outside our boundaries, between the sexes, in schools, and in business) will begin to be seen in a new light.

In the meantime, there will be those who will want to know, Why bother studying action chains or even thinking about behavior in this way when there is already enough complexity with which to contend? Why? Because people held in the grip of action chains can never be free of them unless they see the AC's for what they are. For instance, a friend built a beautiful country hideaway in an isolated New Mexico village. To his dismay, one of the local busybodies, with thousands of square miles to choose from, also bought land and built a house within hailing distance. The last thing in the world my friend wanted was to become involved with this particular widow, even in a superficial way. Things looked grim indeed until he remembered that they were both originally from New England and, since he was already established in the valley, she could not call on him until he had called on her! He never did. The two lived separate and uninvolved lives in sight of each other until his death, many years later.

Had they known of the work of Emanuel Schlegloff,[1] people who have been plagued by indecent phone calls could have discouraged the caller. In analyzing the opening gambits of telephone conversations, Schlegloff discovered that whoever answers the ringing phone is the first to speak. The caller speaks next. The rules are so binding that it is possible to foil the obscene caller by picking up the phone and simply refusing to say hello.

The American is all too familiar with the action chain governing the rules for entertaining friends. How many times have you heard a woman say, "We have had them over twice. Now it's their turn." The chain can be broken by either party.

At a certain point in all AC's, one arrives at a stage at which words are called for. Failure in the use of words short-circuits the chain and frequently leads to violence. This point is illustrated by Melville's[2] Billy Budd.

For those of us who come from the northern European tradition, disputes escalate in stages, starting with nonverbal cues and body messages and proceeding to indirection, verbal hints, verbal confrontation, legal action, and finally force, or physical action. The paradigm is basically the same whether it is a household dispute, neighbors quarreling over a boundary, or management and labor locked in a conflict for power. The labor dispute is like a ballet, in which the steps and stages are well known and it is taken for granted that they are known by everyone. The exception is when the culture or the subculture of the two parties is different. Then the fat *is* in the fire. Incorrect reading of the adumbrative[3] (foreshadowing) sequences of an action chain not only deprives the participants of the steps, stages, and way stations that tell them where they are and permit reconsideration and face-saving withdrawal but, what is more serious, leads to meteoric and unpredictable escalation of disputes to a point of no return. In the animal world, outside intervention that short-circuits action chains usually results in vicious, uncontrolled fighting of a type that is ordinarily rare among animals. In man, the same principles apparently hold. One manifestation of a serious psychosis is the omission of important steps in the chain while jumping precipitously to the final stage. Intercultural disputes have this quality also. In any event, short-circuiting of an action chain is likely to be serious. In courtship, it may end up in rape; in disputes, it can go as far as murder. When cultures meet, because the steps are different few people know where they are.

Take the difference between the Anglo-American and the Spanish-American in New Mexico, a relationship I have observed for over half a century. The descendants of the Spanish conquistadors are sensitive to the slightest suggestion of criticism. Confrontations are therefore to be avoided at all costs. In addition, there is obdurate pride, which must be maintained, and for males there is the added burden of "machismo." Like the Arab, the Spanish-American social organization tends to be flat. School children and adults alike who do not belong to the elite tend to avoid competition or any activity that will set them apart from their own group. Their leaders, in contrast, are expected to be forceful and strong and to show that strength.

In Anglo-American disputes, one progresses by steps and stages—from subtle innuendo and coolness (one must be polite) to messages via a third party, to verbal confrontation, then legal action, and finally force—if nothing has worked and the law is on your side. For the Spanish-American, another system is used. First there is brooding (May's third stage[4]) and, since verbal confrontation is to be avoided, the "If I could have found my tongue, I would not have struck him" law is applied. The first inkling that something is wrong is a show of force. Force or action is to the Spanish-American not a step in a chain but a communication in itself. It is designed to get attention. Later, much later in the process, they resort to the courts.

The Spanish-American pattern was illustrated by an acquaintance, a rancher named Chavez, who was telling his sister of trouble he had with an Anglo neighbor. The Anglo, either deliberately or through ignorance, had fenced several hundred acres of Chavez's land. In discussing this with his sister, Chavez said, "I am going to do it 'their' way this time. I'm not going to tear down that fence. Instead, I'm going to tell my lawyer to fix things up." Up to this point, nothing had been communicated to the Anglo rancher that anything was even wrong. Under normal circumstances, his first inkling of trouble would have been when he discovered his fence cut to ribbons and the posts uprooted.[5]

A more typical Spanish-American reaction is the activities of Reyes Lopez Tijerina, who put up signs laying claim to land, took two state park rangers captive, and raided the Tierra Amarilla courthouse, with tragic consequences. He was signaling for attention to Spanish-American grievances. The Anglo community read it as the last step in a dispute and countered with an arsenal of legal actions.

In attempting to fathom a pattern like this, it is important to keep in mind that several different forces are at work in Spanish-American culture. The first is avoidance at all costs of face-to-face confrontations or unpleasantness with anyone with whom you are working or with whom you have a relationship. Avoidance of unpleasantness can lead to great stress, however. For example, a young Spanish-American boy in Santa Fe was working part time for a hotel cook to whom he was also deeply indebted. One day, he simply failed to turn up, because the hours of his other job had been changed, which resulted in a serious conflict. Rather than having to tell the cook about his problem, he simply left without notice. In another instance, in my own household we once lost a very fine housekeeper because her husband insisted that she come home by 3 P.M. and our hours were nine to four but could have been changed. She could not bring herself to discuss this with my wife, and only indirectly and too late did we learn what the problem was.

Other factors affecting escalation are the incredibly strong ties and loyalties of family and friends in the Spanish-American community. If one person loses his job, the whole family may quit, with the result that disputes have a rather extraordinary interreticulated quality that is difficult for the linear-minded Anglo to sort out. The net effect is for the Spanish-Americans to hold back until they can stand it no longer and then strike out. In the Middle East, where these patterns have their origins, third parties play an important role by intervening in disputes.[6] In the American Southwest, the third-party intervention pattern is no longer present (if indeed it ever was), and the results are bitter confrontations.

The Spanish-Americans of New Mexico fall into the high-context, highly involved group, where there is constant monitoring of the individual's emotional state. But low-context Anglos, not being as finely tuned to other people's moment-to-moment moods, are almost inevitably caught off guard. Looking at the Spanish-Americans' actions, Anglos often assume they are dealing with an "end of the rope" phenomenon, while in reality they are in the middle of an action chain. The Anglo overreacts. One Anglo rancher in Tierra Amarilla, a large, poor county in northwestern New Mexico, who has had his fences cut repeatedly over the years, his valuable horse shot, and his house destroyed by fire, is quite naturally livid on the subject of his Spanish neighbors. He doesn't know or care why they feel the way they do for the loss of their lands, or why they act as they do. Both sides are held in a vise-like grip of their own cultural unconscious; both are at a standoff, and all communication is now parataxic. Neither knows how they got into such a miserable mess nor do they know how to disengage with honor. Both the Anglos and the Spanish-Americans are victims of a culturally engendered situational neurosis that will require extensive treatment before it is cured.[7]

All cultures with which I am familiar follow general ethological principles and have built-in safeguards to prevent disputes from going too far, though such safeguards may not always work. These safeguards apply within the bounds of the culture but, because they are not intellectually understood or made explicit, they seldom function when dealing with outsiders. The European Spanish, having been occupied by the Arabs for over five hundred years, incorporated many Arab culture patterns. It is therefore difficult to understand why the role of the responsible intermediary, so well developed in the Middle East, is not stronger in the Spanish colonial culture of New Mexico. Given the short, rapid escalation of steps so characteristic of high-context cultures, disputes will inevitably become serious unless disinterested outsiders take on the responsible role of a strong and highly committed intermediary. By what process the intermediary role was lost, attenuated, or possibly even failed to be integrated in the Spanish communities of New Mexico, is not known. New Mexico was the furthermost oupost of Spanish culture in North America and hence peripheral in many respects to the mainstream of that culture. To complicate matters further, the Anglo-Americans came in as conquerors following the Mexican-American War in 1846. They destroyed or failed to provide support for many Spanish institutions. Anglos generally do not understand, in fact distrust, the role of the intermediary and don't know how to use it themselves.

While the evidence collected over the years on dispute escalation between these two cultures is convincing, this is not the whole story. However, most of the suffering and ill will can be traced to a failure to read the adumbrative signs of the escalation process on both sides. In most of life's struggles, there are no villains and no heroes, and no one is to blame, because the nature of the cultural unconscious is such that by definition only a few even know it exists.

In the Far East, we find similar but more serious situations, serious because more is involved and the cultural distances are greater. Once while visiting Tokyo, I was invited to lunch with a Japanese friend atop one of the city's new skyscrapers with all of Tokyo spread out below us. Perhaps the choice of setting was deliberate—I will never know—because my host chose the occasion to give me an overview of some of the sticky points in U.S.-Japanese relations. In his own way—indirect but very clear to me—he said that there were certain things that the Americans had missed in Japanese culture and that these things

represented danger points of which Americans were almost totally unaware. We discussed the matter from a variety of angles.
My interest in adumbrative behavior made me anxious to know
more about how people in Japan know where they are in a relationship at a given moment and how they keep tabs on how
things are going.

Again, the high-context rule applies. In face-to-face relations
in Japan, amenities and cordialities are maintained, no matter
how one is feeling. To show one's anger is tantamount to admit-
ting loss of control (and face), unless, of course, *"things have
gone too far."* There are no adumbrative signs to warn of im-
pending disaster, and Americans, as well as many Europeans,
will unconsciously push and push—looking for structure, pattern, and limits. Because they are unfamiliar with the Japanese
system, Europeans are almost inevitably destined to go too far.

We could ask ourselves, of course: How are we supposed to
know? The answer is: Make haste slowly and make use of the
most skillful, subtle interpreter of the culture you can find.

The reader will remember the incident in which I was being
moved around in hotels and even from one hotel to another
without any warning or word from the management. If I had
been using my own cultural system, this could have been taken
to mean that they were trying to communicate something to
me. Fortunately, in this instance I was only partially influenced
by my own culture.

Chinese culture bears certain resemblances to Japanese in
regard to adumbrations. In troublesome situations, one acts as
though nothing had happened. What makes this possible is the
tremendous latitude and great stability of the system. Individuality, minor dissent, and clashes of personality are handled by
pretending that they do not exist. If one acknowledges the
things that happened, then one must take action, and action is
very, very serious. For example, a Chinese father will put up
with a lot from his son without ever saying anything, because
he knows that the boy must express himself but also that the
strength of the family system, rooted as it is in ancestors, will ultimately bring the son around. However, when youth goes ram-
pant, as was the case with the Red Guards, the events are

frequently consciously designed beforehand to achieve specific ends. It is difficult to explain and almost impossible for Westerners to understand how others could stand back and ignore what are to us clear-cut signs. How could the Chinese fail to recognize and respond to acts on their own doorstep (Vietnam) at one moment and be so hypersensitive at another? Yet the Chinese will fail to see when we are serious and will not read and interpret correctly the adumbrative signs in our action chains. When one thinks about it, the process we are involved in is extraordinarily risky—brinksmanship without design. There is a danger for all of us, because neither side can accept the reality of the other's unconscious culture. Any time the members of one culture state that there is no subtlety in another (which is a view that many Chinese apparently have of the United States), it is a clear sign that the subtlety has not become manifest in the course of human transactions, because I know of no culture without subtlety.

Clearly, within the confines of a single culture, disputes, as well as the settlement of disputes, follow reasonably well-established patterns. Otherwise there would be chaos. It is difficult, however, for mankind to come to grips with the fact that there are deep cultural differences that must be recognized, made explicit, and dealt with before one can arrive at the underlying human nature we all share. Given the advanced state of weaponry, if man is not to destroy himself he must begin to transcend his own culture. First, the overt, obvious culture—which it is possible to bridge with patience and good will—but second and more important, unconscious culture—which is much more difficult to transcend.

Recognition of the cultural unconscious is a relatively recent development in Western thought, so recent in fact that understanding out-of-awareness cultural processes is rare. Some of my most learned and erudite colleagues reject the notion that there is even anything to discuss in man's unconsciously structured temporal and spatial system. Talking about unconscious culture in concrete terms is a little bit like talking about writing systems for language prior to the development of writing. The reader should ponder a moment on what it would be like to live ten thousand years ago or more, trying to grapple with the analysis of language. Of course there would be those who verbalized freely, yet were completely unaware of the fact that there was a system that regulated their speech. They would be impatient with anyone who said there was a system. How do I know? Because this is what happens when linguists develop writing systems for languages that haven't had them before. (Remember Ferguson's experience with speakers of colloquial Arabic in Chapter 2.)

Another nonverbal system is the way people walk, which communicates status, mood, gender, age, state of health, and ethnic affiliation. As with some speech parts (the mouth, teeth, and nose, which we share with other mammals), the primary purpose of the legs and body is not communication. Yet people can read volumes from how others walk, particularly if they are well known to the observer.

Aided by graduate students and time/motion analyzers, I have been studying people walking and how they communicate by their walk. There is nothing mysterious about the method. Anyone who has patience and perseverance can do the same thing by playing over and over and over, slow and fast, a frame at a time, movies of many different people walking. The actual analysis is somewhat more complicated and quite tedious. Sorting out the crucial structure points even in a basic system like walking is possible only after you have worked at it a long time. This is because there is the simple act of locomotion and then there is something else. Mae West built her career on that something else.

When determining structure, one must divorce oneself from what is happening on the conscious, explicit, "meaning" level. This explains in part why so little is known about the structure of cultural systems. Also, most people have models that explain practically everything. Much that has been learned about the cultural unconscious conflicts with those models. In addition, the normal route taken when the members of two cultures collide is to explain things in political, economic, operational, or personality terms. These are usually present in any situation, but all are modified by culture, which is seldom examined as a factor in human relations. Finally, when an analysis of any given cultural system has been successfully accomplished, there is a strong tendency to apply that system indiscriminately as though all cultures were alike (the missionaries using English syntax to teach Japanese).

Cultural projection always has been a stumbling block on the path to better understanding. Yet progress in getting rid of cultural projection has been slow. For example, one of the great insights into human behavior and thought occurred at the turn of the century, when Franz Boas[8] and followers Leonard Bloomfield[9] and Edward Sapir[10] discovered as they studied American Indian languages that the generalizations about language (up to that time based on Indo-European languages) were not universally applicable. Boas's insight led to the still only partially accepted practice of approaching each culture anew, as though absolutely nothing was known about its structure. This is still a wise practice.

To some people, linguistic examples may sound esoteric and divorced from the practical realities of life. There is no immediate answer to the businessman who says, "I simply do not believe that whether I sell or not overseas is a matter of manners. So what if I'm a little rude—it's price that counts in the marketplace." He's using cultural projection, and a lot of businessmen do think that way, but it will show up on the bottom line eventually. Nothing could be more practical than being aware of the significance of cultural differences.

This was illustrated to me by my son, who has learned the hotel business from the bottom up. Employees can make or break any hotel, and management may never be able to pin down why things went wrong. One of management's worst offenses is failure to know the substance of the many subcultures that go into making a hotel function. For example, in many hotels bellboys have two jobs: first, carrying luggage in and out, for which they are tipped by guests; second, doing things for front-desk management, such as moving guests from one room to another, checking on supplies or forgotten clothing, etc. They are seldom tipped for the second job. For the first, and primary, job, bellboys rotate like taxis waiting at a stand. The "front boy" is the one at the head of the line, and he is the one who is most visible. A common error of hotel managers, since they frequently do not know how the bellboys' system works, is to ask the bellboy who is most visible to do the second type of job, thereby casting him from his head-of-the-line place and upsetting the rotation system.

The situation just described is an intercultural misunderstanding just like the ones that occur between men and women or between accountants and salesmen in the same firm. Usually there is no language barrier, and large components of the major culture are shared by the people involved. When misunderstandings of this type occur, they are usually attributed to personality or political factors and seldom to the fact that there are at least two different systems involved and there is ignorance on both sides! The principal difference between these situations and true interethnic or intercultural transactions is that the areas of ignorance are larger and the ability of the members of the different cultures to describe how their system works is more limited.

Unfortunately, much of anthropology these days is more concerned with what people say than with what they do, i.e., their folklore of culture. Folklore is folklore and should be treated as such. All one can say when studying any aspect of a strange culture is: there is a system; the people who live by the system can tell you very little about the laws that govern the way the system works (they can only tell you if you are using the system correctly or not); there is little relationship between the manifest way in which the system is expressed (the meanings derived from it) and how it is organized; the system is bio-basic—rooted ultimately in the biology and physiology of the organism; the system is widely shared, yet has within it the capability of distinguishing not only between two or more members of a small group but between hundreds of thousands and even millions of members of a given culture.

A first approximation of a definition of such systems would be as follows: The cultural unconscious, those out-of-awareness cultural systems that have as yet to be made explicit, probably outnumber the explicit systems by a factor of one thousand or more. Such systems have various features and dimensions which are governed by the order, selection, and congruence rules.[11] These rules apply to the formative and active aspects of communications, discourses, perception (in all modalities), transactions between people, and the action chains by which humans achieve their varied life goals. Significant portions of extension systems still function out of awareness. Much of the formation, development, use, and change processes of these extension systems, therefore, fall within the scope of out-of-awareness culture and not only exert a hidden influence on life but are subject to the same rules and laws. The investigation of out-of-awareness culture can be accomplished only by actual observation of real events in normal settings and contexts. It is not amenable to philosophizing—at least at present. Until notation systems apart from language are developed for culture, it is doubtful that the type of revolution occasioned by the development of writing and mathematics will occur. When this happens, however, there is no way of gauging the effect on human consciousness. Culture is therefore very closely related to if not synonymous with what has been defined as "mind."

This chapter has alluded to the slow progress of Western man along the road to human understanding. There are many reasons for the snail-like progress: our scientists haven't yielded as much usable mind/culture data as we would like, for they have been bound by the restraints of their own culture. In one way or other, our educational institutions lie at the root of both the good and the bad. Education influences mental processes as well as how problems are solved. I'm not referring to the content of education—because that can be changed at will—but the structure of the educational process and how it molds our thought processes. Our educational institutions, having taken the bureaucratic road and attained such gargantuan size, have become set in concrete. They are unchangeable. Chapter 12 gives my reasons for thinking so.

12. Imagery and Memory

At what time language developed and how it evolved are not known. What we see is the end product of a long and complex series of evolutionary steps. Along with tool making, language is one of the extension systems that most characterizes human beings—regardless of their stage of economic and political development.

However, the gradual evolution of language was one thing, the realizaton that language is a system another. The knowledge that man not only talks but has rules for talking (grammars) is taken for granted today. Yet when man first became aware of the fact that he talked, a dramatic revolution was set in motion. Language became detached from man and took on a life of its own; it became a system in its own right. From this came writing and writing systems as well as the ability to play with ideas—logic and philosophies. All these developments followed the principle of extension transference and explain in part why intelligence is so closely connected in men's minds with verbal facility. Possibly because language plays such a prominent part in our lives and because of the ET factor, other intellectual systems have been pushed aside. Our problems in education are exacerbated by educational systems and philosophies that stress verbal facility at the expense of other important parts of man's mind, which are either ignored or downgraded. The result is enormous waste of talent and dreadful damage to an unknown but significant portion of our population.

Beginning with the establishment of schools, intelligence and education have become irrevocably linked in men's minds. People who couldn't make it in schools were thought to be dumb. Their lack of performance was invariably associated with failure to master either word or number systems or both. Yet what do intelligence, verbal skills, and education add up to when we take a hard look at man's past as well as his closest relatives in the animal world, the anthropoid apes, who do not talk?

Intelligence, after all, did not begin with man, nor did the mammalian brain begin with schooling. It evolved over a period of millions of years of problem solving in real, life-and-death struggles. What is more, the folk belief that you can't think unless you can put it into words has yet to be demonstrated. In fact, many examples of nonverbal cerebration in both animals and people refute it. The study of our past can teach us a lot about *how* our intelligence has evolved from that of animals. For as anyone who has dealt with animals knows, there are smart and less smart members of any species. Jane Goodall reports chimpanzee behavior that reveals a high order of intelligence and insight.

Figan, a young chimpanzee, showed unusual acumen. Goodall and her husband had placed bananas in the trees in such a way that the larger males could not hog them all and the young and the females had a chance at their share. Goliath, a dominant male, was sitting directly under a banana which he had failed to see but which Figan had spotted. Goodall describes what happened:

> . . . after no more than a quick glance from the fruit to Goliath, Figan moved away and sat on the other side of the tent so that he could no longer see the fruit. Fifteen minutes later, when Goliath got up and left, Figan, without a moment's hesitation, went over and collected the banana. Quite obviously he had sized up the whole situation: if he had climbed for the fruit earlier, Goliath most certainly would have snatched it away. If he had remained close to the banana, he would probably have looked at it from time to time. Chimps are very quick to notice and interpret the eye movements of their fellows, and Goliath would possibly, therefore, have seen the fruit himself. And so Figan had not only refrained from instantly gratifying

his desire but had also gone away so that he would not "give the game away" by looking at the banana.

There was more:

Commonly when a chimpanzee gets up from a resting group and walks away without hesitation, the others will get up and follow. It does not need to be a high-ranking individual—often a female or a youngster may start such a move. One day when Figan was part of a large group and, in consequence, had not managed to get a couple of bananas for himself, he suddenly got up and walked away. The others trailed after him. Ten minutes later he returned by himself and naturally got his share of bananas. We thought this was coincidence—indeed, it may have been on the first occasion—but after this the same thing happened over and over again: Figan led the group away and returned later for his bananas.[1]

People who have had firsthand experience with the reasoning capabilities of animals may still be hesitant to apply what they know to educating children, perhaps because humans are placed in one category and animals in another. We have been detached from the rest of life and seldom see ourselves as part of nature. Konrad Lorenz,[2] the father of ethology, is an exception. His work and that of others[3] show that what we call intelligence is not limited to humans but has its origins in lower life forms. It is widely shared and has played a very prominent part in the survival of many species. For example, the brain-to-body weight ratio (the biologist's basic measure of intelligence) of porpoises and whales is equivalent to that of humans. Porpoises are highly intelligent, but since man has not been able to decode their communication system, there is no way of telling exactly how intelligent they are. Much of what we know of porpoises comes from observations in very limited and stultifying artificial environments. Therefore we have never really been able to observe porpoises long enough and in enough detail in their natural setting to get to know them in the way Goodall knows her chimps. Techniques may never be developed that will make possible years of study of aquatic life in the detail now customary when studying land animals. The problems to be solved are certainly formidable.

Nevertheless, animal studies do show what animals can do without language. And while we have only recently begun to study other animals in their natural state, we are learning more each day. It is not necessary to depend on our still limited knowledge of other life forms. Even more convincing evidence comes from man himself.

Because he was a genius and made so many dramatic contributions to modern physics, the intellectual processes of Albert Einstein came under repeated examination by friends and biographers alike[4] who wanted to know how Einstein did it. He performed poorly in school up to and including his graduate years at the Technological Institute in Zurich. According to Einstein, he did not think in words, nor did his important insights come to him in mathematical terms. Instead, he had physical images coupled with visual images that represented complete entities (systems) which then had to be laboriously broken down and translated into mathematics and words. Fortunately, Einstein discovered early that mathematics (an extension system that works independently of words and is centered in a different part of the brain) was a powerful tool not only for expressing his insights but for communicating with other scientists. However, at times, even mathematics was not enough to make his theories stick, for distinguished and renowned scientists such as Planck and Poincaré resisted Einstein's ideas in spite of his elegant presentations. Apparently they could accept the mathematics, but there was another part of the brain—an integrative part— that said no. Einstein states, in a letter to his friend Professor Heinrich Zangger, that "Planck is blocked by some undoubtedly false preconceptions. . . ."[5]

My own experiences in and out of the academic worlds have forced me to recognize certain things about my own life and the directions it has taken that were in a sense almost predetermined. A low aptitude with words coupled with great curiosity and a practical mind kept me from being swept up and preoccupied with the main stream of philosophical and theoretical anthropology as developed by many of my colleagues. Consequently, I have been involved in a number of projects which brought me into contact with businessmen, lawyers, physicians (mostly psychoanalysts and psychiatrists), diplomats, artists, architects, engineers, designers, and laborers. All have been concerned with the solution of real-life problems.

These experiences, particularly those having to do with teaching and educating, convinced me that people, even within the confines of a single culture, learn in many different ways. In the process of teaching people from many different professions, I have gleaned a good deal that I would not have learned had my career followed more traditional lines.

I do not know what goes into the miracle of learning. I only know that in the United States in recent years we have approached learning ineptly. A teacher can stand on his head and keep students involved, entertained, and interested, but that's hardly the point. Man, the animal with the most highly evolved brain, is above all a learning organism. He is designed to learn. The only questions are: How does he do it? And under what circumstances and settings does he do it best?

So much has been written these days on the subject of education and what is wrong with our schools (much of it both correct and relevant) that one approaches the subject with some trepidation. As an anthropologist, I would naturally look at man in terms of his past, asking myself what kind of an organism he is. How did he get that way? And how does the way in which his sensorium functions affect what happens in a classroom? An unforeseen dividend in my studies of proxemics (man's use of space) was what I learned about man's senses, how he uses them, and what this means in terms of education.

Space and the spatial experience has been the realm of the architect for two millenniums. Architects create both open and closed spaces: cathedrals such as Chartres, Reims, Notre Dame, and the great dome in Florence; squares such as the one at Nancy, San Marco in Venice, and the Piazza della Signoria in Florence. Yet if I had been educated as an architect the chances of my being able to do research, to integrate, and to write a book like THE HIDDEN DIMENSION would be practically nil. Why? Because I would have been brainwashed by the architectural education, which has a bias in favor of visual aesthetics. Most architects think of the spatial experience as primarily visual. As one of them once explained to me, they also think of it in terms of drawings and renderings—that is, two-dimensionally![6] However, behind this relatively simple statement lie some problems of considerable magnitude. One of the talents of architects—the fact that they are great visualizers—separates them from their clients and causes untold pain and agony. Architects can look at a drawing and, using it as a reminder system, reconstruct the spaces quite vividly in their own minds. But few clients have this capacity. Clients have to actually be *in* the space after it is finished before they can experience it. This may explain some of the disasters that come about in urban planning. The non-architects who review the plans do not have the capacity to see what will happen until the highway or the bridge or the building is in place, and by then it is too late.

Chloethiel Woodard Smith, a very gifted architect and friend, has had success in designing for people (as contrasted to designing for other architects). Recognizing the translation problems her colleagues were having, on occasion, she eschewed plans and words and instead put on demonstrations for those involved in a project so they could see what would happen. Considering the placement of a freeway in our nation's capital, she placed chairs strategically on the ground and hired trucks and vans to be parked where the freeway would be. The reality of the high vans accomplished what drawings or words failed to communicate.

The beautiful view of the Potomac was shut off. People develop different sensory modalities either by temperament or training. Many people whose talents and livelihood depend on what is written, live in a paper world and take in little else. In fact, it is difficult to predict what people will perceive or fail to attend. Kevin Lynch, an architect and student of space perception, working at M.I.T. with an English colleague, Don Appleyard,[7] once asked passengers in automobiles driving a selected route on the freeway from Boston to Cambridge to draw at periodic intervals what they saw out the car window. No one drew the automobiles, trucks, or buses. Bridges, underpasses, church steeples, landmarks, yes—but no traffic!

Before working with architects, I had been intimately involved with psychiatrists of the psychoanalytic school, as well as with diplomats. Both are highly verbal and depend for their livelihood and their status on adeptness with spoken and written words. They can take words and translate them into ideas and even emotions. One has to use words well if one wants to communicate with either group. Having become habituated to words after working with these two professions, my first contact with architects came as a shock. It was like working with an entirely new tribe about which I knew nothing. I learned that one had to reach this group via their eyes—with pictures, not words.

The risk one takes in explaining all this is that educators and educational psychologists will jump to the wrong conclusion, because they have known for a long time that, if they augment the spoken word with a visual presentation, communication is improved. The assumption is that the more modalities that are involved in learning, the greater the retention. This approach, however, has implicit in it that all people's central nervous systems are basically the same, and that if they are not, something is the matter. This is not true.

My own deficiencies in this line have taught me a lot. A very low rating on the auditory scale forced me to learn the culture of the word world the hard way. My sister, who was a whiz at words, did exceptionally well in school, but not only because of verbal proficiency. She had an eidetic memory. She could visualize almost anything she had ever seen. During examinations, she carried her crib in her head. She could project any page of text or notebook in her mind's eye and read off what she had written days, weeks, or even months before. My brother, on the other hand, was a near genius with machines and optics but had trouble with words and read only with great difficulty. The educational system washed him down the drain. He experienced considerable misery establishing himself without an education. The miracle is that he was able to succeed in spite of it.

I did not see either of my siblings in a true light until work with architects and product designers opened up a new world for me. One would be hard put to find a less articulate or more gifted and stimulating group. The young designers who attended my classes were deeply involved in how things *work*. They wanted to know principles and were fully aware of a wide variety of systems. Give them a design problem and they would solve it. How often does it cross one's mind that every single man-made thing was once a design problem and was actually consciously designed? The type on this page. The paper. The book itself. The chair one is sitting on. Pencils. Pens. Paper clips. Pots and pans. Clothes, food containers, labels, radios, televisions, magazines, cities and houses, everything.

Because of the highly developed skills of the advertiser, design in the United States has a two-dimensional visual bias. This bias makes it possible to fool the public and is easy to detect in many items—they look fine but don't work. Either they are roughly textured with sharp edges, or they smell bad, or they sound and feel tinny and shabby. People lie with pictures and renderings, even though we don't call it a lie. Did you ever see an architectural rendering of a building and then compare it to the reality? Talk about misrepresentation! Yet we take this form of distortion for granted because we are in the grip of McLuhan's Gutenberg Revolution and extension transference. Truth is printed on a page; reality is pictures. All of which conditions people to a flat, shallow approach to all sensory inputs. We live in an artificial, and for the most part two-dimensional, fragmented, manipulative world of advertising and propaganda. The medium really is the message, particularly in the United States.

My studies of space—how people experience it and create a model of the spatial world in the central nervous system—forced me to acknowledge the perceptual clichés of my culture. These studies revealed the multisensory character of man's existence. The process is somewhat analogous to going from black-and-white to color or from mono to stereo, but much more dramatic. My world became round and deep and real. Full of smells, tastes, textures, heats, sounds, and muscular sensations. Both vision and sound became much more three-dimensional. My design students helped me to realize that man, like all organisms, must not only respond with each of his senses but must be able to store and retrieve multisensory information as well.

All these experiences, research in how man perceives space, fortuitous life experiences, the need to deal with professional groups, clients, and students who image differently in their brains, created a sufficient impact to jolt me out of the restraining perceptual and conceptual bonds of my own culture.[8] I began to ask all my students how they remembered things and how their senses were used in the process of thinking. Most of them of course hadn't the remotest notion of how they thought and remembered, and, as a consequence, they had to go through a long process of self-observation. When they finally did begin to discover something about how their senses were ordered, they invariably jumped to the conclusion that everyone else was just like them, a notion they tenaciously held. One girl with an unusual capacity to visualize insisted that she was in every way exactly like everybody else. This common projection of one's sensory capabilities or lack of them may explain why teachers are frequently impatient with, or unsympathetic to, students who do not have the same sensory capabilities as the teacher. In fact, the degree to which most individuals will tenaciously hold on to the notion that everyone else perceives, thinks, and remembers with the same modalities that he does is remarkable. During a semester-long experiment on proxemics in which advanced students were to teach beginning design students, one pair of students ended the semester with the completely "new" insight that they stored and processed information in very different ways. Each had gone through the frustrating experience of projecting his own sensorium onto the other. One of them finally came to me and said, "I can't get over it! He really *is* different. I'm a word person and he is almost entirely visual."

In order for students to inventory their sensory capabilities, I asked them to, first, rank their senses in order of their dependence on each sense in a memory capacity; and second, to list what they did with each sense in the way of memory. One highly visual student could look at a map once on a cross-country trip and never have to glance at it from that moment on. Another, an auditory-verbal person, could compose and hold in his head up to twenty typewritten pages of text—about five thousand words. Beyond that, he needed an outline.

Another could go down a long ski slope once and remember the muscular sensations associated with every turn, bend, dip, slope, and mogul. He could practice the entire slope while lying in bed. One girl's color memory was so accurate she didn't have to take swatches to stores, while several young men could hear a tune once and then play it "by ear," even years after a performance. One friend can read music from a sheet and hear it in his head. Later, when he hears a live performance, it frequently is not up to his own imaging. Several of my students have weight problems because they can read recipes and taste the final product, which makes them hungry and they overeat. This suggests that some people with weight problems may not be compensatory eaters so much as they are highly developed in the gustatory sense (an overlooked aspect of weight control). We have one friend who is thin because he simply does not like food. His capacity to image tastes—even good ones—is nil. There are those who can image any smell—perfume, the fragrance of their first date, the dank odor of the vegetable cellar in their grandmother's house, and Christmas turkey in the oven.

Finally, I asked my students to describe what they could do creatively with a given sense. Could they design a house without putting pencil to paper, or could they compose music in their heads without benefit of pen or instrument? Beethoven is reported to have been able to image music so vividly that he could compose for the strings, listen to the results, and then feed in the brasses without reference to extensions such as instruments or a written score. His capacity to image auditorily was such that it was a long time before he knew he was growing deaf. Music, to him, evidently was not a passive thing; while he was composing, he did an incredible amount of thumping, bumping, and stamping around in his room.

Nobelist Max Delbruck, while discussing differences such as these, told me that he had recently returned to an old love, astronomy. He was having difficulty, because his visual memory of star charts which he kept near his telescope was not good enough to cover the short time span involved between looking at the charts and checking the stars in the sky. I would have a similar difficulty with words. Another student of mine has practically no capacity to remember either verbal or visual material unless he can attach it to a muscular (proprioceptive) sensation. This may be why it is helpful for students to write out words that they fail to remember or which they misspell.

A young man in one of my seminars, obviously unusually intelligent, had been labeled as retarded as a child because he did so poorly in school. This was puzzling, because he tested well above the average. After repeated visits to different "experts," his family physician suggested that he might have a perceptual problem. That was all. Yet, with this one slender thread of a clue, the boy started working on his own to overcome his difficulty. He soon discovered that he had an uncanny sense that enabled him to remember anything that happened to his body, even the slightest movement, and that he could associate all other senses to these proprioceptive sensations. Such memory is, of course, very helpful when living outdoors but not so helpful in urban living. (He couldn't even remember his way to school, because the car in which he was driven to school provided no feedback to which his body could respond.) Now he drives a sports car with rigid suspension and has no trouble finding his way—he has a physical memory of the road surface!

Most of my young friends used a combination of the senses and separated the auditory into words and music, which is consistent with what is known about the way in which words and music are stored in the brain. The capacity to image creatively inside the head and not have to lean on the crutches of drawing, written text, or models makes a difference to an architect, who can try out a dozen or more solutions to a design problem and, when he has arrived at one that suits him, make a drawing of it. The time required is of course a fraction of that needed if he had to actually make all those drawings. Eric Hoffer, the workingman philosopher, is successful because he can compose and carry text in his head, edit it while working in the field picking peas, and when he has it in the form that suits him, copy the finished product when he gets home at night. Margaret Mead, the internationally famous anthropologist and a prolific writer, is just the opposite. Discussing these processes, she once commented that she conceptualizes blocks of material in her head but does not compose the actual words; i.e., she doesn't edit in her head.

A good memory is a necessity for writers, but some, like Vladimir Nabokov,[9] have remarkably specialized imaging capabilities:

> There are two kinds of visual memory: one when you skillfully create an image in the laboratory of your mind, with your eyes open (and then I see Annabel in such general terms as: "honey colored skin" "thin arms" "brown bobbed hair" "long lashes" "big bright mouth"); and the other when you instantly evoke, with shut eyes, on the dark inner side of your eyelids, the objective, absolutely optical replica of a beloved face, a little ghost in natural colors. (p. 13)[10]

Ex-safecracker Henri Charrière, the author of the remarkable book PAPILLON,[11] was aided in surviving an unheard-of eight years of solitary confinement on Devil's Island by his remarkable capacity to image past events with all his senses. He could walk in the country, breathe the fresh air, smell the flowers, feel the breeze on his face, sit on his mother's soft lap and feel her reassuring caresses. There is no way to imprison such a man. Later, while writing PAPILLON, these same capacities enabled him to re-create the entire prison experience and simply write down what had happened.

Truman Capote[12] has an equally active memory for words and dialogue, which he strengthened and reinforced by training with a tape recorder as a check to be certain that he had not omitted anything. Hemingway was also a word man who attached great importance to getting the right word in the proper context. Mark Twain not only was deeply involved in words but apparently was a good visualizer as well. We know he was an "ear man" because he was sharply critical of James Fenimore Cooper for his sloppy use of words. Twain had an incredible ear for dialogue, and he could also evoke unusually vivid visual images.

In addition to the talents that people are born with, culture has always exerted a dominant influence on memory and thinking. In Iran, for example, schools emphasize verbal memory. Iranian educators do not care how students store and retrieve information just as long as they remember. In earning their living in later life, they must continue to be able to recall great blocks of material even at relatively low organizational levels in the government. The verbal memory system, like many cultural systems, is integrated into the rest of the culture and is felt in all areas of life. Americans who go to Iran frequently lose credibility because they don't appear to "know" anything; that is, they haven't memorized their facts and have to rely on reference material to perform their jobs.

In the eastern-Mediterranean Arab world, children memorize the Koran but they are also given number work, which they practice and play with on their own. The capacity of any street urchin in Beirut to figure exchange rates in his head has never ceased to amaze me.

While working with the Navajo Indians in the early thirties, I found them to have remarkable visual, verbal, and proprioceptive memories. They remembered in incredible detail, using several, if not all, the senses. The Hopi, who were equally gifted, seemed to be more oriented toward words and figures. This gave them an immediate advantage over the Navajos when dealing with the whites.

On Truk, where I did field work immediately following World War II, memory seemed to be oriented toward social transactions, particularly injustices, which apparently were never forgotten.[13] The Trukese place great emphasis on education but seem to find a closer match between the Japanese educational system and their own needs than what the United States provided. This suggests that at some time in the future, educational systems will be examined for what they do best rather than be evaluated by some culturebound theory that is supposed to apply to all peoples.

Psychologists have known for a long time that there are

differences in imaging capabilities. They have, however, been hesitant to do much about it. It was contrary to the dictates of the culture. For example, a California Institute of Technology psychobiologist, Levy-Agresti, working with split-brain epileptics (the nerves connecting the two hemispheres had been severed), discovered that the right hemisphere, which is the non-speaking hemisphere, was much better at identifying the shapes of unseen objects held in the hands. She "theorized" that some people may be more "picture minded" than "verbal minded."[14] Such caution!

It is the rare psychologist who will do what Luria did and invest a significant block of time in the study of a particular gifted individual, even one who had been brain-damaged.[15] In other words, we Americans are oriented toward the sensorily homogenized masses—men and women without any particular talent, or if they have talent, that is what is *not* studied. Consequently, our psychology has not contributed as much to man's knowledge of the range of capabilities of the human species as it should. This is a mistake. Our Einsteins not only lead the way but set things up so that less gifted people can follow. Culture makes the average bright but may also dull the brilliant. Serious and detailed study of the exceptionally gifted is rare, with the exception of symbolizers (words and math). The very fact that they are "not representative" disqualifies them as subjects. Yet, in the few instances in which they have been studied, some important things have been learned about the capabilities of the human sensory apparatus.

One such case is reported by Charles F. Stromeyer III, an M.I.T. psychologist who conducted experiments[16] on a young woman who teaches at Harvard. Elizabeth (not her name) has the dual capacity of being able to project a true image of something she has seen and then alter the image—put leaves on a bare tree or a beard on a clean-shaven face. Because psychologists make a distinction between memory and imaging, a distinction that probably shouldn't be made, testing of good visual imagers has been difficult. The psychologists needed to develop a way of testing Elizabeth's imaging capacity without reference to context—always hard to do. To accomplish this end, Stromeyer used computer-generated stereograms. A CGSG is a series of randomly spaced computer-generated dots that will appear solely as dots if viewed normally but will generate a figure in depth when viewed with both eyes through a stereoscope. Elizabeth, because of her remarkable visual memory, was able to combine the two sets of computer-generated dots without using the stereoscope, i.e., look at one with one eye, and later look at the second with the other eye, combining the two images as though she were looking through a stereoscope and thereby actually generate the figures which the two combined images could produce when viewed simultaneously. Elizabeth viewed a 10,000-dot pattern for a minute with one eye, rested ten seconds, and then viewed the second pattern with the other eye. Without benefit of the stereoscope, by combining the remembered image with the one before her she was able to distinguish the letter T "coming towards me." In a later series of experiments the two sessions were separated by a whole day. Twenty-four hours *after* she looked at the CGSG with her right eye, she was able to see a square floating above the surface when viewing the dots with her left eye. In a double-blind test in which neither the experimenter nor the subject knew the results of the test, Elizabeth was able to reconstruct from memory and fuse two 10,000-dot images separated by a period of three days![17] It would have been possible, of course, to test Elizabeth using old-fashioned stereoscopic postcards, but it would have meant taking her word for the fact that she could generate a three-dimensional view when images for each eye were separated in time. The advantage of the computer-generated dot experiment is that it is impossible to fake.

Elizabeth has an extraordinary capacity to image visually. We do not know how many more are like her and what their distribution in the population is or whether the culture, through the schools, discourages imagers. However, many of my students who had the capacity when young tended to lose it as they got older.

Visual and auditory imaging and memory have been extensively studied using a variety of techniques. However, other forms of memory have been neglected. Good, reliable information on the tactile, proprioceptive, thermal (infrared receptivity and sensing capacities of the skin), interioceptive, and to a lesser degree, olfactory, memory systems is scarce. What could such research reveal? Some people can image smells at will and with them recall memories of past events. A good olfactory memory is essential to pharmacists, chefs, and metallurgists. Yet, American culture places a negative value on both olfaction (witness our preoccupation with deodorants) and touch. Otherwise, manufacturers couldn't get away with producing things that smell so bad. Knowledge of the proprioceptive memory is limited. But to re-experience accurately what the body actually does while performing can be a great asset to dancers, athletes, and musicians. It enables them to correct and improve their techniques in off seasons, to practice without actually being on the field or having the instrument in their hands. There are other facets to body imagery that seem to be even more important, for one of the most important imaging capabilities has to do with the body sense as interpreter of the world. The usefulness of capabilities of this sort was illustrated by the case of an inventor who had made a number of break-throughs in the design of ultra-high-pressure hydraulic valves. The inventor was successful because he was able to imagine in body terms what it would be like to be such a valve holding back all that pressure.[18] My friend Buckminster Fuller apparently thinks with his body. He has, in addition, an unusual verbal memory. Both Fuller's and Einstein's experiencing of the laws of nature contain significant elements of the physical. In fact, systems thinking seems to be related to the capacity to experience functions that are apparently related to the somatosensory motor cortex—recall an image in physical terms.[19]

Additional data on this fascinating subject is described in a volume titled SYNECTICS,[20] which covers a series of reports on the creative process as it occurs in actual problem-solving situations. The scientists and engineers who were studied made minute-to-minute records of what was taking place in their minds and bodies while solving real-life problems in their laboratories. Until each had managed to image the problem physically, new solutions were not possible. A scientist would have to imagine what it felt like to be a pendulum or a spring, just as Einstein imagined what it was like to be a photon traveling through space or how it would feel if one were in an elevator that was constantly accelerating and how that individual could or could not determine whether it was gravity or acceleration that was pushing him toward the floor.

Even the most pedestrian of planning is impossible without some capacity to image creatively. Yet there is no common word or phrase in English for the capacity to image realistically and dynamically, to mentally plan and rearrange the furniture.[21] The poet, the artist, the writer, the sculptor, the architect, the designer, the hostess, the cook, the seamstress, and the carpenter must all be able to image creatively (each in a different combination of senses), combining the components that go to make up their particular art, in ways they are conscious of before the event. Yet, how little is made of this extraordinary capacity in everyday life!

13. Cultural and Primate Bases of Education

There is always an intimate relationship in nature between the form of an organism and its performance. In the absence of knowledge concerning the nature of an organism, it is impossible to properly develop that organism to its greatest potential. This rule applies whether it be animals, man, or one of man's extensions. Most people would consider it a foolish sacrilege to use fine surgical instruments for carpentry, a beautiful Ferrari for a taxicab, Einstein to teach grade-school arithmetic, or Winston Churchill as a magistrate. In nature, this sort of balance between form and function has been worked out to perfection if the animal is to survive. Man—the creator of his own dimension —is still trying to discover what kind of an organism he really is. Knowledge of himself is basic to perfection of his institutions, yet the knowledge that exists and is commonly known is almost entirely composed of folklore. Why haven't we done better? Moved faster? Partly because of culture, partly the complexity. The task of building a foundation of this knowledge is more difficult than for the physical world, because the very tools one uses are a product of the processes under observation. It is almost impossible to find a suitable physical analogue for this problem. Perhaps there is none. Without first mastering culture's unwritten rules, we cannot escape the binding constraints on knowledge of our species which can be seen in all situations and contexts and can be observed wherever human beings interact. Where does one begin such an inquiry?

We could start with any one of the ten basic cultural systems.[1] Space and time, two of the most basic systems, have been discussed elsewhere.[2] Learning is another such system and, as is characteristic of all basic cultural systems, it is interwoven with all the others. Nothing happens that does not involve or influence learning in some way. How one learns is culturally determined, as is what one learns.

Cultures originating in Europe have "institutionalized" learning, and in the process have managed to produce great affronts to man's basic nature. If we are to reverse this process and if progress is to be made in overcoming the hidden grip of culture, more must be known of man's origins, how he came to be what he is as well as his physiological and biological being. What kind of organism was man before he started to develop the massive institutions we see today? First, last, and always, human beings are primates and share many characteristics with the other primates. All of this is directly related in the deepest, most basic sense to how people learn and should be educated. But what should be done?

One promising formula for re-creating education would be to design the education process around what is already known about: how the human nervous system (the part concerned with learning) works, stores, and retrieves information in a variety of sensory modes; man as a primate; the relation of school size to the total experience; and accepting the reality of culture and the necessity of preserving the cultural values of each ethnic group. These four categories of knowledge may seem at first to be quite disparate and unrelated, yet they do seem to hold the key to identifying much that is wrong with education in the United States today.

In considering what kind of organism man is, one inevitably returns to the brain, that incredible, only partially understood organ. It is, after all, very much in the middle of things and has something to do with every aspect of the entire organism. Unfortunately, little of what is currently known about the brain has been of direct use to educators. The connecting links between neurophysiology, neuroanatomy, and psychopharmacology in the everyday world have yet to be forged. There are, however, a few men (all of them different) whose work on the brain or those parts of the brain that are relevant to our discussion is sufficiently comprehensive to provide keystones to the foundation of education for the future. Five men whose work I wish to discuss are: A. R. Luria, K. S. Lashley, K. H. Pribram, Paul Pietsch, and P. D. MacLean. Luria,[3] the Russian neurophysiologist, has made careful studies of how the human brain responds when it is traumatized (wounded or injured in any way) as well as how it recovers its functions. Stanford University's Pribram[4] works on how monkey brains store and organize sensory information. He follows in the footsteps of Lashley but has traveled farther, while Pietsch,[5] a professor at Indiana University, has produced new and impressive evidence on information storage in the brain. MacLean[6] has contributed an appreciation of the phylogeny of certain neurological processes. A score of other distinguished scientists have also devoted their lives to the study of the central nervous system, and their work could be translated and applied to various facets of education. However, as of this moment, in order to maintain some semblance of congruity between levels in this book, it is necessary to restrict ourselves primarily to the work of Luria, Lashley, Pribram, Pietsch, and MacLean.

But let us consider for a moment the European preoccupation with the distinction between mind and brain, because this distinction concerns the core issues of this book—man as a cultural organism and man as a biological organism. There has been for some time a practice among scholars to distinguish between mind and brain; brain being the physiological organ, and mind, what man does with that organ. The descriptions that follow were chosen because they specifically exclude mind, yet reveal functions which, while definitely structured, are popularly and erroneously associated with functions of mind. The mind/brain dichotomy in the absence of a suitable theory of culture has proved to be such a slippery and elusive concept that many American practitioners have simply sidestepped the issue.[7] Yet the physiological organ is deeply altered by experience. How does one go about describing the brain's program before it has been altered? I propose that this state of affairs is an accident of history (our notions grew out of a basically European tradition), coupled with the artificial separations of psychology and anthropology and produced a concept of mind independent of and divorced from a theory of culture. *What has been thought of as mind is actually internalized culture.* The mind-culture process which has evolved over the past four or more million years is primarily concerned with "organization" and, furthermore, the organization of "information" as it is channeled (and altered by the senses) to the brain.[8] Skinner's[9] reinforcement schedules determine what is perceived in the world and what is not. The only thing is that life, not Skinner, defines the rewards and punishments as well as the organization, which constitute a transaction between the organism and the environment. The totality—the man-environment transaction including introjects and extensions—is culture. What anthropologists think and say and what people think and say about culture are independent of the process itself and can be termed metaculture. (Most anthropology is concerned with metaculture, but that is another issue, independent of this discussion.)

A view of the brain that has attracted considerable attention in recent years is propounded by P. D. MacLean.[10] MacLean, a physician, has demonstrated that man has not one but three brains and therefore three natures, which may not always be in step with each other. The three are: an old reptilian brain; an old mammalian brain; and a higher and more recent mammalian brain known as the neocortex. The reptilian brain (the brain stem) takes care of the vital functions and also includes such features as space orientation—territoriality and responses to crowding. Between the old brain and the new brain lies the old mammalian brain, called the limbic system.[11] The limbic system evolved in response to evolutionary pressures for birds and mammals to live in groups. The limbic system makes it possible to experience emotions—pleasure and pain—and to read significance into the environment. It also plays an important role in refining observations in order to handle increasing environmental complexities such as dominance hierarchies. The

third brain—the new brain, or neocortex—lies on top of and sur-
rounds the other brains and has much to do with man's capacity
for symbolic behavior.

And while MacLean and Luria (whose work will be discussed
later) approach the brain quite differently, what MacLean adds
is the notion of depth and age to such activities as the spatial
function. He also shows us that social hierarchies, social group-
ing, and emotion are very basic and that they have been with us
for a long time, perhaps a hundred million years. In case this
seems too simple, remember that there was not a simple imposi-
tion of one primitive brain on another but, rather, a joint evolution as each new brain was added. These functions are integrated, but they sprang from different sources in response to
different challenges. The reptilian foundation was laid down
somewhere in the neighborhood of half a billion years ago, when
reptiles began storing information in their brains for future use.
If there is any single aspect or common feature that underlies all
education and all learning and all cultures, it is the storage and
synthesis of information for future use. How this miracle is accomplished was worked out independently by Paul Pietsch[12]
and Karl Pribram[13] in an impressive series of experiments with
salamanders and monkeys.

The dynamic study of memory, however, began with Karl
Lashley,[14] the famous psychologist who spent a lifetime trying to
locate memory in the brain. He worked with rats, cutting away
sections of the brain to see how much they could remember by
testing their performance in solving problems such as running
mazes. No matter how much of the cerebrum (the old
mammalian brain) he cut away, if there was any left at all, the
rats could still remember. It was impossible to excise memory!
Some hard-nosed scientists found Lashley's results unbelievable.
Like most of us, they wanted everything in its place. However,
nothing in life is inherently neat, and answers come from unexpected sources. It wasn't until more than twenty years after
Lashley began his research on rats that Dennis Gabor, a physicist at the University of London working with light rays as a
means of improving the electron microscope stumbled on the
optical hologram, which earned him the 1971 Nobel prize[15] and

in the process provided a model that helps to explain Lashley's results. The optical hologram is multiple-image storage, or lensless 3-D laser-beam photography. By now, most people have seen or read about holography in the popular press.[16] Cut a hologram in half, in quarters, or reduce it to a mere chip; the image remains—just as memory remained in the rat's brain. The image is not as bright, but it is all there.

Stanford's Pribram was the first to build a theory of memory using a holographic model. Like Lashley, he systematically both excises and stimulates different parts of the brain. Instead of rats, he uses monkeys (over one thousand of them so far). Monkeys, of course, are closer to man than rats and salamanders. Pribram's experiments are highly detailed, subtly contrived, and have required as long as seven years for completion. Yet he found it impossible to localize memory,[17] over the full range of the phylogenetic scale including animals as primitive as salamanders and as advanced as man.

In 1971, another scientist, Pietsch, walked to the podium and addressed anatomists in Dallas, Texas. The title of his paper was "Scrambled Salamander Brains: A Test of Holographic Theories of Neural Program Storage."[18] According to Pietsch, a hologram ". . . does not capture a thingy thing. It captures rules—a harmonic syllogism . . . mathematics in reverse." The idea, even in the physical world, takes getting used to. Holographers can construct acoustical holograms and get the original back—not with sound waves but with light in some other form. The same principle enables organisms with brains, particularly man, to shift instantly, if need be, from one sense modality to another. Just as remarkable are the many different images that can be stored on the same holographic plate; i.e., storage in depth. Yet none of this interferes in the slightest with the specialized and localized functions of the brain. Applications of the principles being discussed are not limited to Lashley and his rats or Pribram and his monkeys. According to Pietsch, one can see the evidence of them as far back as Pavlov.

Holographic thinking is in direct conflict with many of the underlying basic assumptions of our culture, as well as with the content and organization of American education. The reader may wonder how holographic theory explains the centers of the brain, where specific functions are localized: rage, fear, hunger, as well as the visual, auditory, and motor areas of the brain. According to Luria, these are processing and contexting stations, not "storage depots"—they act to classify, context, and pump information in and out but not to house it. But, to return to Pietsch:

At first he was skeptical of the entire holographic notion. Lashley's experiments were inconclusive. Pietsch felt that only by shuffling parts of the brain could you test the holographic theory. This he did. In seven hundred operations, he transferred parts of the brain around like a Las Vegas faro dealer. Regardless of the arrangement of their brain, the salamanders still sensed the presence of their favorite food, tubifex worms, and ate them. As the theory predicted, scrambling the brain's anatomy did not scramble its programs. In order to test the theory further, he chose the brain of a tadpole (a vegetarian) and grafted it in place of the excised salamander brain. In three months the salamander had eighteen hundred encounters with fresh worms, played with them, but did not eat a single tubifex, because this salamander had been provided with a different program.

Pietsch's, Lashley's, and Pribram's studies go a long way to explain the conservatism, once programmed by culture, not only of individual human beings, but of whole cultures as well. This is why it is difficult to change behavior (once formed) and why changes, when they do occur, require so much time.

Looking at the individual in those rare instances in which he tries to restructure his life, it is a common experience of patients and therapists in psychoanalysis to keep having to go over and over and over the same material. Each time a dynamism is analyzed, it is seen in a slightly different light and from a different point of view, and it sometimes appears as though nothing changes. One reason psychotherapy is frequently so slow is that in order to change one thing it is necessary to alter the entire psyche, because the different parts of the psyche are functionally interrelated. Anthropologists have known for a long time that all aspects of culture are interrelated. They also know that to change one thing is to change everything. In fact, it was this very characteristic of culture that started me working on the ideas, theories, and observations set forth in THE SILENT LANGUAGE[19]—everything is interrelated, interdigitated, reflected in everything else, while overt culture is an extension of both mind and brain. Internalized culture is mind.

The implications for education of both brain holography and how culture works are deep and revolutionary. Good-by, compartmentalization of knowledge. Good-by, subjects presented without reference to context. Good-by, periods, quarters, semesters, and time-slicing. Treatment of education that is systematic (in the true sense and not the perverted sense of the word) and comprehensive will eventually come to pass. Since holography permits the storage of entire systems on separate planes, it may well prove easier when someone has been subject to a scrambled, inconsistent learning experience to simply start over again. Because the brain is also situational, a new, coherent program can be learned without interference from the original, scrambled program. There is deep relevance for cross-cultural and minority education in this knowledge, because each culture can be treated as a separate image stored in one of Gabor's holograms. To mix them is like adding a tadpole's brain to the medulla of a salamander. By mixing programs, you may inhibit the student from doing one thing, without providing the means for his doing something else, which has been pretty much the history of our cross-cultural and interethnic education to date.

A. R. Luria's work deals with specialized brain functions rather than memory which is stored holistically in the brain. By studying the loss of specific functions and the patterning of these losses sustained by thousands of individuals with localized brain lesions, Luria has advanced our understanding of how the brain handles information and how the brain itself is structured to perform certain functions *independent of culture*. However, before embarking on a description of specialized brain functions as they relate to the educational process, one of Luria's books, which sheds new light on memory, should be considered. No brains or parts of brains were excised or stimulated; instead, a whole man over a generation's span, was studied. Luria's interest in this man was stimulated by the fact that the man had a perfect memory, which raised some interesting questions.

The creative brain is a forgetting mechanism, as we shall see.[20] Obsessed as we are with the need to memorize facts (instilled in us in schools), few people realize how important it is to be able to forget. The critical nature of forgetting is developed in THE MIND OF A MNEMONIST,[21] the life story of a man who could not forget and remembered everything, and the effect that this had on his life.

Describing his first attempts at testing the mnemonist, Luria writes:

> It was of no consequence to him whether the series I gave him contained meaningful words or nonsense syllables, numbers or sounds . . . verbal or in writing. . . . I simply had to admit that the capacity of his memory had no distinct limits.

But what kind of a mind did this man have? A visualizer, the mnemonist was excellent at solving problems, because he could create images in his head where other people required blocks and objects and figures. However, even simple reading of a written text was a perplexing and frequently difficult process, because he had to contend with images, often conflicting, irrelevant, and confusing, generated by the printed word. His ability to visualize was *too* vivid and too literal. There were other problems as well:

> Poetry, for example, was the most difficult type of reading for him because it calls on higher synthesizing functions in the brain (one has to grasp the figurative meaning in a context rather than a literal meaning of the word). Abstract ideas meant another round of problems and torment. Words and concepts like "infinity" and "nothing" created insurmountable obstacles in his brain. Each time that he tried to master something new, his vivid memory would interfere just as though he were a cripple.

Here we have a caricature of what the average education tries to produce in the young. If the young can do well what many schools require, the mind that results from this process is one with little experience in creative thinking and solving real-life problems.

Without stating it in so many words, American education assumes a brain that compartmentalizes and localizes knowledge, a stimulus-response organ in which a single stimulus leads to a uniform response. Certainly, this is the way everything is taught. Another hidden assumption (discussed in Chapter 12) is that thinking is possible only when using symbols—words and numbers. Yet, according to Luria, the brain functions in several different ways. Some functions (mostly having to do with the senses), are, in contrast to memory storage, actually localized; others are integrative in character. For example, Luria's studies demonstrate how four closely linked functions (analyzing speech sounds, repeating verbal sounds, naming objects, and writing) are actually found adjacent to each other, in a single part of the brain. Clearly, the way activities are functionally or spatially related in the brain is a subject we should know more about. Given the above clustering of functions, it is possible to see why some people have trouble with spelling in those instances in which the orthography (writing system) bears little or no relation to the spoken language, as is the case in English.

Continuing this line of inquiry, we find the following: The frontal part of the brain, the part where synthesis of thoughts and ideas as well as their expression take place, is concerned in part with five surprisingly different but apparently related activities—perception, body movement, performance of planned action, memorizing, problem solving. Body movement! Who would have thought that body movement was related to problem solving? Can't you just see old Miss Quinby telling Johnny, who is having trouble solving a problem in arithmetic, to stop fidgeting! The full significance of this particular cluster both for education and everyday living has yet to be realized and spelled out. If Luria's work is taken seriously, we come up with a much more active learning situation than most of us ever envisage. He found, for example, that if children were not allowed to vocalize sounds and words when they were learning to write, they made six times the number of spelling errors as a control group that did the vocalizing naturally. (Remember, this is Russian, in which the orthography and the spoken language are not confusing and inconsistent, as they are in English.)

Rhythmic movements of the body, and *order* (A follows B), are controlled by the same part of the prefrontal brain. Perhaps someday we will be curing dyslexia by having people dance. Coding sounds into phonemes (the structural units of speech) involves still another part of the brain, located both in the occipital (rear) and parietal (side) lobes, which also control spatial relations between the parts of a letter (grapheme) and the ability to put parts together to form a whole. (Capital F is made of three parts: | — —.) Putting the parts together in the proper order (sequencing) is done in the anterior portion of the left hemisphere. The tertiary parts of the parietal-occipital areas are concerned with spatial analysis. Men with this portion of the brain damaged have trouble differentiating between left and right or telling time from the hands of a clock.

The brain, a synthesizing organ, makes possible purposive behavior, intention, and the formulation of programs. Attention and concentration are regulated in a deep, old part of the brain (the brain stem and reticular formation), yet both are linked with synthesizing and concept formation. The question one must ask is: What effect does an educational system have on concept formation when the educational system does not either demand concentration or hold attention?

In the brain and its organization, one finds a model or, rather, a series of models *of the mental processes men had to perform in the past which were essential to survival.* These models are still relevant to survival in today's complex world. In the normal, alert brain there are, for example, hierarchies of responses that are related directly to input. Weak input plus proper contexting brings weak response, and strong input, strong response. The brain does not shoot a gnat with an elephant gun. Ask yourself how many times a day in the average schoolroom the law of hierarchical responses is violated when the teacher makes mountains out of molehills and vice versa (even the bells would wake the dead).

Frequently, functions that appear to be quite different turn out to be closely related, in the same part of the brain. For example, in the lower-left parietal region are located: orientation in space, which deals with order, a necessity for any type of computing; complexities of grammar; and logic. The implications are mind-boggling. Just take the matter of orientation in space. Consider the effect on young children of designing thousands of school buildings so that they look the same no matter from which angle one approaches, as well as the consequences of school interiors that offer a minimum of orienting cues.[22] One colleague of mine was once taken to a new school in a strange neighborhood when he was very young, and couldn't find his way home for lunch because the two sides of the building were exact duplicates of each other and someone shoved him out the wrong door. In another case reported to me, a small boy wouldn't stop crying in school. After weeks of theorizing and prying and probing, it developed that when they finally asked *him* why, he said that he couldn't find his way to the bathroom!

Or take another, deeper, more significant dimension of this problem. Until quite recently, the English grammar that was taught in the schools bore very little relation to the language as it was used in everyday life. This discrepancy between reality and classroom was because the grammar was based on an outdated and faulty analysis of the language. Descriptive linguists, who really know more than anyone about how the language functions and how it is structured, have been trying for a quarter of a century to update the teaching of English grammar. Only recently have changes based on linguistic science begun to take hold. Again, one must raise a question: If logic and the mastery of the complexities of grammar are functionally interrelated in the brain, what does it do to people when you teach them a grammatical system that has little or no connection with the language they are using, which is taught in spatially ambiguous buildings? Looked at in this light, the pittance devoted to pure research by descriptive linguists (though such research appears to the layman to be all too theoretical) certainly was not wasted. Mixing up the substance of what goes into different steps of the brain's structural hierarchies might explain why it is that common sense is so uncommon!

How does the brain, once damaged, recover its functions? And can we learn anything from this process? Luria discovered that

> . . . training or habituation changes the organization of the brain's activity so that *the brain comes to perform accustomed tasks without recourse to the process of analysis.* That is to say, the task may invoke a stereotype based on a network of cortical zones *quite different from the one that was called on originally* when the performance required the help of analytical apparatus.[23] (italics added)

What this says is that people can be trained to perform in ways that bypass the natural and analytical capabilities of the brain. Without this capacity, culture and the educational institutions it spawned could not have evolved. It was once said that science is the process that makes it possible to make the average man brilliant. From the point of view of the brain, all three are the same thing: education—science—culture. This capacity of the brain, once trained to perform accustomed tasks without recourse to the process of analysis, is both a blessing and a curse. It saves time and simplifies matters immeasurably but can be a dreadful handicap in times of stress and change. Much of what takes place in our schools, our universities, and our institutions is founded on this bypassing capacity of the brain. In light of the above, it is important, particularly in mass societies, that some means be perfected to allow people to function analytically when their nature seems to predispose them to do so.

The above explains (in part) how the central nervous system stores and retrieves information in a variety of sensory modes, and the relationship of this organization to man's institutions. But what about man as a primate, and the relation of school size to man's primate antecedents? Fortunately, something is known both empirically and scientifically about the influence exerted by size on groups and the effect of size on how the groups perform.

Research with business groups, athletic teams, and even armies around the world has revealed there is an ideal size for a working group. This ideal size is between eight and twelve individuals. This is natural, because man evolved as a primate while living in small groups. There are also a variety of compelling reasons why this particular size range is the most productive and efficient.[24] Eight to twelve persons can know each other well enough to maximize their talents. In groups beyond this size the possible combinations of communication between individuals get too complex to handle; people are lumped into categories and begin the process of ceasing to exist as individuals. Tasks that can't be handled by a group of eight to twelve are probably too complex and should be broken down further. Participation and commitment fall off in larger groups: mobility suffers; leadership doesn't develop naturally but is manipulative and political. Professor Roger Barker's[25] study of Kansas rural schools is unequivocal on these points. Yet, how many times is the "eight-to-twelve law" violated? Clearly, group size is not everything, but it is significant. We consistently discriminate against all our children and young people when we subject them to massive learning situations. Much, much more could be said on the relationship of group size to how members relate to each other. But what about another important aspect of learning? Man as a primate.

Observations of primate behavior by California's Professor Sherwood Washburn have deep implications for education. Washburn carefully recorded the time spent in the natural state, by different primate groups, on sleeping, looking for food, resting, being social, playing, and the like. Young primates spend most of their time playing—play performs important adaptive and survival functions. Because our culture has not considered play important, studies of this subject are recent. Washburn[26] states:

> Play is important in the development of all mammals . . . juvenile monkeys play for years . . . an investment of thousands of hours of time, energy and emotion. . . . Play is pleasurable to the young primate, and the joy of almost countless repetitions leads to the attainment of adult skills. . . . Through play (emotional, repetitious, from within) children prepare for the adult life of their culture. Separation of education from life

. . . is new in the history of primates. In the American school
there is no view of adult life. . . . In schools *discipline* is sub-
stituted for the internal drive to learn . . . to be a part of culture. *Through a profound misunderstanding of primate biology
the schools reduce the most intelligent primate to a bored and
alienated creature.* (italics added)

The failure to understand the significance of play in maturing
human beings has had incalculable consequences, because play
is not only crucial to learning but (unlike other drives) *is its
own reward.* Following from this, one would assume that one of
the greatest faults in modern education is overstructuring, which
does not allow for play at every point in the educational process.

Washburn also shows that primates learn primarily from their
peers, not from adults. Yet, few schools are organized according
to these principles. Large classes force teachers into becoming
disciplinarians. In this sense, school life is an excellent preparation for understanding adult bureaucracies: it is designed less
for learning than for teaching you who's boss and how bosses
behave, and keeping order.

To return to our primate nature, man evolved as an extremely
active species, and his need to constantly exercise his body is
ever-present and profound. Sitting regimented at desks according to predetermined, fixed schedules is no way to treat a
primate capable of running up to a hundred miles in one day.
Man is possibly the toughest and most adaptable species in the
world, one who has dominated the globe—he can chase and kill
any other animal—yet in light of the capacity as well as the need
for activity, the way children are treated in schools is sheer
madness. Those who can't sit still are stuck with the hyperactive
label and treated as anomalies and frequently drugged. (Perhaps
it is those who can bring themselves to sit still who are the
anomalies—monuments to the tremendous adaptive capabilities
of the human species.) Our schools are a vignette of how man,
in the development of civilization and its core institutions, has
managed to ignore or disregard some of the most compelling
aspects of his own nature. But how long can we go on this way?
The young today seem to be less inclined to accept these incon-

gruities. Even parents are beginning to look critically at all aspects of education. Unfortunately, few educators are equipped to contribute to new dimensions so badly needed in education.

We have discussed man's primate past as well as the physiological and neurological design of the human organism, which creates a biological base on which all education should rest, but we have said nothing about culture and the fact that education is deeply rooted in culture. In the United States, whites are most typically brought up in some version of the northern European tradition. This makes problems for everyone else, because educators, like the missionaries of the past, practice an unconscious form of cultural imperialism which they impose indiscriminately on others. In certain contexts, the structures of culture and education are synonymous, and we can learn about one by studying the other. I refer not so much to content as to how learning is organized, how it is presented, its setting, the language used, and the people who teach it, the rules by which they play, as well as the institutions themselves. Those features of education that are synonymous with culture are very unlikely to change when the educators start innovating, when they try open and closed classrooms, permissive and non-permissive discipline, fast and slow tracks, reforming curriculum, and the like. This point is crucial, and its importance is frequently overlooked.

For example, the classroom atmosphere of a Navajo school run by Navajos at Rough Rock, in Arizona,[27] is totally different from most American classrooms. Small children are much more independent. They are less controlled and regulated. An examination of the minute-to-minute operation of the classroom shows that the pace is slower than in white schools. This description fits my own experiences with Navajos forty years ago.

We in the West are convinced that we have a corner on reality—a pipeline to God—and that the other realities are simply superstitions or distortions brought about by inferior or less developed systems of thought.[28] This gives us a "right to free them from ignorance and make them like us." The dazzling success of our technology, as well as our understanding of the physical world, has blinded Europeans and Americans alike to the complexities of their own lives and given them a false sense of superiority over those who have not evolved their mechanical extensions to the same degree. Science is our new religion, and in many instances, like old religions, it has served man well up to a point. But it has been put on a pedestal, and its pronouncements and rituals are commonly taken as dogma.

Certainly, our schools have come in for their share of criticism and, while I do not want to beat a dead horse, there are some points that might be made from the anthropological viewpoint. For example, one hears a lot about the need to motivate students to learn, indicating that the strength of the drive to learn is not generally understood. The fact is that the sexual drive and the learning drive are, if one can measure the relative strength of such disparate urges, very close to each other in the power they exert over men's lives.[29] Sex insures the survival of the species; it is not essential to the survival of the individual, whereas learning is absolutely necessary to insure the survival of the individual, and the culture, and the species. It is man's way of growing, maturing, and evolving. Somehow, in the United States we have managed to transform one of the most rewarding of all human activities into a painful, boring, dull, fragmenting, mind-shrinking, soul-shriveling experience.

A key factor in explaining the sad state of American education can be found in overbureaucratization, which is seen in the compulsion to consolidate our public schools into massive factories and to increase to mammoth size our universities even in underpopulated states. The problem with bureaucracies is that they have to work hard and long to keep from substituting self-serving survival and growth for their original primary objective. Few succeed. *Bureaucracies have no soul, no memory, and no conscience.* If there is a single stumbling block on the road to the future, it is the bureaucracy as we now know it. So far, no one has come up with an answer to bureaucracy except proliferation. The educators have been particularly susceptible to the irresistible pull of the sirens of superorganization. After all, theirs is the biggest business in the United States.

We have enshrined organization at the expense of the individual, and in so doing have forced the individual into molds that are not appropriate. All this is arbitrary. Organization is arbitrary and therefore can also be changed and adapted to individuals. As to the purposes that lie behind education, much too much emphasis has been placed on monetary success. Too much money has gone into buildings! With a different game plan, the job could have been done for less. Right now, professors and teachers are being used inefficiently because their work is structured too tightly. The guiding philosophy of education has within it the implicit notion and culturally patterned belief that a teacher's job is to *transmit* a body of knowledge to students. But many people learn better by teaching others, not by listening to professors. As currently organized, most universities are very expensive ways of educating professors. Primates, as we have said, do most of their learning from peers, and man is no exception. In fact, the whole notion of teaching is very recent when viewed against the backdrop of man's past.

Implicit in the U.S. educational pattern are large rewards to the highly articulate and those who can work with figures—little else pays off. Consequently, students are often left stranded, overworked, or eliminated by the system not because they don't have brains and talent, but because their particular skills do not fit this system—a system, incidentally, that was modeled after the Prussian Army by Horace Mann, first commissioner of education in Massachusetts. The system badly needs updating.[30] Also, schools at different levels serve different purposes: Up to high school, the idea is to provide everyone an opportunity to "make it" and let nothing interfere with the process. College is for those who have made it and let nothing take that away. Graduate school is to keep both systems going.

The implicit philosophy of most secondary schools is interesting and demonstrates why schools are poor educationally but good agents of society. First, everything must be done according to the clock and the calendar. Ear-shattering bells, even in universities, remind you not only of every hour but that there is an administration that runs things. Class periods, of course, bear no known relationship to the time required to deal with a given subject, to say nothing of the particular state of the class at the moment the bell rings. (They may be just getting warmed up.)

The first lesson the student learns is the culturally important point that schedules are sacred and rule everything.

The second most crucial point is that bureaucracies are for real and are not to be taken lightly. The organization is placed above everything else. Later, and to their regret, many people discover that jobs are just like school except that the teacher has now become the boss, so nothing has really changed.

Third, education is a game in which there are winners and losers, and the game has little relevance to either the outside world or to the subject being studied. How the subject is divided and taught is usually completely arbitrary, without reference to internal consistency.

Four, size is valued. Big schools are considered better than little ones. (They provide more services.) The pressure to consolidate is unending regardless of how much time is spent in buses or the conclusive evidence that smaller schools (six hundred or less) produce happier and more productive, socially conscious, responsible citizens. Barker[31] studied the effect of the size of the school on participation in school activities as well as emotional maturity of the students. In small schools, students participated more, it meant more to them, they were more tolerant of others (p. 197), they formed closer, more lasting relationships, were more effective in group processes, could communicate better, performed six times more in responsible positions (only 2 per cent didn't fill responsible positions, as compared with 29 per cent in the large school), they were absent less often, were more dependable, tended to volunteer more often, were more productive, were more articulate, and found their work more meaningful. In other words, the small schools produced better citizens, who tended to be more satisfied with their lives and were more competent in every way.

What is easily missed in all this is that consolidation is not restricted to schools but found on all sides—particularly in business and government. Everything is getting bigger: automobiles, airplanes (747's and 707's), buildings (World Trade Center, Sears Tower, John Hancock Building), and cities. We are living in an age of giants. Yet everything that is known about man's needs points in the other direction. It is like a disease: since everyone has it, we think nothing of it. The problem, of course, is that vulnerability increases with size and it therefore becomes necessary, as Galbraith has pointed out,[32] to "manage" the environment, which makes for great rigidity and suppression of the individual as well.

Another guiding principle is that the American system of education is assumed to be the best in the world and equally applicable to all peoples and must therefore be imposed upon them—American Indians, central-city blacks, Puerto Ricans, Spanish-Americans, and Mexican-Americans—without regard to their own culture. Fortunately for all concerned, minorities in the United States are beginning to demand a say in the education of their children. Two of the most notable experiments are the Navajo schools at Rough Rock, Arizona (previously mentioned), and at Ramah, New Mexico. Both have Indian boards of directors and are run by the Indians, both combine traditional Navajo language and culture with a normal "white" curriculum. Both have been savagely attacked not only by the state and by Bureau of Indian Affairs educators, but also by the educational "big guns" in the Midwest and the East.

Educational systems regardless of country or culture have often been exported as complete packages in the past—the French in Syria, Lebanon, and Indo-China, and the Japanese in the mandated territories of the Pacific. Once established and functioning, these systems have proved to be extraordinarily stable and difficult to change. If possible, they are even more resistant to change (in any but superficial ways) than farmers in traditional societies, usually thought to be the most persistent and resisting group in the world. It is this basic inertial stability of education that Illich,[33] Holt,[34] Herndon,[35] Kozol,[36] and Hentoff[37] have found to be so unmanageable and unwieldy.

To take one's view of man from current folklore—no matter how prestigious the source—can be risky at best and downright foolish at worst. By studying man's past and examining the behavior of related species, it is possible to achieve new insights into the nature of man, such as the fact that he is a playing animal. One of the most important and basic mechanisms for internalizing the patterns needed in later life is play—a discovery that runs counter to much practice and most belief concerning how children learn. Man is not only one of the world's greatest players but he is also a species that evolved with a tremendous capacity for activity. Sitting still in confined places is one of the worst punishments that can be inflicted on the human species. Yet this is what we require of students in school.

In any discussion of education, something must be said about the organ that is being educated (the brain). Not only do different students remember and integrate information with different sensory modalities, but the new information about the brain itself reveals some amazing things about how the whole process of education should be accomplished. It is possible to look forward to a time when the relevance of insightful, integrated, synthesizing studies of both the brain and the mind will make their impact on education. The impact will be revolutionary indeed. The fact that the brain is, among other things, a forgetting organ is seldom recognized in schools. The holographic synthesizing capabilities of the brain explain both culture and why it is so difficult to get people to change once they have internalized a mode of behavior.

Self-awareness and cultural awareness are inseparable, which means that transcending unconscious culture cannot be accomplished without some degree of self-awareness. Used properly, intercultural experiences can be a tremendous eye opener, providing a view of one's self seldom seen under normal conditions at home. Like all opportunities for growth and self-knowledge, the mere thought can be somewhat frightening. Of course, it all depends on how deeply one chooses to go, because opportunities for learning about the cultural self occur at all levels, ranging from the details of pronunciation of language to largely dissociated or poorly developed parts of the personality, the way people move—their tempo and rhythm—the way they use their senses, how close they get to each other and the type of bonds they form, how they show and experience their emotions, their images of what constitute maleness and femaleness, how hierarchical relationships are handled, the flow of information in social systems, the definitions of work and play, how the psyche is organized (the relationship of the id, ego, and superego), where the ego is situated, as well as much more. All are deeply personal and controlled by culture. Such structural features as action chains, situational frames, extensions and how one uses them, all affect each of us very deeply. But not as deeply or as intimately as the way in which culture directs the organization of the psyche, which in turn has a profound effect upon the ways people look at things, behave politically, make decisions, order priorities, organize their lives, and, last but not least, *how they think.*

14. Culture as an Irrational Force

Coping with and explaining irrationality in oneself and others is not easy, for it appears to be an intrinsic part of life. Sadly, irrationality does not yield to logic. This is true to such an extent that one wonders how we ever got this particular pair (logic and irrationality) juxtaposed as though they were polar opposites. The explanation lies in the concept of logic, which is an invention of Western culture dating back to Socrates, Plato, and Aristotle.[1] "Logic" enables men to examine ideas, concepts, and mental processes by following low-context paradigms.

Having had a number of experiences in my lifetime with cultures as disparate as the Japanese and the Navajo, neither of which finds the Western system of logic effective, convincing, or acceptable as a way of arriving at a decision, I am not at all convinced that there is anything sacred in logic. I find nothing wrong with the mental processes of either culture. Both have highly reliable ways of arriving at correct decisions as well as testing the validity of those decisions. Both use much larger, more inclusive frames than our linear, low-context, logical frames.

The reason man does not experience his true cultural self is that until he experiences another self as valid, he has little basis for validating his own self. A way to experience another group is to understand and accept the way their minds work. This is not easy. In fact, it is extraordinarily difficult, but it is of the essence of cultural understanding. A by-product of such acceptance is a glimpse of the strengths and weaknesses of one's own system.

Experience has taught me not to trust logic and certainly not to use my culturally patterned way of thinking to make a point to someone of another culture.

The core of the problem may be that Western philosophies and beliefs are pictures in men's minds as to the nature of what is. Because of extension transference, the pictures are taken for reality when all they are is an idea or explanation. Such pictures and explanations are real in one sense, because they are constructions of the human mind and they tell us a lot about how that mind works as a product of a given culture. But they are *not* the mind and they are not the real world either. They are, in Poincaré's term, "conventions." Such conventions are nevertheless essential models on which some behavior can be based. If, however, one treats them as reality, they are impossible to transcend or even examine except in their own terms. Also, Western philosophies are restricted to working with words, and if one is to use words wisely and with validity, it is essential to know what the particular word system itself does to man's thought processes. To do this, you must know how language structures thought, as elucidated so clearly by Whorf.[2] Further, some way of including context must be found; philosophies can be meaningful only to the people who create them. If they have meaning to others, that meaning is forever altered by both the internal and external contexting these other people bring with them. The ideas and concepts of the Chinese philosopher Confucius mean one thing to the Chinese, something else to Westerners. In these terms, what we conceive as logic is rational only in very limited contexts in the West.

Ultimately, what makes sense (or not) is irrevocably culturally determined and depends heavily on the context in which the evaluation is made. The result is that people in culture-contact situations frequently fail to really understand each other. I would suspect that at least some of the problems encountered in the protracted peace negotiations throughout history could have been traced to matters of this sort.

Years ago, when I was working with the Navajo and the Hopi Indians in Arizona, there were continual struggles and misunderstandings because the cultural gulf separated three systems

(Navajo, Hopi, and white American). None of them made sense to the others. The white Oraibi school principal of the twenties simply could not understand why unused land belonging to clan X at the foot of the mesa lay fallow while members of clans Y and Z walked twenty miles to their fields. Ultimately his meddling in Hopi affairs created such a crisis that he had to leave the reservation while it was straightened out. Deeply eroded Hopi institutions already weakened by repeated encounters with white culture were hanging on the ropes. The school principal's white logic was unconsciously self-serving. It made him feel superior to the Indians, because he would have better sense than to walk twenty miles when one mile would do. What he did not understand was that the "logic" of the Hopi system was based on maintaining the integrity of the system and all the relationships that went with it. To rend the fabric of Hopi social and religious institutions made very little sense. Tilling one's own ancestral fields was a small price to pay for peace—which the Hopi had a hard enough time maintaining without some white government employee stirring things up.

The reasoning that lay behind the white man's sheep-reduction program of the thirties or the earlier extinction of the Navajo horse was unfathomable to the Navajo.[3] The whole thing was patently insane from the Navajo point of view. The strait-laced whites were unconsciously deeply threatened by the attachment of the Navajos to their horses and the fun they had racing them. By destroying those beautiful horses, they also destroyed an important part of Navajo life.

One does not have to limit oneself to cultural interfaces to encounter the bizarre, the parataxic, or the insane. Much is inherent in any given culture, particularly when cultures become as complex as in the United States. There are several forms of irrationality, and in listing them one inevitably succeeds in producing something to offend everybody.

Classifying the irrational is not for the purpose of stepping on people's toes but, rather, is an indicator of the relative difficulty to be encountered when confronted with a given type of irrationality. Some types are more difficult to cope with than others, while some are impossible to correct.

Situational irrationality is easier to cope with than neurotic irrationality, which is harder to deal with than cultural irrationality. Perhaps this is because irrationality seldom looks irrational from the inside. Yet the most sane behavior may turn out to be completely nutty if in trying to preserve institutions the means used results in their downfall. Some forms of the irrational can be traced to overintellectualizing at the expense of the nonverbal. We see this in the seventeenth-century thinking of Descartes, who enshrined logic and, by so doing, achieved a dominant place in Western thought. Even on the strictly personal level, all of us have had experiences in which something made sense to one part of our personality and complete nonsense to another. The irrational constitutes a significant portion of normal behavior.[4] It is time for Western man to accustom himself to that fact. Instead of denying it in ourselves and others, we should take a healthier attitude and accept that in all men, all institutions, and all cultures, as well as all relationships, there are inevitably things that don't make sense and are counterproductive. At times these elements are insignificant, but at other times they are overwhelming.

There are at least six varieties, situations, or levels in which it is possible to observe the irrational, the nonproductive, the self-defeating, or the counterproductive at work. The classification given here is, of course, a first approximation.

The initial form of irrationality is *situational*, ranging from impulse buying to the behavior of automobile drivers when traffic is bad. Something in the situation causes people to behave counterproductively. Much of modern technology as well as social-science research is directed toward understanding and correcting situational ills, and much of our faith in this type of research and in technology as well can be traced to situational successes. One example is traffic control on highway approaches to toll gates. Psychologists discovered that stripes painted on the road will slow down oncoming traffic. Wide stripes are used at the beginning of the approach and the stripes become closer together as cars enter the gates. This is very effective in reducing speed.

The second type is *contextual* irrationality, which comes from the application or projection of the logic of one context onto another. When people get overly technical, applying a classroom system of logic to social conversation, the effect is to stop the flow of conversation dead in its tracks. Contextual irrationality—using logic or rules of one context in the place of another—is a common form of interpersonal manipulation and exploitation popular among intellectuals and academicians.

Neurotic irrationality has been well documented by the psychoanalytic movement. All of us have some aspect of our personality in which our behavior does not contribute either to our personality ideal or to our own welfare. Yet we seem powerless to change. In other aspects of our lives, we may behave quite reasonably. Power, money, property, sex, children, work and play, careers, and violence are a few of the areas in which we have trouble. Neurotic irrationality is ubiquitous and sufficiently difficult to treat so that many psychiatrists and psychoanalysts are inclined to stop looking for the source of human ills once they have dealt with the intrapsychic dimension. There are, however, forces at work in the culture that cause many individuals to behave in what would otherwise be considered an irrational manner. In fact, the British psychoanalyst Laing[5] holds that the culture itself is not just neurotic but psychotic and that when people go insane it is a response *to* the culture. My friend Humphry Osmond, also a psychiatrist, says, "Presumably those people whose culture is repugnant to them are liable to become neurotic, deviant or psychopathic because they are constantly being exposed to something which distresses them."

Bureaucratic and *institutional* irrationality occur because, of all man's institutions, bureaucracy in all cultures has a tremendous potential to be counterproductive. This drive toward inefficiency may be a direct consequence of blind adherence to procedure, but it also stems from bureaucratic needs for self-preservation, and a vulnerability to pressure groups. The combination is unbeatable. The bureaucracy is as subject to extension transference as any human system I know. Established to serve mankind, the service function is soon forgotten, while bureaucratic functions and survival take over. Each reader will have his own examples: welfare systems that break up homes and create dependence; taxation that hits the poor and robs the middle class of incentives to work; building codes that are wasteful, inefficient, discriminatory, and archaic; hospitals where nurses awaken patients to give them their sleeping pills; dams where none are needed. The list goes on and on. By their very nature, bureaucracies have no conscience, no memory, and no mind. They are self-serving, amoral, and live forever. What could be more irrational? Changing them is almost impossible, because they function according to their own rules and bow to no man, not even the President of the United States. Custom, human frailties, and the will to power keep our bureaucracies going. When speaking of bureaucracies I include big business, philanthropic and educational institutions, churches, and government on all levels. Paradoxically, most bureaucracies are staffed largely with conscientious, committed people who are trying to do the right thing, but they are powerless (or feel powerless) to change things. None of which would be so serious if it weren't that these are the very institutions on which we depend to solve all major problems. Some answer must be found to bureaucracy. It is not social injustice capitalized upon by political leaders that causes revolutions. It is when bureaucracies become so top-heavy and inefficient they are incapable of serving the needs of the people, that governments fall.

Cultural irrationality is deeply entrenched in the lives of all of us, and because of culturally imposed blinders, our view of the world does not normally transcend the limits imposed by our culture. We are in effect stuck with the program culture imposes. Theoretically, a culture in which there was proper adjustment to the environment would be one in which the irrational was at a minimum. At least, this is the fantasy of the West— that there are people somewhere who live simple, straightforward lives, usually in exotic places, who wear no clothes and who are free from sexual and materialistic hangups. At least some cultures wiped out by the technologically advanced nations do appear to have approached such a balance. The Eskimos are frequently cited as having developed a very refined technical and behavioral response to each other as well as to their environment. The early descriptions of Eskimo life would lead one to believe that this was so. Nevertheless, analysis of their myths and dreams recorded while much of their culture was still intact left a deep impression on me and the uneasy feeling that, below the surface, the Eskimo, like most of mankind, was still in the process of trying to adjust his culture to himself. The surface problem in analyzing any culture is that people maintain rather stereotyped pictures of themselves that may not fit the multiple facts, levels, and dimensions of which all cultures are composed.

Today in the United States we are still struggling to throw off the yoke of the Protestant ethic. Our enshrinement of time and the way in which we allow our lives to be fragmented is frightening. The whole process of extension transference is highly irrational. Ethnocentrism is inevitably characterized by irrational elements and, as long as it is widely shared, it is impossible to combat. Individuals sometimes do lose their prejudices, but whole groups are slow to change and in many instances give up one prejudice only to take on another.[6] Individual irrationality is thought of as a product of the particular psychodynamics of the person, whereas cultural irrationality is widely shared and therefore often thought to be normal. Our attitudes toward consumption and material goods and our apparent lack of interest in curbing waste at a time when our resources are running out is clearly insane. But because we share the insanity with others and get little help from our institutions or leaders, this insanity goes virtually unchecked in spite of valiant efforts of the environmentalists. After all, you can't stop progress! Or can you?

Understanding man, understanding culture, and understanding the world and unraveling the irrational are inseparable aspects of the same process. Culturally based paradigms place obstacles in the path to understanding because culture equips each of us with built-in blinders, hidden and unstated assumptions that control our thoughts and block the unraveling of cultural processes. Yet, man without culture is not man. One cannot interpret any aspect of culture apart from, and without the co-operation of, the members of a given culture.

Unfortunately, for a variety of reasons (some of them political), it is becoming increasingly difficult in America to work at

the interface between cultures. Recently, an unusually percep-
tive colleague of Spanish descent told me that almost without
exception the attempts of social scientists to describe Spanish-
American culture, particularly in New Mexico, were "rip-offs"—
egregious distortions in which most of the statements made
were either wrong or out of context. These statements, he said,
gave an Anglo intellectual's view of Spanish-American culture,
which is about as relevant as an unmarried uncle's view of how
to discipline his sister's children. Since the men and women responsible for these studies are for the most part both well
trained in Anglo-American social science methodology and well
motivated, one can only assume that there is something basically wrong with the way in which social science research is
often conducted.

One source of error seems to lie in two assumptions: that an
outsider can, within a matter of months or even years, adequately understand, explain, and describe a foreign culture; and
that he can transcend his own culture. These errors in theory
and practice were not at first evident to Europeans, who, reinforced by their conviction of superiority and the correctness of
their methods, carried their own stereotypes with them and
explained everyone else in the world to other Europeans without
having to face the people whose lives and institutions they had
been describing. Since Europeans shared stereotypes with colleagues and laymen alike, many interpretations of foreign cultures were taken at face value.[7] I am not for a moment suggesting or implying that social scientists in the field were neither
gifted nor sincere. I am only saying that their own peer groups as
well as the public had a view of other people that was characteristic of European cultures.

I used to see these processes at work in the U. S. State Department whenever there was an attempt to get at the reality of
another political/cultural system. The careers of distinguished
men like John Stewart Service (who knew China so well) ran
aground on the reefs of cultural, as well as political, barriers.
This did not go unnoticed by less venturesome and less talented
foreign service officers. With few exceptions, no matter where
one looked, custom and fashion determined what was to be

reported to Washington and what was not, to say nothing of what was made public. For the most part, the distortions were not deliberate; they were unconscious.

There is, as far as I know, no way out of the dilemma of the cultural bind. One cannot normally transcend one's culture without first exposing its major hidden axioms and unstated assumptions concerning what life is all about—how it is lived, viewed, analyzed, talked about, described, and changed. Because cultures are wholes, are systematic (composed of interrelated systems in which each aspect is functionally interrelated with all other parts), and are highly contexted as well, it is hard to describe them from the outside. A given culture cannot be understood simply in terms of content or parts. One has to know how the whole system is put together, how the major systems and dynamisms function, and how they are interrelated. This brings us to a remarkable position; namely, that it is not possible to adequately describe a culture solely from the inside or from the outside without reference to the other. Bicultural people and culture-contact situations enhance the opportunity for comparison. Two other situations that expose culture's hidden structure are when one is raising the young and is forced to explain things, and when traditional cultural institutions begin to crumble as they are now doing. The task is far from simple, yet understanding ourselves and the world we have created—and which in turn creates us—is perhaps the single most important task facing mankind today.

15. *Culture as Identification*

"Life is a continuous process of consolidation and detachment."

E.T.H.

From birth to death, life is punctuated by separations, many of them painful. Paradoxically, each separation forms a foundation for new stages of integration, identity, and psychic growth. This introduces a subject in which everyone is involved, in which one finds a meeting ground, a point of synthesis, of the intrapsychic and cultural processes. None of us asks either to be born or to die. Yet both are natural and inevitable separations of the person from an all-encompassing environment. Between the two lie many other separations, each accompanied by new awareness. There is a time when the baby has not yet distinguished between his own body and the nurturing breast. During that time, he experiences himself and his small universe as a unit. Even at this primitive and simple level, life is not always serene, for when the breast does not function—does not present itself—and hunger strikes, frustration and rage at this uncontrollable part of the self-universe are commonly observed. Eventually, the baby learns that he and mother are separate beings and have independent existences. Yet, the experience of the separation is frequently not clear-cut; it is much more indefinite and obscure than many of us once believed. (If there is a boundary at all, or when there is ambiguity as to where the boundary lies, people experience difficulty.) Sullivan,[1] for example, builds much of his theory of the development of the self around the notion that the infant only gradually and in stages separates mother's feelings, as contrasted with her physical being, from his own. When mother is warm, comforting, and giving, the infant feels good. When mother is distracted or anxious, the child's emotions reflect this state. The process of separating mother's emotions or those of other significant persons from our own emotions can be protracted, and to some extent it is never really complete, even though this may be denied.

Richard Hughes,[2] in his remarkable little book A HIGH WIND IN JAMAICA, writes a poignant example of the identity–separation process in his description of Emily's discovery of herself. Emily, a captive of pirates, is on one of the last of the sailing ships with her brothers and sisters. The children had been on the boat for some weeks and had explored every inch of the schooner. Life had settled down to a routine. Hughes's description follows:

> And then an event did occur, to Emily, of considerable importance. She suddenly realised who she was.
>
> There is little reason that one can see why it should not have happened to her five years earlier, or even five later; and none, why it should have come that particular afternoon.
>
> She had been playing house in a nook right in the bows, behind the windlass (on which she had hung a devil's-claw as a door-knocker); and tiring of it was walking rather aimlessly aft, thinking vaguely about some bees and a fairy queen, when it suddenly flashed into her mind that she was *she*.
>
> She stopped dead, and began looking over all of her person which came within the range of her eyes. She could not see much, except a fore-shortened view of the front of her frock, and her hands when she lifted them for inspection; but it was enough for her to form a rough idea of the little body she suddenly realised to be hers.
>
> She began to laugh, rather mockingly. "Well!" she thought, in effect: "Fancy *you*, of all people, going and getting caught like this!—You can't get out of it now, not for a very long time: you'll have to go through with being a child, and growing up, and getting old, before you'll be quit of this mad prank!"
>
> Determined to avoid any interruption of this highly important occasion, she began to climb the ratlines, on her way to her favourite perch at the masthead. Each time she moved an

arm or a leg in this simple action, however, it struck her with fresh amazement to find them obeying her so readily. Memory told her, of course, that they had always done so before: but before, she had never realised how surprising this was.

Once settled on her perch, she began examining the skin of her hands with the utmost care: for it was *hers*. She slipped a shoulder out of the top of her frock; and having peeped in to make sure she really was continuous under her clothes, she shrugged it up to touch her cheek. The contact of her face and the warm bare hollow of her shoulder gave her a comfortable thrill, as if it was the caress of some kind friend. But whether the feeling came to her through her cheek or her shoulder, which was the caresser and which the caressed, that no analysis could tell her.

Ray Bradbury's[3] DANDELION WINE also contains a wonderfully appropriate passage on *being alive*. To be truly alive in a culture like our own, one must grow up, and while growing up involves meeting a multitude of challenges, the full impact of the process does not come home until one has "cut the apron strings" and established oneself as independent of one's parents. The degree to which this process is complete varies with the individual and from culture to culture. In many cultures, the bonds with the parents, grandparents, and even ancestors are not severed but are maintained and reinforced. I am thinking of China, Japan, the traditional Jewish family of central Europe, the Arab villagers, the Spanish of North and South America, and the Pueblo Indians of New Mexico, to mention only a few. In these cultures, one separates himself from childhood. The child moves into the larger and more real world of the adult, but he does not, even under normal circumstances, establish an identity separate from that of his community.

We have considered briefly the separations of self from mother's bosom, from parents' emotional state, and from one's group. How many other kinds of separation crises are there? There are many, and they can take several forms, such as separations on a large scale, involving whole populations. The West has given up belief in the Bible creation myth in exchange for Darwin's new world view of evolution. But this process of separation from one's creation myths is not and probably never will be totally complete, for as this is being written a controversy rages in California over "equal time" for the "creationists" in education that has even usurped the pages of the academicians' own magazine, *Science*.

And while all these events may seem natural and normal and familiar to most educated people, it had not occurred to me until recently, while working on a theory of identification, that the world of man divides into cultures whose members cut the apron strings and those whose members do not. At this point, it is difficult to assess the impact of such differences on our lives except to say that they must be very great indeed.

I believe that man in the aggregate resists separations, that he has more things in his life to be separated from than he can ever achieve, and that one of life's important strategies, albeit an informal, out-of-awareness strategy, has to do with what one is going to give up: appetites of every conceivable variety, neurotic dynamisms, ambition, greed, dependence on material things, security of a home with parents, the need for power and dominance over others, quick temper, lust, hard belief in a single religion to the exclusion of all others, nationalism, a single view of science, and many others.

We should not deceive ourselves; the separation of oneself from an uncontrolled dynamism is not easy, if only because many dynamisms are a function of habit. These are simply illustrations.

The woman who has a compulsion to buy shoes or is powerless to resist sweets shares addiction with the alcoholic. Neither individual can, in operational terms, maintain a clear-cut line between herself and a particular part of the environment. It is as though a hidden tentacle reaches out from body to candy or liquor. This is what is so insidious about environmentally imbedded dynamisms. A man can wrestle and struggle and fume and rage against himself but, like the baby who is powerless to control either mother's breast or her emotions, he is caught up in a hopeless struggle against an undifferentiated part of the self that is still extended into the environment. Or he may unconsciously shift from alcohol to religion or to food from cigarettes and still be just as irrevocably tied as before.

What might be termed the identity-separation-growth dynamisms, which can also be classed as boundary-ambiguity syndromes, are not all the same. In fact, they cover a host of different events. The separation from mother's womb in birth and the separation from physical things in death are existential in nature. Growth and development of the ego as a differentiated dynamism is also existential and therefore natural, but lacking the inevitability of birth and death. (The ego does not *have* to develop and be centered in a particular part of the psyche.) The child soon learns that he can't touch the moon no matter what.

Dynamisms such as greed, envy, or the anxiety occasioned by separation from hearth, home, and mother, while frequently neurotic, can also be *cultural*. It is in the nature of the human situation for man to have to overcome the anxiety occasioned by separations of both types—the neurotic and the cultural.

Addictions are biochemical in nature, and while they may have neurotic elements, are manifestly physiological, which should not mean that they are any less serious or difficult to contend with than other forms of boundary ambiguities.

There is also a type of boundary ambiguity in which the senses do not function normally; here there are perceptual aberrations. One class of such *perceptual* aberrations has to do with the perceived body boundary that expands or contracts, so that the self is actually perceived (not conceived, but perceived) as occupying an entire room. Perceptual distortion of this sort can place an unbearable burden on the psyche, as can auditory distortions (such as hearing voices). Two quite different psychiatrists, Humphry Osmond[4] and Harold Searles,[5] have contributed much to understanding the complex, ill-defined, and poorly understood disorder labeled schizophrenia as a function of altered perceptions.

In an entirely different context, a recent study has demonstrated that there are no generally accepted, valid criteria for making a diagnosis of schizophrenia, where separations are made artificially, with little reference to the real world. I am referring to Professor David Rosenhan's three-year study of mental institutions in all parts of the United States,[6] described earlier. As the reader may remember, Rosenhan and his colleagues went to hospitals and simply said they heard voices—unclear voices saying words like "empty," "hollow" and "thud"—nothing else. Their case histories were their true case histories, yet without exception each was classified as psychotic (schizophrenic) by mental hospitals on little evidence. In this instance, the capability of most of the workers in the mental health fields to draw *valid lines* to separate the so-called psychotic from the so-called normal was ambiguous at best.

Perceptual aberrations are not restricted to psychoses but can also be *situational* in character, particularly in instances of great stress, excitation, or drug influence. In another book, Richard Hughes[7] provides an excellent description of a normal man under stress experiencing the same thing as the schizophrenic suffering from body-boundary ambiguity.

August has just entered his gun room after a damp return from the moors. The body of a dead child rests on the shoulder of his dewy oilskins. He scans the walls of the warm, friendly room, filled with mementos of people and times past.

> Then his eyes shifted. In a corner of the room stood the collection of his fishing-rods. Their solid butts were set in a cracked Ming vase like arrows in a quiver; but he felt now as if their wispy twitching ends were tingling, like antennae—his antennae. Above them the mounted otters'-masks on the peeling walls grinned. The tiny wisp of steam from the ever-simmering kettle on the round cokestove seemed to be actively inviting the brown teapot that stood on the shelf above—the loaf, and the knife, and the pot of jam. In short, these guns and rods of his, and even the furniture, the kettle and the loaf had suddenly become living tentacles of "him." It was as if he and this long-loved gunroom were now one living continuous flesh. It was as if for the time being *"he" was no longer cooped up entirely within his own skin: he had expanded, and these four walls had become now his final envelope. Only outside these walls did the hostile, alien "world" begin.* (italics added)

Perceptual distortions, the failure to separate the body envelope from the surroundings or the incorporation of outside stimuli (the hearing of voices and seeing visions) are definitely cultural. The Plains Indian had to have a vision before he could become either a warrior or a medicine man. *Culture has always dictated where to draw the line separating one thing from another.* These lines are arbitrary, but once learned and internalized they are treated as real. In the West a line is drawn between normal sex and rape, whereas in the Arab world it is much more difficult, for a variety of reasons, to separate these two events. Language provides another instance. One finds that individuals in the northern part of the United States—speakers of middle-class English—draw a line around the spoken sound short "e" as in "pen" and another line around short "i" as in "pin." In the South along the eastern seaboard, these two sounds merge, so that when somone says, "Hand me the p_n," the hearer will ask, "The writin' pein or the stickin' pein?" There is such a thing as "black" English, which is different syntactically and in other ways from "white" English. One of the differences is that the blacks will recognize or distinguish between types of discourse that whites do not. One distinction that blacks make is between the times that they are "signifying" and when they are not. Signifying is using the language in such a way that the speaker communicates to the hearer indirectly and by analogy a message that is different from the manifest content of the conversation and in many instances would make sense only to the hearer. Ethnic blacks (as contrasted with acculturated middle- and upper-class blacks), also rap, sound, play the dozens, woof, mark, loud-talk, shuck, and jive.[8] Whites "signify" too, but they don't have a word for it and when confronted will frequently deny that something they said had carried two or more implications, and what is more, that the second meaning was what the conversation was really all about. Recent research in the Spanish communities of northern New Mexico reveals that the line between mental health and mental illness is not at all as clear-cut as it is in the "Anglo" community, where mental health is seen as a quality of the person, more or less independent of the situation. The Spanish New Mexican is apt to see behavior as highly situational. The idea that a given "person" is mentally ill is a completely foreign notion. What they see is that the individual *in* a certain set of circumstances acts peculiarly or gets violent. So they try to keep the individual away from or out of situations that are not good for him while rejecting the notion that *he* is mentally ill.

There are still people in the West who draw lines between individuals on the basis of skin color or ethnic affiliation, while in Europe it is much more likely that social class will divide people. Also, in the Western world in a deeper sense we draw a line around the individual and say this is our basic entity—the building block of all social relations and institutions. "Men" compete against each other, while churches compete for the stewardship of their souls. None of this can be applied to the Pueblo Indian, for something akin to lineages in the Pueblo are the viable unit. No human being outside of these groups has significance independent and distinct from the group. The Pueblo view of the group as the basic unit is difficult if not impossible for the average European to comprehend, because he lacks the experience of having grown up in such a group. For the Pueblo Indian, the idea of competition between men is therefore repugnant and foreign, with the result that everything in the white man's schools is subversive and threatens the very core of his existence. It is like having different parts of the psyche in competition. When this happens, the individual can only suffer. The Pueblo have cast a larger net. For this reason, arbitrarily separating the Indian from his context comes very close to destroying him— which the white man has repeatedly done his best to do, whether or not he knows it.

What is included in a given boundary is inevitably culturally determined and therefore completely arbitrary. We in the West take the many entities that are enclosed in a single skin and supported by a single system of bones and muscles and say that this is one thing—a person. This brings me to my next point, which concerns the way in which a part of the psyche works that is totally at variance with folk beliefs concerning where the lines are drawn vis-à-vis the person. That is, current lore provides us with a picture of personality boundaries that is at variance with the facts and, because it is at variance, causes no little trouble among people.

The process I am about to describe is related to but not identical with what is known in psychoanalytic circles as "identification"[9] and is a key concept in the process of transcending culture.

Currently, there are differences in opinion among psychiatrists concerning how identification works and what it is. I will limit my discussion to those things I have discovered personally, in the course of my own psychoanalysis, that have worked for me and that I have observed working in those I know well. In the context of this discussion, identification will take two forms: as an individual dynamism that is more or less unique or characteristic of a particular person; and as a manifestation, and probably one of the chief manifestations, of culture. The fact that I draw this particular line is a function of the world in which I was reared, and as is the case with all classifications, the lines drawn are quite arbitrary. There will be cultures in which the distinction does not occur at all or would seem unnatural as well as those cultures that draw additional lines. The subject of identification also illustrates the problems that are created when an individual has been drawing lines in inappropriate ways, for any number of reasons. Because, in the course of conducting daily transactions, this individual may make distinctions that are inconsistent with what is actually happening.

At the beginning of this chapter, I spoke of cutting the apron strings and inferred by implication to the need of the growing young adult to establish his own identity independent of the parent. That is, I was looking at the separation process from the point of view of the child. (I am using "child" in the generic rather than the developmental sense.) Popular psychiatric theory as well as professional practice in the West has focused our attention on these early relationships. In fact, we see them as setting the basic pattern for later life and often spend a good deal of time and money trying to work out the complex relationships that each of us had with parents and siblings when we were young. All of this is well and good up to a point, but whatever it was that happened to us as children has happened, and while it is sometimes helpful to know these things, there is nothing any of us can do to alter or change in any way the parents we had or how they treated us. This brings me to a different source of psychic malaise that is more and more common because it is exacerbated by the times.

In contrast with the Freudian "child in the man" syndrome that looks to the past, we find that an area of psychic tension, discomfort, and grief that has recently been recognized as pivotal to adult mental health is the relationship of middle-aged parents to their children as these children approach and discover adulthood. During the 1960s one read a good deal about the "generation gap."[10] But seldom does one find adequate insightful descriptions of why parents become so upset by the behavior of their children. The answer lies in the presence as well as the discontinuities of individual and cultural identification.

Before examining problems posed by the generation gap, let us further define identification. Identification has many meanings—from documents that establish one's identity to such expressions as "Jones has been closely identified with his company" and "The audience identified with the actor in his role as Hamlet." Students may unconsciously transfer the feelings they have toward their parents to their teachers and behave toward them as if they were their parents. One dictionary defines the psychoanalytic position on identification as "the transference reaction of one person with the feelings or responses relevant to another. . . ."[11]

None of these definitions quite convey what I have in mind (although Melanie Klein's[12] "projective identification" comes closest) when I consider the relationship of parents to their young (individual identification) or to individuals in intercultural transactions (cultural identification). It is necessary, therefore, to still further refine the term identification to include those feelings that one has about parts of the self or aspects of the personality that have been "dissociated," and how one handles these feelings. Dissociation (Sullivan[13]) means those behavior patterns, impulses, drives, and dynamisms that were for one reason or another disapproved of in our childhood by persons very significant to us. Thus, for a variety of reasons, a child may have had a deep resentment of and therefore a need to bully a younger sibling. When the bullying was observed by mother and others, who severely punished the child and made him or her feel guilty and ashamed, the punishment and feelings of guilt did not bear on the underlying need to bully, which therefore remained intact and unchanged. According to Sullivan, the result is that the bullying persists (because the need is still there) but is dissociated from the self, so that self-respect can also be maintained. One continues to bully when the occasion arises, but the bullying is sealed off from conscious awareness; therefore, dissociated acts have a "not me" quality to them. In other cultures and contexts, the dissociation process is handled by explaining a given act as though it were due to forces or personalities or influences outside of the self (Geraldine, on the Flip Wilson Show, "The Debbil made me do it"). When one is acting under the rule of dissociated impulses, everybody *except* the individual himself knows and perceives what is happening. The individual who is stingy and mean in certain relationships will persist in perceiving himself as generous and kind. Similarly the individual who has trouble getting close to people may compensate for this deficiency with a pseudo friendliness and overt joviality (a common cultural trait, characteristic of many Americans, that is recognized all over the world). Or take the case of the man who feels he should be careful and cautious and take good care of things because as a child he was repeatedly told to do so by his parents. Such people will frequently manifest surface neatness but be rather sloppy and lazy underneath; they will not see themselves this way, for the sloppiness and laziness will be dissociated.

When a parent suffering from these or other dissociations sees his child—usually one of the same sex—struggling with something he has himself dissociated or experienced difficulty with, he is apt to become anxious or angry and to be unnecessarily hard on the youngster. Without knowing he has done so, the parent will treat the child as himself (and people *are* very hard on themselves in dissociated areas, because they are acting as their own parent). Not only does one treat the child as oneself, but unconsciously includes the child inside the psychic envelope, so that the child becomes an extension of the self with all that implies, including the extension-transference process described in Chapter 2. The process is reminiscent of one's former reactions to mother's breast, when it was wanted but was not present, which occurred at that stage in life when the universe and the self were one.

Once it is known that identification with the offspring is the source of difficulty and discomfort and agony, it is possible for the parent to take a new tack, which is to "empathize" deeply with the struggling young person, which takes care of the natural concern one experiences and at the same time frees the offspring to be himself. It is crucial that the parent recognize that his difficulties are not really with his offspring but with a dissociated part of the self and are traceable to the identification process. In these terms, it is easy to see why parents and children have trouble with each other, and children, without knowing why, can be deeply resentful when they have to bear the brunt of parental identification at the very time when they are struggling to establish their own identity. This is a difficult task at best, even in a culture that does cut the apron strings.

What is interesting about the process we are discussing is that it is *not* restricted to one's children but will apply to anyone in one's entourage or inventory of friends and associates who is experiencing certain difficulties. Part of the frustration experienced can be traced to anger at oneself for not being able to cope with a dissociated aspect of one's personality and at the same time to defeat from being denied the experience of an important part of the self.

An additional source of feelings of inadequacy can be traced to the normal feelings people have when they can't make something work (ranging from mechanical gadgets, automobiles, social relations, computers, to such bureaucracies as the post office and the telephone company). No matter what one does or how hard one tries, it is exasperating when the system doesn't produce. The source of rage on the part of minority groups in our society is not only that they are treated badly, which they frequently are, but that they can't seem to get the system to work for them. Like the father who identifies with his son's problems, they don't know which buttons to push or how to push them.

So far, I have spoken of dissociated negative traits. However, it is just as likely that positive traits such as love, warmth, compassion, and creativity will be dissociated. I once knew a mother who was made very anxious and envious by any sign of success in her children—in fact, in anyone with whom she was associated. For others to succeed was a sin, because it diminished her worth. It is not hard to imagine the handicap under which these children struggled in the competitive culture of the United States. Having internalized aspects of mother, the problems they then had to cope with were their own dissociated strivings for success and the difficulty of dealing with successful people.

Let us now go beyond the individual to deal with groups. Paradoxically the identification process as described here is one of the strongest cements that bind cultures into cohesive wholes. It is analogous to the forces that bind the nucleus of the atom together.

One would infer from all of this that the important part of culture exists safely hidden below the level of conscious awareness. Why, for example, are people so insistent that others conform to the mores of the group? Why are they made so uncomfortable and anxious if they don't? One image that comes to mind at this point is the tremendous amount of psychic energy and concentration that goes into feeding an infant with a spoon. Watch mothers do this. There are several kinds of maternal patterns, and in the one I am thinking about, the mother opens her mouth and goes through all the motions she wants the child to make. In this case, while she may not be aware of anything that she is doing, the acts themselves are *not* dissociated, which is one of the differences between individual and cultural types of identification. In general, however, the process of identification, whichever type it is, is normally out of awareness or unconscious.

I recently observed a highly intelligent, sophisticated woman going through agonies over the fact that her daughter, who also was a very talented and intelligent person indeed, did not observe amenities that were so important to the mother. Having observed this pattern in action for a considerable length of time and empathizing with the pain it occasioned, I took the risk of telling my friend that I thought she had an identification problem with her daughter and that the two personalities were in a partial sense intermingled, which was painful to both of them. I suggested that it was necessary to draw a new boundary around the self that excluded the daughter, because whatever the daughter was to do with her life, only she could do.

In another instance in which I personally was involved, I found myself becoming deeply annoyed and threatened by a man of my own age who happened to have great personal difficulties in human relations. The sources of these difficulties were complex; one aspect, at least, had to do with ambiguities in regard to his own image. The result was that in order to perform at all, he felt comfortable only (because of his extreme narcissism) when controlling others. Not only did he need to be the center of attention, but he felt compelled to tell everyone else what he or she could or could not do, down to and including small details of daily life. Instead of empathizing with his problem, I discovered, to my surprise and chagrin, that I felt defeated and anxious. Our relationship was such that, for the moment at least, escape was impossible. The reader may think at this point that such a person is more to be pitied than spurned, and he would be right. My problem, however, was not with my friend but with my own feelings. The source of my discomfort was that it was impossible to reach or influence him in any ordinary sense. There was no way. It wasn't until I realized that I had an identification problem and that the source of my discomfort was not in this other man but really in myself that I was able to make some progress in our relationship. I had failed to draw a line separating me from him and was treating him as a recalcitrant, somewhat obnoxious, bumbling part of myself that wouldn't behave.

The paradoxical part of the identification syndrome is that until it has been resolved there can be no friendship and no love —only hate. Until we can allow others to be themselves, and ourselves to be free, it is impossible to truly love another human being; neurotic and dependent love is perhaps possible, but not genuine love, which can be generated only in the self.

The processes being discussed here are much more common than might be supposed, and since the function of maintaining some behaviors out-of-awareness is to keep things safely hidden —safe from change and beyond the reach of reason—any behavior that falls in the out-of-awareness category will be highly persisting in man.

In most people—those who are reasonably well acculturated so that they can function according to the informal rules controlling the various and sundry groups that go to make up their lives—one finds a high degree of sensitivity and responsiveness to the identification needs of others. These are people one gets along with, who don't raise ripples in the pond of life, who give extraordinary consistency to the informal culture of any given group. Which brings us to intercultural and interethnic encounters. Theoretically, there should be no problem when people of different cultures meet. Things begin, most frequently, not only with friendship and goodwill on both sides, but there is an intellectual understanding that each party has a different set of beliefs, customs, mores, values, or what-have-you. The trouble begins when people have to start working together, even on a superficial basis. Frequently, even after years of close association, neither can make the other's system work! The difficulties I and others have observed persist so long and are so resistant to change that they can be explained only in psychological terms: people are in and remain in the grip of the cultural type of identification. Without knowing it, they experience the other person as an uncontrollable and unpredictable part of themselves. I used to see this years ago in Iran, where, at the time, bullying was an accepted and frequent mode of interaction with those who were not in one's own entourage and who were weaker, less powerful, or less influential than oneself. No amount of explanation could convince Americans that the Iranians were not behaving badly and dispel the extreme discomfort they experienced when they saw a more powerful or influential Iranian bullying a weaker one in public. I have also observed the identification process at work in American businessmen in Japan, where they ignore Japanese successes and American failures and persist in telling the Japanese how to do business the American way.

In America, we encounter interethnic identification in another form. Here the groups have lived together, in many instances for generations. They no longer have the goodwill (so fleetingly and quickly dispelled) that one finds when traveling. Instead, there is a deep emotional involvement of the type observed in the family where there is a generation gap. Again, the only thing that explains the feelings and the behavior that one observes is that there is a significant identification factor on all sides. Individuals who are willing to let others be themselves without paying a dreadful price for it are very rare indeed. There has been some progress here and there, yet one seldom hears the remark: "The trouble I have with him is me."

Possibly the most important psychological aspect of culture—the bridge between culture and personality—is the identification process. This process, which works admirably when change is slow but wreaks havoc in times of rapid change such as we are currently experiencing, is most certainly a major impediment to cross-cultural understanding and effective relations among the peoples of the world. Man must now embark on the difficult journey beyond culture, because the greatest separation feat of all is when one manages to gradually free oneself from the grip of unconscious culture.

Notes

Introduction

1. I don't mean that there aren't talented people who make good beginnings. What I am talking about is being deeply contexted in these highly sophisticated, incredibly complex cultures.
2. Hardin (1968)
3. The commons themes are expanded in a book, EXPLORING NEW ETHICS FOR SURVIVAL: THE VOYAGE OF THE SPACE SHIP "BEAGLE," by Garrett Hardin (1972).
4. De Grazia (1962)
5. By being in control of a situation I do not mean in a power sense. I only mean to be in control of all or most of the communication systems, verbal and nonverbal, so that the individual can make himself felt, be a factor in the equations of life.
6. Kesey (1962)

CHAPTER ONE · *The Paradox of Culture*

1. Fromm (1951)
2. No matter what point of departure one uses, symbols inevitably have both a shared and an individual component. No two people ever use the same word in exactly the same way, and the more abstract the symbol, the greater the likelihood of a sizable individual component.
3. New York *Times*, February 20, 1970
   The island, Ruffle Bar, is situated in Jamaica Bay about five miles southwest of Kennedy International Airport.

4. Remarks attributed to a representative of the American Society for the Prevention of Cruelty to Animals (ASPCA). A New York *Times* story on February 23, 1970, described the capture of the dog and repeated the statement about the "happy home."

5. Note the imagery, not commonly the type reported, coming from the mouths of "New York's finest." I am also sure that there was no thought of the implications of the metaphor, which unconsciously links the sentiments of the police with the dog's situation.

6. New York *Times*, April 23, 1970
   In this instance, public pressure and indignation were sufficient to cause the National Parks Service to change its policy. As of this writing the NPS has actually started sponsoring kite-flying contests.

7. Laing (1967)
   Fromm (1959) also speaks of ". . . the dark period of . . . insanity we are passing through."
   The notion that the world is mad is not restricted to the psychiatrists and psychoanalysts. Ada Louise Huxtable, the architecture critic, writes in the New York *Times*, March 15, 1970, ". . . one *practical* decision after another has led to the brink of cosmic disaster and there we sit, in pollution and chaos, courting the end of the earth. Just how practical can you get?" (italics added)

8. Such other insanities as the war in Vietnam, President Nixon's Watergate scandals, spending more on outer space than on the cities and housing or more on an unwanted supersonic transport (keeping twenty thousand people awake for each passenger carried) are so vast and grandiose that the mind boggles at the enormity of the outrages that man can commit against himself. Somehow, the dog's plight not only symbolizes man's drive to be himself, but it is also on a scale that one can comprehend.

9. Galbraith holds that the New Economics will also reflect the view that it is not the consumer, but business and government bureaucracies that determine the economic state of the nation. (1967) (1973)

10. In making this statement I do not mean to imply that "linear" and "comprehensive" are being used as synonyms for "irrational" and "rational." Sequential, or linear statements are

suited to solving certain kinds of problems, whereas comprehensive processes are better adapted to other kinds. *What is
irrational is using one where the other is required,* just as it
is irrational to use a sports car to pull a plow or a tractor to
race with. You can do both, but it doesn't make sense.

11. McLuhan (1960) (1962)
Buckminster Fuller and Marshall McLuhan, both in public ut-
terances and in their writings, have distinguished between two
different ways of thinking. McLuhan talks about linear and
non-linear thinking, Fuller about comprehensive and non-
comprehensive thinking. The distinction popularized by
McLuhan and Fuller is also made by less widely known but
highly respected academicians. A recent article in *Science*,
November 28, 1969, by Beryl L. Crowe, comes to the same
conclusion that I have reached: namely, that the answer to
some of our most basic problems *lies in the way we think.*
Crowe also quotes Aaron Wildavsky (1964) concerning a
comprehensive study of the budgetary process whereby the
government ". . . proceeded by a calculus that is *sequential*
and *incremental* rather than *comprehensive.*" (italics added)
Crowe (1969)

12. Sapir (1931)
13. Kluckhohn and Leighton (1946)
14. Hall (1959)
15. Polychronic time (P-time), as the term implies, is nonlinear.
Everything happens at once. Some jobs and occupations are
more polychronic than monochronic. Whole cultures, such as
those encountered in the Middle East and Latin America, are
polychronic. Hall (1959)
16. Anyone studying priorities in the United States at virtually any
level has only to examine time allocations. Some things that
we *say* are important are not so important as they seem (the
time fathers spend with children, for example). Furthermore,
the relationship of the number of events to time is linear,
sequential, and fixed. You can increase the number of events
only by decreasing the time allotted to each, since each event
is a transaction and has an attack or warm-up phase as well as a
decay or terminating phase. A theoretical point is reached
where productive time (the time between warm-up and terminating) drops to zero and no business is done. To get
around this M-time, executives are forced to delegate respon-

sibility to others also in the grip of the time process. This not only forces M-time people to add layers to bureaucracies *but* sets a theoretical limit on the size of all bureaucracies.

17. There are people who are neurotic or for other reasons reverse this schedule, frittering their lives away. To us, one of the most important things to learn is how to use our time.

18. Hall (1966a)

CHAPTER TWO · *Man as Extension*

1. Gilliard (1962) (1963)
2. Gilliard, personal communication (1963)
3. Most of what has been gleaned of these processes has been learned from studying the capacity of germs and insects to adapt to poisons developed by man to keep them under control. Flies and mosquitoes, for example, evolve forms resistant to DDT even in a few seasons.
4. Marshall McLuhan used to talk about innering and outering (processes he could see at work in man), and few people knew what he meant until he began speaking in terms of extensions —a term he borrowed from the author—in *The Gutenberg Galaxy* (1962).
5. Joyce (1939)
6. Korzybski (1948)
   Johnson (1946)
7. La Barre (1954)
8. Luria (1966)
9. Luria (1972)
10. Whorf (1956)
11. Sapir (1921) (1931) (1949)
12. Hoffmann and Dukas (1972)
13. Labov *et al.* (1968)
14. Also see Scribner and Cole (1973)
15. Hardin (1972)
16. Martin (1972)
17. Andreski (1973)
18. Fuller (1969)
19. Toffler (1970)
20. McHale (1972)

21. Scribner and Cole (1973)
22. Holt (1964) (1967)
23. Kozol (1967)
24. Illich (1970a) (1970b)
25. Chomsky (1968)
26. Hall (1959)
27. Hoffmann and Dukas (1972)
28. The extension-omission side of even one cultural system has not, to my knowledge, been described.
29. Wiener (1954)
30. This point was recognized intuitively by the Taos Indians, who for years would not even allow piped water or electricity into their village.

CHAPTER THREE · *Consistency and Life*

1. For a more complete treatment of culture as a communication, see my THE SILENT LANGUAGE (1959).
2. A lifetime of dealing with the subtleties of intercultural communication has convinced me that the strength and persistence of these habitual behaviors are almost beyond belief. These behaviors are closely identified with the self—the good self, the socially responsible self, which wants to do right and to fit in—and are synonymous with social competence. However, in intercultural situations, when other people call attention to these hidden responses and perceptual differences, suggesting that the world is not as one perceives it, these observations can be unsettling. To do so is to suggest that a person is incompetent, not properly motivated, ignorant, or even infantile. The mere mention of patterns or the suggestion that there are such things threatens some people's individuality. Older parts of the psyche are mobilized—the parts that were active when growing up and that represent the internalized authority of the parent and the past. To counteract the effect of dynamisms from the past, one has to remind oneself that one's image of others is largely made up of projections of various parts of one's own personality including one's psychic needs, which are treated as though they were innate. For example, it is difficult for Americans who like freedom from binding institutional ties to believe that many Japanese would actively seek

to submerge themselves in business or government bureaucracy for life. "How could anyone subject himself willingly to such a paternalistic life?"

3. Powers (1973)
4. See Chapters 1 and 9 of THE SILENT LANGUAGE.

CHAPTER FOUR · *Hidden Culture*

1. Dore (1973) and Robert Cole (1973)
2. Honorifics are suffixes added to words that signal to the listener that the speaker recognizes his higher status.
3. Morsbach (1973)

CHAPTER FIVE · *Rhythm and Body Movement*

1. Bronowski (1974)
2. The term syncing is new, a product of the late mid-twentieth century. Etymologically, it comes from synchrony but has taken on a special, more technical meaning rooted in film making. The *Film Editing Handbook* (Churchill, 1972) gives sync, sync'd, and syncing as the preferred spellings for these forms. One says, "to be in or out of sync."
3. Condon (1974), Condon and Ogston (1967), Condon and Sander (1973) (1974)
4. The body synchronizers have not been identified as physiological areas in the central nervous system, nor do we know whether they are under internal or external control. They are "isomorphic with the articulated structure of . . . speech." Condon and Sander (1974)
5. Condon (1974), Condon and Ogston (1967), Condon and Sander (1973) (1974)
6. Birdwhistell (1970)
7. A closed score works out as planned—like putting a man on the moon. An open score evolves, as is the case with good jazz. Halprin (1969)
8. Condon and Sander (1974)
9. Ibid.
10. Ibid.

11. Proxemics refers to man's use of space as an aspect of his culture; i.e., conversational distance, planning, and use of interior spaces, town layout, and the like. See my The Hidden Dimension (1966).

12. In a recent, as yet unpublished, study of locomotion, significant differences between the walk of Anglo Americans and Spanish Americans were discovered. To the Spanish, the Anglo has an uptight, authoritarian walk unless he is just ambling. To the Anglo, the Spanish American male walk looks more like a swagger than a purposeful walk.

13. Ekman and Friesen (1969)

14. Eibl-Eibesfeldt (1972)

15. Ekman and Friesen (1969)

16. Personal communication from Professor Paul Bohannan.

17. The Hidden Dimension, Chapter VII, "Art as a Clue to Perception."

18. Nierenberg and Calero (1973)

19. The literature on North American black culture is extensive and varied. It includes: highly informative, sensitive biographies of such men as Malcolm X (1965) and Claude Brown (1965); the more sociological studies, of which Liebow's *Tally's Corner* and Herskovits and Herskovits' classical anthropological studies (1936) (1947) are representative, as well as subtle and detailed linguistic studies of Labov (1966) and Labov *et al.* (1968), Mitchell-Kernan (1972), Stewart (1965) (1967), and others too numerous to mention here.

20. Worth and Adair (1972)

Chapter Six · *Context and Meaning*

1. The Hidden Dimension discusses this quality of culture in more detail.

2. Meier (1963)

3. Man also imposes a selective screen between the conscious part of his mind and the unconscious part. Sullivan (1947) and Freud (1933).

4. Whorf (1956)

5. Polanyi (1968)

6. Sullivan (1947)

7. The linguist Noam Chomsky (1968) and his followers have tried to deal with the contexting feature of language by eliminating context and going to so-called "deep structure." The results are interesting but end up evading the main issues of communication and to an even greater extent stress ideas at the expense of what is actually going on.

8. For further information on Chinese, see Wang (1973).

9. Bernstein (1964)

10. Eiseley (1969)

11. I do not agree with Eiseley's generalizing about all of mankind, because activism, like everything else, has to be taken in context. As we will see, LC cultures appear to be more vulnerable to violent perturbations than HC cultures.

12. Saul Bellow's (1974) article on the role of literature in a setting of changing times is also relevant to this discussion. Bellow makes the point that for some time now there has been a conscious effort on the part of avant-garde Western intellectuals to obliterate the past. "Karl Marx felt in history the tradition of all dead generations weighing like a nightmare on the brain of the living. Nietzsche speaks movingly of 'it was,' and Joyce's Stephen Dedalus also defines history as a 'nightmare from which we are trying to awaken.'" Bellow points out, however, that there is a paradox that must be met, for to do away with history is to destroy one's own part in the historical process. It is reasonably certain, however, that what these men were trying to do was to redefine context in order to reduce its influence on men's actions. Simply to do away with the past would lead to an incredibly unstable society, as we shall see.

13. Black culture is much higher on the context scale than white culture, and one would assume from our model that riots do not have the same meaning for blacks as they do to the white society in which the blacks are imbedded.

14. Birren (1961)

15. For further details on this fascinating set of experiments, see Land (1959).

16. These distinctions are completely arbitrary and are for the convenience of the writer and the reader. They do not necessarily occur in nature. The inside-outside dichotomy has been struck down many times, not only by the perceptual transactionalists (Kilpatrick, 1961) following in Dewey's footsteps but in my own writings as well. Within the brain, experience (culture)

acts on the structure of the brain to produce mind. It makes little difference *how* the brain is modified; what is important is that modification does take place and is apparently continuous.

17. Buder (1967)
18. See Hall (1966a) for a comprehensive treatment of man's relationship to the spaces he builds as well as a bibliography on the subject.
19. Barker (1968) and Barker and Schoggen (1973)
20. The interested reader will find it worthwhile to consult Barker's works directly.
21. Kilpatrick (1961)
22. Hall (1966a)
23. Toffler (1970)
24. McLuhan (1964)

CHAPTER SEVEN · *Contexts, High and Low*

1. Boorstin (1973)
2. Some English anthropologists have chosen this one to the virtual exclusion of all others.
3. Slovenko (1967)
4. Ibid.
5. McCormick (1954)
6. This is the reason why "summaries" of President Nixon's Watergate tapes would not do. Judge Sirica needed the whole context in order to make a judgment of any given remark or statement, which shows that occasionally an American jurist recognizes the need for contexting information in order to make a judgment.
7. Occasionally, the rich, the highly placed, and the powerful, such as ex-Vice-President Agnew, will get away with plea bargaining and avoid jail. Or in some cases, an individual will be judged incompetent to stand trial, which is, of course, prior to the trial and hence not really relevant to our discussion, which is of trials in different cultures.
8. This does not mean that, when there is a market that is not being met by French businessmen, an American like Levitt the builder cannot move in and take over, just as small foreign cars filled a hole in the American market. It is only when there is

competition for a given market that knowledge of and adherence to local custom is a prerequisite to success.

9. The American in Japan can get some feeling of how basically different it would be to be Japanese if he keeps his eyes open, for he frequently finds the Japanese system both foreign and threatening. This should not mean that the system doesn't work and work very well, only that it is not generally understood by Westerners or even found believable when it is understood.

10. When I first read Snow Country, this scene really puzzled me. I had to let the entire situation as described by Kawabata do the contexting for me. Taken out of context, the scene was meaningless. Taken in the context of Japanese culture, which plays down any overt expression of emotion in human relations, the scene as portrayed by Kawabata has an unbelievable impact.

11. Keene (1968)

12. La Barre (1954)

13. La Barre (1962)

Chapter Eight · *Why Context?*

1. Warren and Warren (1970)

2. Choice of words seemed to matter very little; the results were the same.

3. For the interested professional, the Warrens' experiments, coupled with the context rule, provide an alternate explanation to Bateson's (1956) hypothesis that there is something specific *in* the message itself that suggests the missing part. Internal contexting as it is used here takes care of the whole notion of redundancy (Hockett, 1966; Shannon, 1951; Osgood, 1966) and is more in line with a transactional approach. In fact, W. S. Condon's (1974) studies of synchrony would seem to disprove the redundancy principle in human information processing. It would appear that the concept of redundancy is an artifact that has been used to take the place of contexting in natural systems; i.e., without context, something like redundancy is needed. With it, the whole system works together to maintain a synchronous balance between the many different communication levels. It is possible that the 50 per cent redun-

dancy that Shannon (1951) noted in printed English can be explained by the fact that one is dealing with a second-generation extension—the printed word—in a relatively low-context culture. It would be interesting to discover whether the same figure would hold for a high-context extension such as written Chinese.

4. Johnston and McClelland (1974)
5. For more on mimicry and camouflage, see ANIMAL CAMOUFLAGE (Portmann 1939).
6. Lettvin, Maturana, McCulloch, and Pitts (1959)
7. Gouras and Bishop (1972)
8. A good photograph is one in which the photographer has increased the context.
9. In large parts of Latin America, all common diseases are classed as either "hot" or "cold," which tells the practitioner how to treat the patient as well as what foods to give him, since all foods are also classified as either "hot" or "cold." Herbs are classified according to their curative value as well as by other features significant to the daily life of the Indians.
10. Raven, Berlin, and Breedlove (1971)
11. Szent-Györgyi (1972)
12. Holden (1971)
13. Dubos. Talk given at Arden House, New York, Wenner-Gren Foundation Conference on Medicine and Anthropology in 1961. For further discussion along this same line, see Dubos (1965) (1968).
14. How much more involved can you get than creating an entire experimental situation for organisms even as intelligent and responsive as the Norway rat?
15. Skinner (1971)
16. Hsu, personal communication.

CHAPTER NINE · *Situation—Culture's Building Block*

1. The reasons for this are various:
   a. The situational dialect of the classroom is not the SD of the street or anywhere else, except the classroom.
   b. Pronunciation often gets in the way, because there are features of all languages that have not been analyzed. These are the ones that don't get taught.

c. Words must be used properly in context (see the selection law: Hall, 1959). My aunt once went to town in Grenoble to buy a sweater for skiing. The clerk was puzzled because she asked for a man who sweats!

d. Possibly the most serious criticism of the way language is taught, by asking children to learn vocabulary and grammar and combine the two, is that the brain doesn't work that way. The same method was tried in aircraft identification in World War II. The type of wing, tail, fuselage, and number of motors was worked out and presented to aircraft spotters. In practice, they found they couldn't combine the parts fast enough.

2. Situational dialects are also known as "co-ordinate language systems." See "Learning Language in Total Situations." In Osgood and Sebeok with Diebold (1965).

3. I had a wonderful opportunity to learn all over again the impact of the SD on the outsider on a recent trip to Australia. After a meeting, we were trying to arrange travel which had been handled by one of the secretaries, who had left work for the day and gone home. I couldn't find her name in the phone book and asked an Australian colleague if he knew her phone number. He replied, "She's not on the phone." I said, "I don't know how you know whether she's using the phone or not, but I still need her number." He said, "She's not on the phone." This continued until I said, "Quite frankly, I don't know what in hell you are talking about," at which point he said, "Oh, excuse me for using Australian slang. She has no telephone."

4. Drucker (1970), Chapter 1, page 6.

5. Lorenz (1952)

6. See Chapter 3 of THE SILENT LANGUAGE, "The Primary Message Systems," for a more complete exposition of criteria used in identifying basic situations.

7. "On Being Sane in Insane Places," Rosenhan (1973).

CHAPTER TEN · *Action Chains*

1. Hall (1966a) and Calhoun (1962)
2. Tinbergen (1952)
3. Sullivan (1947)

4. Recently in the United States there has been a flurry of inter-
    est in talking to plants. Whether this has any effect that can
    be differentiated from the added care and attention that ac-
    company such talk is not known. The point about the Hopi is
    that they include all of nature in the same category as people.
5. Castaneda (1968) (1971) (1972)
6. Leyhausen (1965) in Lorenz and Leyhausen (1973)
7. Spite patterns in the Middle East are a common feature of ev-
    eryday life. People who live in the area and know the patterns
    are very careful not to get the Arabs aroused to the point at
    which spite comes into play. For they will cut off their nose to
    spite their face. This point was made fourteen years ago (Hall,
    1959) and is a necessary component of any system of under-
    standing Arab psychology. Patterns such as these are difficult
    for Americans to reconcile with their own pragmatism.

    See Hall (1966a) for a picture of a four-story house in Bei-
    rut not much thicker than a wall that was built to spite a
    neighbor by cutting off his view of the sea. Lebanese inform-
    ants told me of another house in the middle of a neighbor's
    land that was completely surrounded by a spite wall so the
    inhabitant couldn't see over at all!
8. Spitz (1964)
9. Freud once postulated coitus interruptus as the key factor in
    the development of neuroses. Freud was writing in a very
    special context, in times that were very different from today.
    We still have neurosis but about the only place one encounters
    coitus interruptus today is in a blue movie. Regardless of
    whether Freud was right or wrong, he recognized the
    seriousness of the uncompleted act at the time he wrote. In a
    sense, all sex is the example par excellence of an action chain,
    and there are few adults who have not had the frustrating ex-
    perience of a broken chain during sex.
10. May (1972)
11. For an elaboration of this view see Chapter 1; also, my book
    THE SILENT LANGUAGE.
12. For an excellent description of this ritual, see Bennis,
    "Searching for the 'Perfect' University President," *The Atlan-
    tic* (April 1971), which describes what Bennis went through
    while being considered for the presidency of Northwestern
    University.

CHAPTER ELEVEN • *Covert Culture and Action Chains*

1. Schlegloff (1968)
2. Melville (1961)
3. Adumbration is the term given to those foreshadowing action chains that reveal to either of the two parties in an interaction or to a third party that events are escalating.
4. May (1972)
5. There will be some Spanish-Americans who don't live in New Mexico or who have been Anglicized and who don't recognize this pattern. It is slowly dying out as the two cultures come closer together.
6. Hall (1959)
7. The cultural unconscious is at work in Israeli-Arab disputes. Arabs I know used to say unabashedly, "One Jew can lick twenty Arabs." Later, after the Six-Day War, I heard them say, "We weren't fighting Jews. We were fighting Europeans!" One must read this statement in context, because Jews have lived as villagers throughout the Middle East for thousands of years. And it is experience with these indigenous Jews that forms the basis of much of Arab expectations for insight, understanding, and performance on the part of the Israelis. The Arabs expect to have their position understood, and it is quite clear that other considerations are in the forefront of Israeli thinking. Neither side sees the other for what they are. At least the Arabs seem to be discovering that they are dealing with European culture and not Middle Eastern culture. The risk that is taken by the Israelis in their continued defeats of the Arabs is that, each time, the Arabs learn more and more and improve their performance. The lessons are expensive but they are lessons nonetheless. If there ever were two peoples who had everything to gain and nothing to lose from understanding each other, it is the Arabs and the Israelis.
8. Boas (1911)
9. Bloomfield (1933)
10. Sapir (1949)
11. Hall (1959)

CHAPTER TWELVE · *Imagery and Memory*

1. Lawick (1971)
2. Lorenz (1952) (1955) (1966)
3. The ethologist has replaced the old-fashioned naturalist as a student of other life forms. While there are many who have added materially to our understanding of other life forms, I would mention Hediger (1950) (1955) (1961) and Tinbergen (1952) (1958) as two thinkers whose work has made a wide impact.
4. Hoffmann and Dukas (1972)
5. Ibid.
6. Extension transference again. It is possible to see the extension-transference process at work in the awarding of architectural prizes. The basis for making awards is drawings and renderings, in some instances before the building has even been built. To answer this, the juries that make the awards will state that it is impossible to visit all the buildings and that the two-dimensional representations are all they need to judge a building, which may be true if aesthetics is the sole criterion.
7. Appleyard, Lynch, and Myer (1964)
8. All of which made my cross-cultural experiences much more real.
9. Nabokov (1958)
10. Note how Nabokov localizes his two types of visualizing: the laboratory of the mind and the "dark inner side" of the eyelids.
11. Charrière (1970)
12. Capote (1965)
13. I am not referring to the type of injustices suffered by U.S. Indians and blacks or other minorities, but injustices the Trukese foisted on each other.
14. *Newsweek*, November 11, 1960, p. 94.
15. Luria (1968) (1972)
16. Stromeyer (1970)
17. *Scientific American*, March 1970, p. 62.
18. This case was reported by a colleague who had worked for the inventor for some time and was able to observe and discuss his imaging capabilities with him.
19. Also see Julesz (1969)

20. Gordon (1961)
21. The word "imagine," if used in the original sense, would do. As currently used, "imagine" does not conjure up the appropriate images.

CHAPTER THIRTEEN · *Cultural and Primate Bases of Education*

1. Interaction and Materials
   Association and Defense
   Work and Play
   Bisexuality and Learning
   Space and Time (Hall, 1959)
2. Hall (1959)
3. Luria (1966) (1970)
4. Pribram (1969) (1971)
5. Pietsch (1972a) (1972b)
6. MacLean (1965)
7. A recent, 500-page review, *Readings in Psychology Today* (Julesz, 1967), does not contain a single reference to mind in its index.
8. Understanding the transition from senses to brain, and their function in structuring mind, has always been an important, in fact crucial, link in the chain of understanding mankind. It is a media/message, form/content sort of thing which keeps being brought home in many ways. Only recently, Lewin (1974) reared kittens separately in carefully controlled environments where the sensory inputs were structured in such a way that one set perceived only horizontal lines while another only vertical lines. Later, when these same, otherwise identical, kittens were moved to the real world, the perceptual habits imprinted during the experimental phase of their lives persisted. The two sets of kittens lived in two different perceptual worlds—that is, one was blind to vertical lines such as chair legs, sides of windows, and door frames, while the other was blind to horizontals (walls and all vertical lines would be there, but ceilings, floors, lintels, and sills wouldn't)—a demonstration in miniature of both mind and culture.
9. Skinner (1953)
10. MacLean (1965)
11. Esser (1971) calls it the social brain.

12. Pietsch (1972a) (1972b)
13. Pribram (1969) (1971)
14. Lashley (1929)
15. Gabor (1972)
16. Pennington (1968)
17. For detailed descriptions of Pribram's work, the reader is referred to an excellent article in *Scientific American* (1969) as well as his book (1971).
18. Pietsch (1972b)
19. Hall (1959)
20. Forgetting, like memory, is highly situational in character.
21. Luria (1968)
22. Admittedly, today one finds the so-called "open" classroom, but also the windowless school—an educators' gimmick developed in an attempt to deal with some of the more serious uncorrected faults in education. It is useful, if you are a teacher, to be able to move the furniture, and children like to be able to sit on the rug. But this is not my point. For years and years, all schools looked alike.
23. Luria (1970), p. 78
24. Tiger (1969). Also see a popularization by Antony Jay (1971), and Ardrey (1970), pp. 321–31.
25. See Barker (1968) for the effect of size of schools on performance.
26. Washburn (1973a)
27. Collier *et al.* (1974)
28. We are not alone in this. Most cultures are suffused with beliefs in the superiority of their own system. It is one of those things that was valuable and sensible in times past but has long outlived its usefulness.
29. Comparing the two is like comparing the lungs and the liver. Both are needed for survival, but they perform different functions.
30. Mann was a great believer in organization and thought that the Prussian Army was the most perfect organization produced by mankind for molding human beings.
31. Barker (1968)
32. Galbraith (1967)
33. Illich (1970a) (1970b)
34. Holt (1964) (1967) (1969)
35. Herndon (1968)

36. Kozol (1967)
37. Hentoff (1966)

CHAPTER FOURTEEN · *Culture as an Irrational Force*

1. Logic was first systematically expounded in Aristotle's *Organon*.
2. Whorf (1956)
3. The Navajo horse was apparently the only remaining descendant on the North American continent of the Spanish conquistadors' remarkable horses. These tough little animals (half Arab, half Barb) were bred for the rigors of the conquest. There were no better horses for the Navajo country. In South America, the relatives of the Navajo pony are the famous pampas horses used for herding cattle and for polo.
4. As a Westerner, I feel I can speak for my own kind. Men in other parts of the world, reared in other cultures, must deal with their own forms of the irrational.
5. Laing (1967)
6. Hall (1947)
7. Anthropologists are not alone, but share with other scientists a predisposition to be culturebound. It is a rare scientist indeed who does not look at everyday life as one thing and the theories and methods of his discipline as completely separate. This is because science is learned in schools and laboratories. Science teachers deliberately set up a dichotomy between "science" and everyday life, some of which is valid and some not. The schoolroom, the laboratory, and everything produced by science bear the stamp of culture. Even English and American laboratories are different in many subtle respects.

CHAPTER FIFTEEN · *Culture as Identification*

1. Sullivan (1947)
2. Hughes (1961b)
3. Bradbury (1969)
4. Osmond (1959)
5. Searles (1960)
6. *Science,* January 1973

7. Hughes (1961a)
8. Mitchell-Kernan (1972)
9. Meisner (1970)
10. Mead (1970)
11. The dictionary in this instance so oversimplifies Freud's thinking as to result in a gross distortion. To Freud, identification meant the internalization of what he termed objects (i.e., people or aspects of behavior) into the ego or ego structures in such a way as to structurally modify the ego. The stress in this instance is on the term internalization. See Meisner (1970).
12. Klein (1951)
13. Sullivan (1947)

Bibliography

ADAIR, JOHN. See Worth.

ANDRESKI, STANISLAV. *Social Sciences as Sorcery*. New York: St. Martin's Press, Inc., 1973.

APPLEYARD, DONALD; LYNCH, KEVIN; and MYER, JOHN R. *The View from the Road*. Cambridge, Mass.: M.I.T. Press, 1964.

ARDREY, ROBERT. *Social Contract: A Personal Inquiry into the Evolutionary Sources of Order and Disorder*. New York: Atheneum Publishers, 1970.

AUDY, J. R. "Significance of the Ipsefact in Ecology, Ethology, Parasitology, Sociology, and Anthropology." In A. H. Esser (ed.). *Behavior and Environment: The Use of Space by Animals and Men*. Proc. of an internat. sympos. at 1968 Meeting of AAAS, at Dallas, Tex. New York and London: Plenum Press, Inc., 1971.

BARKER, ROGER G. *Ecological Psychology*. Stanford, Calif.: Stanford University Press, 1968.

——; and SCHOGGEN, PHIL. *Qualities of Community Life*. San Francisco: Jossey-Bass, Inc., Publishers, 1973.

BATESON, GREGORY. "The Message: This Is Play." In *Group Processes: Transactions of the Second Conference*. New York: Josiah Macy, Jr. Foundation Publications, 1956.

——; JACKSON, D. D.; HALEY, J.; and WEAKLAND, J. H. "Toward a Theory of Schizophrenia," *Behavioral Science*, Vol. 1, pp. 251–64, 1956.

BELLOW, SAUL. "Machines and Story Books," *Harper's Magazine*, Vol. 249, pp. 48–54, August 1974.

BENEDICT, RUTH. *Chrysanthemum and the Sword: Patterns of Japanese Culture*. Boston: Houghton Mifflin Company, 1946.

——. *Patterns of Culture.* Boston: Houghton Mifflin Company, 1934.

BENNIS, WARREN G. "Searching for the 'Perfect' University President," *The Atlantic,* Vol. 227, No. 4, April 1971.

BERLIN, BRENT. See Raven.

BERNSTEIN, BASIL. "Elaborated and Restricted Codes: Their Social Origins and Some Consequences." In John J. Gumperz and Dell Hymes (eds.). THE ETHNOGRAPHY OF COMMUNICATION, *American Anthropologist,* Vol. 66, No. 6, Part II, pp. 55–69, 1964.

BIRDWHISTELL, RAY L. *Kinesics and Context.* Philadelphia: University of Pennsylvania Press, 1970.

——. *Introduction to Kinesics.* Louisville, Ky.: University of Louisville Press, 1952.

BIRREN, FABER. *Color, Form and Space.* New York: Reinhold Publishing Corp., 1961.

BISHOP, PETER O. See Gouras.

BLAKE, PETER. *God's Own Junkyard.* New York: Holt, Rinehart & Winston, Inc., 1964.

BLOOMFIELD, L. *Language.* New York: Henry Holt & Company, Inc., 1933.

BOAS, F. Introduction, *Handbook of American Indian Languages.* Bureau of American Ethnology, Vol. 40, 1911.

BOORSTIN, DANIEL J. *The Americans: The Democratic Experience.* New York: Random House, Inc., 1973.

BRADBURY, RAY. *Dandelion Wine.* New York: Bantam Books, Inc., 1959.

BREEDLOVE, DENNIS. See Raven.

BRONOWSKI, J. *The Ascent of Man.* Boston: Little, Brown & Company, 1974.

——. "The Principle of Tolerance." *The Atlantic,* December 1973.

BROWN, CLAUDE. *Manchild in the Promised Land.* New York: The Macmillan Co., Publishers, 1965.

BUDER, STANLEY. "The Model Town of Pullman: Town Planning and Social Control in the Gilded Age," *Journal of the American Institute of Planners,* Vol. 33, No. 1, pp. 2–10, January 1967.

CALERO, H. H. See Nierenberg.

CALHOUN, JOHN B. "Population Density and Social Pathology," *Scientific American,* Vol. 206, No. 2, February 1962.

CAPOTE, TRUMAN. *In Cold Blood.* New York: Random House, Inc., 1965.

CASTANEDA, CARLOS. *Journey to Ixtlan.* New York: Simon & Schuster, Inc., 1972.

———. *A Separate Reality.* New York: Simon & Schuster, Inc., 1971.

———. *The Teachings of Don Juan: A Yaqui Way of Knowledge.* Berkeley: University of California Press, 1968.

CHARRIÈRE, HENRI. *Papillon.* New York: William Morrow & Co., Inc., 1970.

CHOMSKY, NOAM. *Language and Mind.* New York: Harcourt, Brace & World, Inc., 1968.

———. *Aspects of a Theory of Syntax.* Cambridge, Mass.: M.I.T. Press, 1965.

CHURCHILL, HUGH B. *Film Editing Handbook: Technique of 16mm Film Cutting.* Belmont, Calif.: Wadsworth Publishing Co., Inc., 1972.

COLE, MICHAEL. See Scribner.

COLE, ROBERT E. *Japanese Blue Collar.* Berkeley: University of California Press, 1973.

COLLIER, J.; LARTSCH, M.; and FERRERO, P. *Film Analysis of the Rough Rock Community School* (MS), 1974.

CONDON, W. S. "Communication and Order, the Micro 'Rhythm Hierarchy' of Speaker Behavior." In J. T. Harries and E. Nickerson. *Play Therapy in Theory and Practice.* In press.

———. "Synchrony Demonstrated Between Movements of the Neonate and Adult Speech," *Child Development.* In press, submitted July 1973.

———; and OGSTON, W. D. "A Segmentation of Behavior," *Journal of Psychiatric Research,* Vol. 5, pp. 221–35, 1967.

———; and SANDER, L. W. "Neonate Movement Is Synchronized with Adult Speech: Interactional Participation and Language Acquisition," *Science,* Vol. 183, No. 4120, January 11, 1974.

CROWE, BERYL L. "The Tragedy of the Commons Revisited," *Science,* Vol. 166, pp. 1103–7, November 28, 1969.

DE GRAZIA, SEBASTIAN. *Of Time, Work and Leisure.* New York: Twentieth Century Fund, 1962.

DENNISON, GEORGE. *The Lives of Children.* New York: Random House, Inc., 1969.

DE TOCQUEVILLE, ALEXIS. *Democracy in America.* New York: Harper & Row, Publishers, 1966.

DIAMOND, I. T.; and HALL, W. C. "Evolution of the Neocortex," *Science*, Vol. 164, pp. 251–62, April 18, 1969.

DILLARD, J. L. *Black English: Its History and Usage in the United States*. New York: Random House, Inc., 1972.

DORE, RONALD. *Japanese Factory*. Berkeley: University of California Press, 1973.

DRUCKER, PETER. "Schools Around the Bend," *Psychology Today*, Vol. 6, No. 1, June 1972.

———. *Technology, Management and Society*. New York: Harper & Row, Publishers, 1970.

DUBOS, RENÉ. *Man, Medicine, and Environment*. New York: Frederick A. Praeger, Inc., Publishers, 1968.

———. *Man Adapting*. New Haven, Conn.: Yale University Press, 1965.

EIBL-EIBESFELDT, I. "Similarities and Differences Between Cultures in Expressive Movements." In R. A. Hinde (ed.). *Non-Verbal Communication*. London: Cambridge University Press, 1972.

EISELEY, L. "Activism and the Rejection of History," *Science*, Vol. 165, p. 129, July 11, 1969.

EKMAN, PAUL. "Universals and Cultural Differences in Facial Expression of Emotion." In *Nebraska Symposium on Motivation*, 1971, J. Cole (ed.). Lincoln: University of Nebraska Press, 1972.

———; and FRIESEN, W. V. "Nonverbal Leakage and Clues to Deception," *Psychiatry*, Vol. 32, No. 1, pp. 88–106, 1969.

———; and ELLSWORTH, PHOEBE. *Emotion in the Human Face*. New York: Pergamon Press, 1972.

ELLSWORTH, PHOEBE. See Ekman.

ESSER, ARISTIDE H. "Social Pollution," *Social Education*, Vol. 35, No. 1, January 1971.

FERRERO, P. See Collier.

FREUD, SIGMUND. *New Introductory Lectures on Psychoanalysis*. New York: W. W. Norton & Company, Inc., 1933.

FRIESEN, WALLACE V. See Ekman.

FROMM, ERICH. *Sigmund Freud's Mission*. New York: Harper & Brothers, 1959.

———. *The Forgotten Language*. New York: Rinehart & Company, 1951.

FROMM-REICHMANN, FRIEDA. *Principles of Intensive Psychotherapy*. Chicago: University of Chicago Press, 1950.

FULLER, R. BUCKMINSTER. *Untitled Epic Poem on the History of Industrialization.* New York: Simon & Schuster, Inc., Publishers, 1970.

———. *Operating Manual for Spaceship Earth.* Carbondale, Ill.: Southern Illinois University Press, 1969.

GABOR, DENNIS. "Holography, 1948–1971," *Science,* Vol. 177, pp. 299–313, July 28, 1972.

GALBRAITH, JOHN KENNETH. *Economics and the Public Purpose.* Boston: Houghton Mifflin Company, 1973.

———. *The New Industrial State.* Boston: Houghton Mifflin Company, 1967.

———. *The Affluent Society.* Boston: Houghton Mifflin Company, 1958.

GILLIARD, E. THOMAS. "Evolution of Bowerbirds," *Scientific American,* Vol. 209, No. 2, pp. 38–46, August 1963.

———. "On the Breeding Behavior of the Cock-of-the-Rock (Aves, *Rupicola rupicola*)," *Bulletin of the American Museum of Natural History,* Vol. 124, 1962.

GORDON, WILLIAM J. J. *Synectics: The Development of Creative Capacity.* New York: Harper & Row, Publishers, 1961.

GOURAS, PETER; and BISHOP, PETER O. "Neural Basis of Vision," *Science,* Vol. 177, pp. 188–89, July 14, 1972.

HALL, EDWARD T. "Art, Space and the Human Experience." In Gyorgy Kepes (ed.). *Arts of the Environment.* New York: George Braziller, Inc., 1972.

———. "Human Needs and Inhuman Cities." In THE FITNESS OF MAN'S ENVIRONMENT, *Smithsonian Annual II,* Washington, D.C.: Smithsonian Institution Press, 1968. Reprinted in *Ekistics,* Vol. 27, No. 160, March 1969.

———. *The Hidden Dimension.* Garden City, N.Y.: Doubleday & Company, Inc., 1966(a).

———. "High- and Low-Context Communication." Paper presented at the annual meeting of the American Anthropological Association in Pittsburgh, Pennsylvania, November 1966(b).

———. *The Silent Language.* Garden City, N.Y.: Doubleday & Company, Inc., 1959.

———. "Race Prejudice and Negro-White Relations in the Army," *American Journal of Sociology,* Vol. 3, No. 5, March 1947.

HALL, W. C. See Diamond.

HALPRIN, LAWRENCE. *The RSVP Cycles.* New York: George Braziller, Inc., 1969.

HARDIN, GARRETT. *Exploring New Ethics for Survival: The Voyage of the Spaceship "Beagle."* New York: Viking Press, 1972.

———. "The Tragedy of the Commons," *Science,* Vol. 162, pp. 1243–48, December 13, 1968.

HEDIGER, H. "The Evolution of Territorial Behavior." In S. L. Washburn (ed.). *Social Life of Early Man.* New York: Viking Fund Publications in Anthropology No. 31, 1961.

———. *Studies of the Psychology and Behavior of Captive Animals in Zoos and Circuses.* London: Butterworth & Co. (Publishers) Ltd., 1955.

———. *Wild Animals in Captivity.* London: Butterworth & Co. (Publishers) Ltd., 1950.

HENRY, JULES. *Culture Against Man.* New York: Random House, Inc., 1963.

HENTOFF, NAT. *Our Children Are Dying.* New York: The Viking Press, Inc., 1966.

HERNDON, JAMES. *The Way It Spozed to Be.* New York: Simon & Schuster, Inc., Publishers, 1968.

HERSKOVITS, M. J.; and HERSKOVITS, F. S. *Trinidad Village.* New York, Alfred A. Knopf, 1947.

———. *Suriname Folk-lore.* New York: Columbia University Press, 1936.

HINDE, R. A. (ed.). *Non-Verbal Communication.* London: Cambridge University Press, 1972.

HOCKETT, C. F. "The Problem of Universals in Language." In Joseph H. Greenberg (ed.). *Universals of Language.* Cambridge, Mass.: M.I.T. Press, 1966.

HOFFER, ERIC. *Working and Thinking on the Waterfront.* New York: Harper & Row, Publishers, 1969.

———. *True Believer.* New York: Harper & Brothers, 1951.

HOFFMANN, BANESH; and DUKAS, HELEN. *Albert Einstein Creator and Rebel.* New York: The Viking Press, Inc., 1972.

HOLDEN, CONSTANCE. "Psychologists Beset by Feelings of Futility, Self-Doubt," *Science,* Vol. 173, No. 4002, p. 1111, September 17, 1972.

HOLT, JOHN. *The Underachieving School.* New York: Pitman Publishing Corporation, 1969.

———. *How Children Learn*. New York: Pitman Publishing Corporation, 1967.

———. *How Children Fail*. New York: Pitman Publishing Corporation, 1964.

HORNEY, KAREN. *Our Inner Conflicts: A Constructive Theory of Neurosis*. New York: W. W. Norton & Company, Inc., 1945.

———. *The Neurotic Personality of Our Time*. New York: W. W. Norton & Company, Inc., 1937.

HSU, FRANCIS L. K. *Americans and Chinese*. Garden City, N.Y.: Natural History Press, 1970.

HUGHES, RICHARD. *The Fox in the Attic*. New York: Harper & Row, Publishers, 1961(a).

———. *A High Wind in Jamaica*. New York: New American Library, 1961(b).

ILLICH, IVAN. *Celebration of Awareness: A Call for Institutional Revolution*. Garden City, N.Y.: Doubleday & Company, Inc., 1970(a).

———. "Why We Must Abolish Schooling," *New York Review of Books*, Vol. 15, No. 1, July 2, 1970(b).

JAY, ANTONY. *Corporation Man*. New York: Random House, Inc., 1971.

JOHNSON, VIRGINIA E. See Masters.

JOHNSON, WENDELL. *People in Quandaries: The Semantics of Personal Adjustment*. New York: Harper & Brothers, 1946.

JOHNSTON, JAMES C.; and MC CLELLAND, J. L. "Perception of Letters in Words: Seek Not and Ye Shall Find," *Science*, Vol. 184, pp. 1192–93, June 14, 1974.

JOYCE, JAMES. *Finnegans Wake*. London: Faber & Faber, Ltd., 1939.

———. *Ulysses*. New York: Random House, Inc., 1934.

JULESZ, BELA. "Experiment in Perception." In *Readings in Psychology Today*. Del Mar, Calif.: CRM Books, 1967.

JUNG, C. G. *Psychological Types*. New York: Harcourt, Brace & Company, 1923.

KAWABATA, YASUNARI. *Snow Country*. New York: Alfred A. Knopf, 1957.

KEENE, DONALD. "Speaking of Books: Yasunari Kawabata," *New York Times* Book Review, December 8, 1968.

KESEY, KEN. *One Flew over the Cuckoo's Nest*. New York: The Viking Press, Inc., 1962.

KILPATRICK, F. P. *Explorations in Transactional Psychology* (contains articles by Adelbert Ames, Hadley Cantril, William Ittelson, and F. P. Kilpatrick). New York: New York University Press, 1961.

KLEIN, MELANIE. *The Psychoanalysis of Children.* London: Hogarth Press, Ltd., 1951.

KLUCKHOHN, CLYDE; and LEIGHTON, DOROTHEA. *The Navajo.* Cambridge, Mass.: Harvard University Press, 1946.

KORZYBSKI, ALFRED. *Science and Sanity: An Introduction to Non-Aristotelian Systems and General Semantics* (3d. ed.). Lakeville, Conn.: Int. Non-Aristotelian Library Publishing Co., 1948.

KOZOL, JONATHAN. *Death at an Early Age.* Boston: Houghton Mifflin Company, 1967.

LA BARRE, WESTON. "Paralinguistics, Kinesics and Cultural Anthropology." In T. A. Sebeok, A. S. Hayes, and M. C. Bateson (eds.). *Approaches to Semiotics.* The Hague: Mouton & Co., N.V., Publishers, 1962.

——. *The Human Animal.* Chicago: University of Chicago Press, 1954.

LABOV, WILLIAM. *The Social Stratification of English in New York City.* Washington, D.C.: Center for Applied Linguistics, 1966.

——; COHEN, PAUL; ROBINS, CLARENCE; and LEWIS, JOHN. *A Study of the Non-Standard English of Negro and Puerto Rican Speakers in New York City.* Vol. II, pp. 76–152. New York: Dept. of Linguistics, Columbia University, 1968.

LAING, R. D. *The Politics of Experience.* New York: Ballantine Books, 1967.

LAND, EDWIN H. "Experiments in Color Vision," *Scientific American,* Vol. 200, No. 5, May 1959.

LARTSCH, M. See Collier.

LASHLEY, KARL SPENCER. *Brain Mechanisms and Intelligence: A Quantitative Study of Injuries to the Brain.* Chicago: University of Chicago Press, 1929.

LAWICK, JANE (GOODALL) VAN. *In the Shadow of Man.* Boston: Houghton Mifflin Company, 1971.

LEIGHTON, DOROTHEA. See Kluckhohn.

LETTVIN, J. Y.; MATURANA, H. R.; MC CULLOCH, W. S.; and PITTS, W. H. "What the Frog's Eye Tells the Frog's Brain," *Proc. Inst. Radio Engrs.,* Vol. 47, p. 1940, 1959.

LEWIN, ROGER. "Observing the Brain Through a Cat's Eyes," *Saturday Review/World*, October 5, 1974.

LEYHAUSEN, PAUL. "On the Function of the Relative Hierarchy of Moods (as Exemplified by the Phylogenetic and Ontogenetic Development of Prey-Catching in Carnivores)" (1965). In Konrad Lorenz and Paul Leyhausen, *Motivation of Human and Animal Behavior*. New York: Van Nostrand-Reinhold Co., 1973.

LIEBOW, ELLIOT. *Tally's Corner*. Boston: Little, Brown & Company, 1967.

LORENZ, KONRAD. *On Aggression*. New York: Harcourt, Brace & World, Inc., 1966.

——. *Man Meets Dog*. Cambridge, Mass.: Riverside Press, 1955.

——. *King Solomon's Ring*. New York: The Thomas Y. Crowell Co., 1952.

LURIA, A. R. *The Man with a Shattered World*. New York: Basic Books, 1972.

——. "The Functional Organization of the Brain," *Scientific American*, Vol. 222, No. 3, March 1970.

——. *The Mind of a Mnemonist*. New York: Basic Books, Inc., Publishers, 1968.

——. *Higher Cortical Functions in Man*. New York: Basic Books, Inc., Publishers, 1966.

LYNCH, KEVIN. See Appleyard.

MALCOLM X and HALEY, ALEX. *The Autobiography of Malcolm X*. New York: Grove Press, Inc., 1965.

MARTIN, MALACHI. "The Scientist as Shaman," *Harper's Magazine*, Vol. 244, No. 1462, pp. 54–61, March 1972.

MASTERS, WILLIAM H.; and JOHNSON, VIRGINIA E. *Human Sexual Response*. Boston: Little, Brown & Company, 1966.

MATURANA, H. R. See Lettvin.

MAY, ROLLO. *Power and Innocence*. New York: W. W. Norton & Company, Inc., Publishers, 1972.

——. *The Meaning of Anxiety*. New York: The Ronald Press Company, 1950.

MC CLELLAND, J. L. See Johnston.

MC CORMICK, CHARLES T. *Handbook of the Law of Evidence*. St. Paul, Minn.: West Publishing Company, 1954.

MC CULLOCH, W. S. See Lettvin.

MC HALE, JOHN. *World Facts and Trends*. New York: Collier Books, 1972.

MAC LEAN, P. D. "Man and His Animal Brains," *Modern Medicine*, Vol. 95, p. 106, 1965.

MC LUHAN, MARSHALL. *Understanding Media*. New York: McGraw-Hill Book Co., Inc., 1964.

———. *The Gutenberg Galaxy*. Toronto: University of Toronto Press, 1962.

———. "The Effect of the Printed Book on Language in the 16th Century." In *Explorations in Communication*. Boston: Beacon Press, Inc., 1960.

MEAD, MARGARET. *Culture and Commitment: A Study of the Generation Gap*. Garden City, N.Y.: Natural History Press/ Doubleday, 1970.

MEIER, RICHARD. "Information Input Overload: Features of Growth in Communications-Oriented Institutions," *Libri* (Copenhagen), Vol. 13, No. 1, pp. 1–44, 1963.

MEISNER, W. W. "Notes on Identification Origins in Freud," *Psychoanalytic Quarterly*, Vol. 39, pp. 563–89, 1970.

MELVILLE, HERMAN. *Billy Budd*. New York: New American Library, 1961.

MITCHELL-KERNAN, CLAUDIA. "Signifying and Marking: Two Afro-American Speech Acts." In John J. Gumperz and Dell Hymes (eds.). *Directions in Sociolinguistics*. New York: Holt, Rinehart & Winston, Inc., 1972.

———. *Language Behavior in a Black Urban Community*. Berkeley: Monographs of the Language-Behavior Research Laboratory, No. 2, February 1971.

MONTESSORI, MARIA. *The Montessori Method*. New York: Frederick A. Stokes Company, 1912.

MORSBACH, HELMUT. "Aspects of Nonverbal Communication in Japan," *Journal of Nervous and Mental Disease*, October 1973.

MYER, JOHN R. See Appleyard.

NABOKOV, VLADIMIR. *Lolita*. New York: G. P. Putnam's Sons, Inc., 1955.

NIERENBERG, G. I.; and CALERO, H. H. *How to Read a Person Like a Book*. New York: Pocket Books, 1973.

NUTINI, HUGO. "The Ideological Bases of Levi-Strauss's Structuralism," *American Anthropologist*, Vol. 73, No. 3, June 1971.

OGSTON, W. D. See Condon.

OSGOOD, C. E. "Language Universals and Psycholinguistics." In Joseph H. Greenberg (ed.). *Universals of Language*. Cambridge, Mass.: M.I.T. Press, 1966.

——; and SEBEOK, THOMAS A. (eds.). *Psycholinguistics: A Survey of Theory and Research Problems*. With A. RICHARD DIEBOLD. A *Survey of Psycholinguistic Research, 1954–1964*. Bloomington, Ind.: Indiana University Press, 1965.

OSMOND, H. "The Relationship Between Architect and Psychiatrist." C. Goshen (ed.). In *Psychiatric Architecture*. Washington, D.C.: American Psychiatric Association, 1959.

PENNINGTON, KEITH S. "Advances in Holography," *Scientific American*, Vol. 218, No. 2, February 1968.

PIETSCH, PAUL. "Shuffle Brain," *Harper's Magazine*, Vol. 244, No. 1464, pp. 41–48, May 1972(a).

——. "Scrambled Salamander Brains: A Test of Holographic Theories of Neural Program Storage." (Abstract of paper presented at American Association of Anatomists conference, 85th session, Southwestern Medical School, University of Texas, April 3–6, 1972), *The Anatomical Record*, Vol. 172, No. 2, February 1972(b).

PIRSIG, ROBERT. *Zen and the Art of Motorcycle Maintenance*. New York: William Morrow & Co., 1974.

PITTS, W. H. See Lettvin.

POLANYI, M. "Life's Irreducible Structure," *Science*, Vol. 160, pp. 1308–12, June 21, 1968.

PORTMANN, ADOLF. *Animal Camouflage*. Ann Arbor: University of Michigan Press, 1959.

POWERS, WILLIAM T. "Feedback: Beyond Behaviorism," *Science*, Vol. 179, pp. 351–56, January 26, 1973.

PRIBRAM, KARL H. *Languages of the Brain* (Experimental Psychology Series). Englewood Cliffs, N.J.: Prentice-Hall, Inc., 1971.

——. "The Neurophysiology of Remembering," *Scientific American*, Vol. 220, No. 1, pp. 73–86, January 1969.

PROVINE, WILLIAM B. "Geneticists and the Biology of Race Crossing," *Science*, Vol. 182, pp. 790–96, November 23, 1973.

RAVEN, PETER H.; BERLIN, BRENT; and BREEDLOVE, DENNIS E. "The Origins of Taxonomy," *Science*, Vol. 174, pp. 1210–13, December 17, 1971.

ROE, ANNE; and SIMPSON, G. G. (eds.). *Behavior and Evolution*. New Haven, Conn.: Yale University Press, 1958.

ROSENHAN, D. L. "On Being Sane in Insane Places," *Science*, Vol. 179, pp. 250–58, January 19, 1973.

ROSSI, PETER H. "Ripe for Change" (review of Anthony G. Oettinger and Sema Marks. *Run, Computer, Run*. Cambridge, Mass.: Harvard University Press, 1969), *Science*, Vol. 167, p. 1607, March 20, 1970.

SANDER, L. W. See Condon.

SAPIR, EDWARD. *Selected Writings of Edward Sapir in Language, Culture and Personality*. Berkeley: University of California Press, 1949.

———. "Conceptual Categories in Primitive Languages," *Science*, Vol. 74, p. 578, 1931.

———. *Language: An Introduction to the Study of Speech*. New York: Harcourt, Brace & Company, 1921.

SCHLEGLOFF, EMANUEL. "Sequencing in Conversational Openings," *American Anthropologist*, Vol. 70, No. 6, pp. 1075–95, December 1968.

SCHOGGEN, PHIL. See Barker.

SCRIBNER, SYLVIA; and COLE, MICHAEL. "Cognitive Consequences of Formal and Informal Education," *Science*, Vol. 182, pp. 553–59, November 9, 1973.

SEARLES, H. *The Non-Human Environment*. New York: International Universities Press, 1960.

SEBEOK, THOMAS. See Osgood.

SHANNON, C. "Prediction and Entropy of Printed English," *Bell System Technical Journal*, 30, pp. 50–65, 1951.

SINGER, P. "Philosophers Are Back on the Job," New York *Times* Magazine, June 7, 1974.

SKINNER, B. F. *Beyond Freedom and Dignity*. New York: Alfred A. Knopf, Inc., 1971.

———. *Science and Human Behavior*. New York: The Macmillan Co., 1953.

SLOVENKO, RALPH. "The Opinion Rule and Wittgenstein's Tractatus," *Etc.: A Review of General Semantics*, Vol. 24, No. 3, pp. 289–303, September 1967.

SMITH, H. L., JR. "Descriptive Linguistics and Language Teaching." In E. W. Najam (ed.). MATERIALS AND TECHNIQUES FOR THE LANGUAGE LABORATORY, *International Journal of American Linguistics*, Vol. 28, No. 1, Part II, 1962.

SPITZ, RENÉ A. "The Derailment of Dialogue: Stimulus Overload, Action Cycles, and the Completion Gradient," *Journal of the American Psychoanalytic Association*, Vol. 12, No. 4, October 1964.

STEWART, W. A. "Sociolinguistic Factors in the History of American Negro Dialects," *The Florida FL Reporter*, Vol. 5, No. 2, pp. 1–4, 1967.

——. "Urban Negro Speech: Sociolinguistic Factors Affecting English Teaching." In R. Shuy (ed.). *Social Dialects and Language Learning*. Champaign, Ill.: National Council of Teachers of English, 1965.

STROMEYER, CHARLES F., III. "Eidetikers," *Psychology Today*, Vol. 4, No. 6, November 1970.

SULLIVAN, HARRY STACK. *Conceptions of Modern Psychiatry*. New York: William Alanson White Psychiatric Foundation, 1947.

SZENT-GYÖRGYI, A. "Dionysians and Apollonians," *Science*, Vol. 176, p. 966, June 2, 1972.

TIGER, LIONEL. *Men in Groups*. New York: Random House, Inc., 1969.

TINBERGEN, NIKO. *Curious Naturalists*. New York: Basic Books, Inc., 1958.

——. "The Curious Behavior of the Stickleback," *Scientific American*, Vol. 187, No. 6, December 1952.

TOFFLER, ALVIN. *Future Shock*. New York: Bantam Books, Inc., 1970.

TRAGER, GEORGE L. "Paralanguage: A First Approximation," *Studies in Linguistics*, Vol. 13, pp. 1–12, 1958.

TURNBULL, COLIN M. *The Forest People*. New York: Simon & Schuster, Inc., 1961.

VAN ZANDT, HOWARD F. "Japanese Culture and the Business Boom," *Foreign Affairs*, January 1970.

WANG, WILLIAM. "The Chinese Language," *Scientific American*, Vol. 228, No. 2, February 1973.

WARREN, RICHARD M.; and WARREN, ROSLYN P. "Auditory Illusions and Confusions," *Scientific American*, Vol. 223, No. 6, December 1970.

WASHBURN, S. L. "Primate Field Studies and Social Science." In Laura Nader and Thomas W. Maretzki (eds.). *Cultural Illness and Health*. Washington, D.C.: American Anthropological Association, 1973(a).

——. "The Promise of Primatology," *American Journal of Physical Anthropology*, Vol. 38, No. 2, pp. 177–82, March 1973(b).

——. "Evolution of Primate Behavior." In Francis O. Schmitt (ed.). *The Neurosciences: Second Study Program* (pp. 39–47). New York: The Rockefeller University Press, 1970.

WHORF, BENJAMIN LEE. *Language, Thought, and Reality*. New York: The Technology Press of M.I.T. and John Wiley & Sons, Inc., 1956.

WIENER, NORBERT. *The Human Use of Human Beings* (2nd, rev. ed.). Garden City, N.Y.: Doubleday Anchor Books, 1954.

WIGMORE, JOHN HENRY. *A Treatise on the Anglo-American System of Evidence in Trials at Common Law* (3rd edition, ten volumes). Boston: Little, Brown & Company, 1940.

WILDAVSKY, AARON. *The Politics of the Budgetary Process*. Boston: Little, Brown & Company, 1964.

WORTH, SOL; and ADAIR, JOHN. *Through Navajo Eyes: An Exploration in Film Communication and Anthropology*. Bloomington: Indiana University Press, 1972.

Index

Index
of
IDEAS and
techniques of
TRANSCENDENCE

1. an INDIVIDUAL
    cannot
  thru introspection   p. 28
    and   pp. 39–48, 61–73, 100, 185–86, 193,
  Self-examination   205–6, 211, 216–17
    understand himself
      or
  the forces that
    mold his life,
      without
    understanding
  his CULTURE.

2. CULTURES
    won't
  change unless   pp. 62–64, 177
    everyone
      changes.
  There are:
    neurological-biological   pp. 36–38, 61–64, 102–4, 176–78
    political-economic-historic pp. 106–7, 181–82, 184, 219
      and
        CULTURE-   pp. 105–12, 122, 184
          PSYCHODYNAMIC
  reasons for this.

3. CULTURE
    is
  dictatorial   pp. 28, 30, 145–47, 151, 193
    unless
  understood and examined.

4. "It is
   not
   that MAN
      must
   be in sync   pp. 16–19, 35, 119–21, 125, 151–52,
      with,   165–66
   or adapt
      to
   his CULTURE
      but
   that CULTURES grow
      out of sync
         with
            MAN."
   When this
      happens
   PEOPLE
      go crazy
   and

   THEY DON'T KNOW IT.   pp. 9, 16, 131–32, 155, 213
5. In order
      to
   avoid
      mass insanity
         PEOPLE
   must learn   pp. 143–44
      to   178–80
   transcend   187–95
      and
   adapt their
      CULTURE
         to the times
            and to their
   biological organisms.

6. To accomplish
      this task,
         since
   introspection
      tells you nothing,
         man needs   pp. 146–47
   the EXPERIENCE
      of
   other CULTURES.
      I.e.
   to survive, all
      CULTURES   pp. 36, 49, 71–74
   need each other.

INDEX OF THEMES

INDEX

AUTHOR'S INDEX